The Complete All-Color Guide to
House Plants Cacti & Succulents

William Davidson and T. C. Rochford

House Plants illustrated by Henry Barnett
Cacti and Succulents illustrated by June Baker

Galahad Books Galahad Books New York

ACKNOWLEDGEMENTS

The publishers would like to thank Mr J. E. Bolton of
Altcar Road, Formby, Merseyside for allowing Mrs
June Baker to make use of his extensive collection of
cacti and succulents for artist's references. We would
also like to thank Thomas Rochford and Sons Limited
for supplying plants for the same purpose and for the
reference for the illustration of hydroculture equipment
which appears on page 18.

Published by Galahad Books
a division of A & W Promotional Book Corporation
95 Madison Avenue, New York, NY 10016

Library of Congress Catalog Card No. 76–11283
ISBN: 0–88365–364–8

Filmset in England by Tradespools Ltd., Frome,
Somerset, in 9 on 11 pt. Monophoto Times
Colour reproduction by
Culver Graphics Litho Ltd., Buckinghamshire
Printed and bound in England by
Jarrold and Sons Ltd., Norwich, Norfolk

Contents

(continued on page 6)

Cacti and Succulents

True Cacti with Areoles

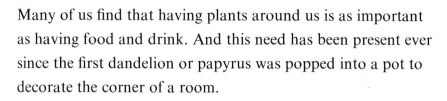

Introduction

Many of us find that having plants around us is as important as having food and drink. And this need has been present ever since the first dandelion or papyrus was popped into a pot to decorate the corner of a room.

In recent years there has been a vast increase in the number and range of plants available for growing indoors, and it is safe to assume that there is a correspondingly large increase in the number of gardeners and plant lovers generally who are deriving great pleasure from growing plants in pots. For many, it would seem, indoor plants become as important as – sometimes even more important than – their pets, even to the point where they are fussed over and chatted to in the certain belief that they will grow and perform better as a result. When one sees their plants, who can deny that there might be something in their point of view.

There has also been a corresponding escalation of interest in the more specialized cultivation of cacti and succulents, some of which can be grown as house plants but most of which are better suited for greenhouse or conservatory cultivation. They are indeed enthusiasts' plants in the real sense of that term, with the fascination coming from the achievement of growing them successfully and in getting them to flower.

What we have attempted to do in this book, with the help of our two artists, June Baker and Henry Barnett, is to describe and illustrate a fully representative range of the finest and most desirable species and varieties of a very large number of genera. One thing which has also been fully allowed for is the convenience of readers in that the descriptions and cultural advice are always immediately below the relevant illustrations. In addition, the plants are grouped together logically, either from the viewpoint of ease or otherwise of cultivation (in the case of the house plants) or ease of identification in the case of cacti and succulents.

Over the last two decades, progress and innovation have been very much a part of the indoor-gardening scene. Not only have many fine new plants been introduced, but improvements in growing techniques and the availability of specially formulated composts have made it much easier to achieve success. One of the latest developments has been hydroponics, or soilless culture. This has been made possible at domestic level by the development of ion-exchange fertilizers which reproduce the buffering effect of soil. Hydroculture, as it is called, means that the house-plant owner no longer has to gauge the watering and feeding of the plants so accurately.

One thing which can confidently be predicted is that the interest in both these groups of plants will continue to increase. We hope that this book will make some small contribution towards your enjoyment of them over the years.

Thomas C. Rochford

Common Names with their Botanical Equivalents

A

Aaron's Beard, *Opuntia leucotricha*
African Violet, *Saintpaulia*
African Wind Flower, *Sparmannia africana*
Amazon Lily, *Eucharis grandiflora*

B

Baby's Tears, *Helxine soleirolii*
Bamboo, *Bambusa*
Bastard Jasmine, *Cestrum*
Bay Tree, *Laurus nobilis*
Beavertail Cactus, *Opuntia basilaris*
Bellflower, *Campanula*
Bird's Nest Fern, *Asplenium nidus*
Bird of Paradise Flower, *Strelitzia reginae*
Bishop's Cap Cactus, *Astrophytum*
Black-eyed Susan, *Thunbergia alata*
Boston Fern, *Nephrolepis exaltata bostoniensis*
Bottle Brush, *Callistemon*
Busy Lizzie, *Impatiens*
Butterfly Flower, *Schizanthus*

C

Calamondin Orange, *Citrus mitis*
Cape Heath, *Erica*
Cape Ivy, *Senecio macroglossus*
Cape Jasmine, *Gardenia jasminoides*
Cape Primrose, *Streptocarpus*
Cast Iron Plant, *Aspidistra lurida*
Castor Oil Plant, *Ricinus communis*
Century Plant, *Agave*
Chenille Plant, *Acalypha hispida*
Chimney Bellflower, *Campanula pyramidalis*
Chin Cacti, *Gymnocalycium*
Chiotilla, *Escontria chiotilla*
Christmas Cactus, *Zygocactus truncatus*
Cigar Plant, *Cuphea platycentra*
Clog Plant, *Hypocyrta glabra*
Coconut Palm, *Cocos nucifera*
Coffee, *Coffea arabica*
Copperleaf, *Acalypha wilkesiana*
Coral Berry, *Ardisia crispa*
Corncob Cactus, *Euphorbia mammillaris*
Creeping Fig, *Ficus pumila*
Creeping Devil Cactus, *Machaerocereus eruca*
Croton, *Codiaeum*
Crown of Thorns, *Euphorbia milii, E. splendens*
Cups and Saucers, *Cobaea scandens*

D

Date Palm, *Phoenix*
Devil's Tongue, *Ferocactus corniger*
Donkey's Ears, *Sansevieria*
Drunkard's Dream, *Hariota salicornioides*
Dumb Cane, *Dieffenbachia*

E

Earth Stars, *Cryptanthus*

F

False Aralia, *Dizygotheca elegantissima*
Fiddle-leaf Fig, *Ficus lyrata*
Fig, *Ficus*
Flaming Dragontree, *Dracaena terminalis*
Flamingo Plant, *Anthurium scherzerianum*
Freckle Face, *Hypoestes sanguinolenta*

G

Garrambulla, *Myrtillocactus geometrizans*
Geranium, *Pelargonium*
German Ivy, *Senecio mikanioides*
Golden Barrel Cactus, *Echinocactus grusonii*
Goose-foot Plant, *Nephthytis*
Grape Ivy, *Rhoicissus rhomboidea*
Gum Tree, *Eucalyptus*

H

Hare's Foot Fern, *Davallia canariensis*
Hart's-tongue Fern, *Phyllitis scolopendrium*
Heath, Cape, *Erica*
Heather, *Erica*
Hedgehog Cactus, *Echinocereanae, Echinocactanae*
Heliotrope, *Heliotropium*
Herringbone Plant, *Maranta leuconeura erythrophylla*
Hot-water Plant, *Achimenes*
Houseleek, *Sempervivum*

I

Italian Bellflower, *Campanula isophylla*
Ivy, *Hedera*
 Cape, *Senecio macroglossus*
 German, *Senecio mikanioides*
 Grape, *Rhoicissus rhomboidea*

J

Jade Plants, *Crassula arborescens,*
   C. portulacea, C. lactea
Jasmine:
   Bastard, *Cestrum*
   Cape, *Gardenia jasminoides*
   Madagascar, *Stephanotis floribunda*
Jelly Beans, *Sedum pachyphyllum*

K

Kaffir Lily, *Clivia*
Kangaroo Vine, *Cissus antarctica*
King of Tree Philodendrons, *Philodendron
   eichlerii*

L

Lady's Fingernail, *Neoregelia spectabilis*
Laurel, Spotted, *Aucuba japonica*
Lemon, *Citrus*
Lemon-scented Verbena, *Lippia citriodora*
Living Stones, *Lithops*
Lobster Claw, *Clianthus*
Lollipop Plant, *Pachystachys lutea*

M

Madagascar Jasmine, *Stephanotis
   floribunda*
Maidenhair Fern, *Adiantum*
Medusa's Head, *Euphorbia caput-medusae*
Mind-your-own-business, *Helxine
   soleirolii*
Money Trees, *Crassula arborescens,
   C. portulacea, C. lactea*
Morning Glory, *Ipomoea*
Moses-on-a-raft, *Rhoeo discolor*
Mother-in-law's Armchair, *Echinocactus
   grusonii*
Mother-in-law's Tongue, *Sansevieria*

N

Norfolk Island Pine, *Araucaria excelsa*

O

Old Man Cactus, *Cephalocereus senilis,
   Espostoa lanata*
Old Lady Cactus, *Mammillaria hahniana,
   M. lanata*
Oleander, *Nerium oleander*
Orange, *Citrus*

P

Palms, *Kentia, Neanthe, Phoenix*
Parlour Palm, *Kentia fosteriana*
Parasol Plant, *Heptapleurum arboricola*
Partridge Breasted Aloe, *Aloe variegata*
Pasacana, *Trichocereus pasacana*
Passion Flower, *Passiflora*
Peacock Plant, *Calathea makoyana*
Peyote Cactus, *Lophophora williamsii*
Pick-a-back Plant, *Tolmiea menziesii*
Pineapple, *Ananas*
Pitahaya, *Carnegiea gigantea*
Poinsettia, *Euphorbia pulcherrima*
Polka Dot Plant, *Hypoestes sanguinolenta*
Polka Dots, *Opuntia macrodasys albispina*
Pomegranate, *Punica granatum*
Pony-tail Plant, *Nolina recurvata*
Poor Man's Orchid, *Schizanthus*
Prayer Plant, *Maranta leuconeura
   kerchoveana*
Prickly Pear, *Opuntia*
Primrose, Cape, *Streptocarpus*
Princess of the Night, *Selenicereus
   pteranthus*
Purple Heart, *Setcreasea purpurea*

Q

Queen of the Night, *Selenicereus
   grandiflorus*

R

Rabbit's Tracks, *Maranta leuconeura
   kerchoveana*
Rat's-tail Cactus, *Aporocactus
   flagelliformis*
Red-hot Cat's Tail, *Acalypha hispida*
Rubber Plant, *Ficus elastica*

S

Saguaro, *Carnegiea gigantea*
Screw Pine, *Pandanus veitchii*
Sensitive Plant, *Mimosa pudica*
Shrimp Plant, *Beloperone guttata*
Silk Oak, *Grevillea robusta*
Snake Plant, *Sansevieria*
Snow in Summer, *Cerastium tomentosum*
Song of India, *Pleomele reflexa variegata*
Spanish Moss, *Tillandsia usneoides*
Spider Cactus, *Gymnocalycium denudatum*
Spider Plant, *Chlorophytum*
Spotted Laurel, *Aucuba japonica*
Spurge, *Euphorbia*
Stag's Horn Fern, *Platycerium*
Stick Cactus, *Euphorbia tirucallii*
Stonecrop, *Sedum*
Strawberry Cactus, *Echinocereus
   enneacanthus, E. salm-dyckianus*
Sweetheart Plant, *Philodendron scandens*
Swiss Cheese Plant, *Monstera*

T

Three-men-in-a-boat, *Rhoeo discolor*
Tiger Jaws, *Faucaria tigrina*
Turk's Head Cactus, *Melocactus maxonii*

U

Umbrella Plant, *Cyperus*

V

Variegated Yam, *Dioscorea discolor*
Venus Fly Trap, *Dionaea muscipula*
Verbena, Lemon-scented, *Lippia citriodora*

W

Wax Plant, *Hoya*
Weeping Fig, *Ficus benjamina*
White Sails, *Spathiphyllum*
Whitsun Cactus, *Schlumbergera gaertneri*
Winter Cherry, *Solanum capsicastrum*

Y

Yam, Variegated, *Dioscorea discolor*

House Plants

William Davidson

Choosing House Plants

House plants are acquired in a number of ways: many as the result of making a definite purchase, others are bought on the spur of the moment, some are grown from cuttings offered by a friend or arrive as gifts. When choosing a plant for yourself it is possible to take into account the all-important aspect of home conditions, but with gifts all that can be hoped for is that the donor has made some allowance for the sort of conditions that the plant is likely to meet in its new home, as there is not much joy to be had from introducing tender plants to cold conditions that are going to be totally alien to them.

Quality plants may be a little more expensive, but they are usually the better buy in the long run. The general tidyness of the plant – clean pot, clean leaves, absence of pests and diseases, and growth that is neatly tied in position – will be an indication that the grower of that particular plant had its well-being in mind, and you can rest assured that it will give more satisfaction than the cheaper plant that has an untidy and uncared-for look. The place of purchase is also worthy of consideration, the warm shop or greenhouse that offers plants some protection from the elements will have better produce than the retailer who markets his plants from the pavement outside his shop.

General Care of House Plants

On paying for his plant almost every purchaser will ask the inevitable question 'How do I look after it?' If only the supplier could be exactingly precise and give the ideal needs for all his various plants in the way of temperature, light, feeding and, in particular, the precise amount of water required. If only he could then he would save us all a great deal of trouble.

Light. Many of the plants we can be reasonably specific about, but the majority must be covered by more general advice. And in this respect room conditions that are light, airy and reasonably warm [minimum temperature 13°C (55°F)] will offer plants a much better chance of prospering than conditions that are wet and cold, or hot and dry. In fact, the worst possible conditions are a combination of high temperature and dry atmosphere, because not only are pests more prevalent then but the plants' resistance is much lower. To alleviate the effects of a dry atmosphere some way must be found of increasing the humidity; this can be helped by plunging the plant pots to their rims in moist peat or standing them on a layer of gravel which is kept moist.

Good light should not necessarily be interpreted as exposure to direct sunlight, as the majority of indoor plants will be adversely affected if stood in direct sunlight for long periods. The sunny windowsill is fine

13

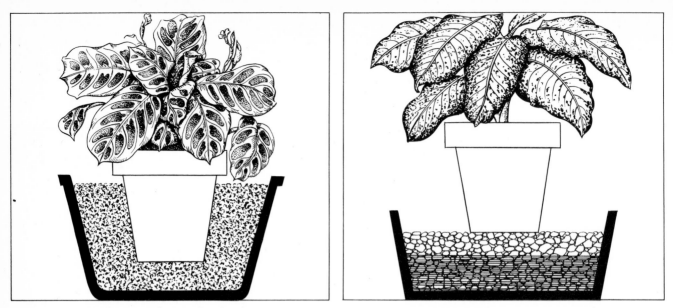

Two ways of increasing humidity: left, plunging the pot in peat; right, standing the pot on moist gravel

in winter when the heat of the sun is less intense, but most plants will suffer as a result of strong summer sun beating down on them. Plants with variegated or highly coloured foliage, such as the croton, will require lighter positions than plants with purely green foliage. Here again, however, we have exceptions as most of the marantas and calatheas have colourful foliage but it is essential that they are not exposed to direct sunlight.

Rooms with small windows offering poor light would also be ill suited to all but the toughest of indoor plants, such as the green-leaved *Philodendron scandens* and *Rhoicissus rhomboidea*. Should there be no alternative to badly lit conditions then it is better to forget about plants and think of other ways of improving the appearance of the home surroundings.

Watering. How much, how often, from the top, from the bottom of the pot, hard or soft water, in the morning or the evening? These are only some of the questions that are asked on the difficult subject of proper watering. All sorts of devices are available for assisting the novice when it comes to watering, but few of them compare with putting a finger in the compost to test whether it is wet or dry. The most important advice concerning watering is to warn the wielder of the watering can that more plants die as a result of over-watering than ever die as a result of drying out, so it is advisable to err on the side of dry rather than wet conditions. When the compost is permanently sodden then the roots in the pot become inactive and in time rot and die. However, once again there are exceptions, such as cyperus and azalea, that will quickly decline if the compost dries out for any length of time.

Plants may be watered from the top or the bottom; it makes little difference provided the compost is thoroughly saturated each time the pot is watered.

Small amounts of water do little more than moisten the top inch of compost and merely serve to tantalize rather than water the plant. With the flowering plants such as saintpaulia it is important that water is kept off the leaves and flowers; the flowers in particular will develop brown patches and die off rapidly should they become wet.

When contemplating going on holiday the collection of indoor plants can be something of a problem. Neighbours and friends are often apprehensive about the prospect of caring for someone else's treasured plants; and the apprehension is often justified when the returning holidaymaker finds that his prize collection has been reduced to a mass of dead and dying leaves. When leaving plants for someone else to care for give

Most house plants, except those with hairy leaves, benefit from being sprayed over with water

them precise instructions concerning the amount of water and fertilizer required by each plant. The neighbour can then take on the onerous task with a little more confidence! For short absences the plants can be placed on a bed of wet sand in a basin.

Despite the damage that may be caused to flowering plants, the majority of foliage plants will benefit from being regularly sprayed over with a fine mist spray – a treatment that will also help to combat the dry conditions prevailing in centrally heated rooms. Wherever possible, when watering or spraying, it will be advisable to use rain water, as hard tap water is less suitable and will leave a lime deposit on the leaves. Not everyone has facilities for collecting rain water, but all is not lost as hard tap water can be softened by immersing a small hessian sack of peat in a bucket or tub of water. Chemically softened water should never be used for plants.

Cleaning and General Hygiene

Indoors it is inevitable that plant leaves will become dust covered and much less attractive if something is not done to keep them clean. There are many different types of leaf-cleaning agents on sale which may be sprayed on to the leaves or applied with a sponge or damp cloth, but not all of them are suitable for all plants. Therefore, care must be exercised when using these products for the first time to ensure that plants are not susceptible to whatever the concoction may be. For example, some of the spray-on leaf cleaners will damage many plants if applied during periods of low temperature. And, surprisingly, the kentia palms and aspidistras, both of which have leaves that would seem to be as tough as those of any indoor plant, are especially vulnerable to damage. So it would seem sensible that any new leaf-cleaning product should be tried on part of the plant in the first instance and left for a week or so to see what reaction there may be. Overdoing the leaf cleaning only gives plants an unnaturally glossy appearance so it is better to use a sponge moistened in water most of the time and to treat plants with specialized leaf cleansers only occasionally. Soft new leaves should never be handled as they bruise very easily until they stiffen up.

All indoor plants should be cleaned over and generally tidied up periodically as it is inevitable, no matter how competent the grower, that brown leaves will appear. These do nothing for the appearance of the plant, so have them off and put them in the bin! Untidy plant growth can, of course, be tied into place at any time but we are often asked to advise on the best time for pruning indoor plants. For the vast majority of purely foliage plants any time is a good time – healthy plants come to very little harm as a result of having a few odd branches trimmed off to improve their appearance.

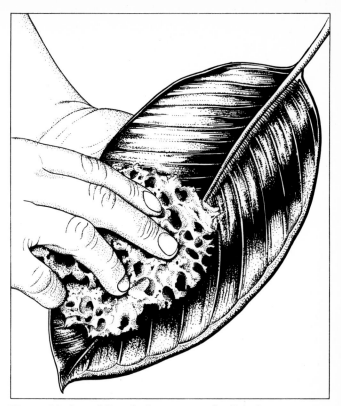

Plants with glossy foliage look more attractive if the leaves are regularly washed

Pests and Diseases

Sickly plants, like sickly people, are much more prone to disease and general maladies than are healthy ones. So it is important to make every effort to maintain plants in the best possible condition, and not to hang on to them for too long when they do show signs of deterioration. Either remove sick plants to an isolation area away from other plants or, better still, be courageous and dispose of them when they begin to show obvious signs of severe ill health.

Rather than wait for the pests to arrive and then treat them, it is often wise to give a precautionary treatment with a general insecticide that will keep the majority of pests under control. This is certainly sensible in respect of the minute red spider mite that is seldom detected before the plant is suffering considerably as a result of its presence. For indoor plants the spray-on type of insecticide is the most effective and the easiest to handle. When applying it take the precaution of wearing rubber gloves and treat the plants out of doors on a still warm day. The plants should be left out in the shade until the insecticide has dried before they are brought indoors again. An essential requirement when applying insecticides in liquid form is to ensure that the plant is thoroughly saturated on both sides of the leaf – soaking the undersides of the leaves is really much more important than wetting the top sides.

Red spider mite is especially prevalent on ivies but is likely to affect all plants in hot, dry conditions. It occurs

15

mainly on the underside of the leaves and is almost invisible without the aid of a lens but can be detected as it causes the leaves to take on a very dry appearance and to become brown around their edges.

Greenfly (Aphid), the familiar garden pest, usually attacks the soft new growth of the plant and is not difficult to eliminate.

Mealy bug is a powdery white insect that wraps its young in a cottonwool-like substance and is usually found in such places as the twining growth of stephanotis, amongst the overlapping leaves of aglaonema, or tucked into the angle of leaf and stem on other plants. The best way of controlling it is to apply methylated spirits with a soft brush directly on to the pest.

Whitefly is one of the most persistent pests, and is usually found on the undersides of leaves of many plants, pelargoniums in particular. Some recent insecticides are claimed by their manufacturers to kill whitefly; total elimination is not easy but persistent spraying of the undersides of leaves will maintain a reasonable measure of control. If only a few plants of modest size are affected then they can be placed in a sealed polythene bag for twenty-four hours. This will kill the mature fly but the treatment must be repeated to catch any hatching from eggs.

Scale insects are brown or flesh coloured and cling to leaves and stems like miniature limpets as they slowly suck the life out of the plant. They can be eradicated by being wiped off with a sponge that has been soaked in malathion insecticide. Be sure to wear rubber gloves while doing this.

Compost and Potting

If the whispered comment 'What about potting?' is anything to go by, then one almost feels that there must be some sort of mystique about the simple operation of transferring a plant from one size pot to another slightly larger one. Perhaps there is something rather special about it when you only have one or two plants. However, a few simple rules are all that are required to do this successfully.

Pot only healthy plants, never sick ones.

Pot on into a pot only slightly larger than the one the plant is currently growing in.

For preference, potting should be carried out in late spring or early summer.

Use a properly prepared compost made for the job and not something dug up from the garden.

Pots. Clay pots will need a few pieces of broken pot (crocks) in the bottom to prevent the solitary drainage hole becoming blocked with compost. But, as is more likely these days, when using plastic pots there is no need for crocks in the bottom as plastic pots are amply supplied with drainage holes.

Method. The new pot should allow for about 1 in (2·5 cm) of new compost all the way round the root ball and the same in the bottom. Except in a few isolated cases the new compost should be of a peaty nature, and a mixture of two parts of John Innes potting compost No. 2 and one part of sphagnum peat will usually give

An easy method of potting on. A pot of the size that the plant is currently growing in is placed inside one of the new size and compost is added

The smaller pot is lifted out to leave a space in the compost which is equivalent to the area of the plant's root ball

the desired results. After potting, water the compost thoroughly then keep on the dry side to give the new roots a chance to get on the move. If plants are properly potted in late spring then there should be no need to feed the plant until early the following spring when the new season's growth begins to develop. Every second year is frequent enough to pot on plants that have been growing indoors, but it is often wise to pot larger plants that seem to be overgrown almost as soon as they are acquired. With some plants, such as sparmannia and strelitzia, which grow very vigorously it may eventually become necessary to trim the roots in order to keep them within the bounds of a 10-in (25-cm) pot. One very simple way of doing this is to water the plant well before removing it from its pot and, with a strong sharp knife, to cut away completely the lower section of the root system. Using the same pot, put crocks in the bottom, fresh compost on top of the crocks (an amount equivalent to the depth cut from the plant) and simply set the plant on top of the new compost. If this operation is carried out in early summer the plants will quickly root into the new mixture, gaining a new lease of life and seldom batting an eyelid in spite of the apparent harshness of the treatment.

For strong-rooting plants that are likely to be in their pots for some length of time it is essential that the potting compost should have some body in it. In this respect the John Innes mixtures cannot be bettered, but these will vary considerably from one producer to the next and it may be necessary to add peat to the mixture if it seems to be too thin – that is if it trickles through the hand like sand.

The plant is removed from its present pot and is placed in the space created by the removal of the smaller pot. The compost is firmed with the fingers

Hydroculture – Growing Plants without Soil

For those who want it, home gardening can now take advantage of a new method of growing plants which has been developed from hydroponics – the science of growing plants in water with fertilizers added.

To grow plants in this way the procedure at the moment is to start by sowing seed or propagating cuttings in compost in the conventional manner, and then to convert the plants to hydroponic culture (hydroculture) when they are established. In time the amateur grower will be able to convert his own plants, but at the moment it is done by the nurseryman in warm glasshouses on specially constructed benches.

When converting plants every vestige of soil is washed from the roots and the plant is then placed in a net pot in the bottom of which there is a shallow layer of Hydroleca. While the plant is held centrally in the pot the remaining space is filled with more Hydroleca, there being no need to ram or push the material into position. (Leca is a specially prepared granule that is used in the making of lightweight concrete, while Hydroleca is a special grade that is intended solely for use in hydroculture. The special grade is a smaller and more uniform pebble about the size of a shelled hazelnut, and is especially useful for its capillary action which is a necessary requirement for growing plants in water successfully.)

It takes about one month to convert the average indoor plant from soil growing to water growing and a further six to eight weeks for it to become reasonably established before being dispatched to the retailer. Prior to dispatch the net pot is placed in a watertight outer container, which should not be much larger than the net pot unless a number of plants are being grouped in the same outer container, as with office planters for example.

The outer container should have a water level indicator and a filler tube (see diagram overleaf). Water for replenishing the container can be poured over the Hydroleca or down the filler tube, but it is important when adding fertilizer that this should go down the filler tube only and be washed in – this will ensure that it finds its way directly into the water at the bottom of the container. When feeding plants, only specially manufactured fertilizers designed solely for use in hydroculture should be used, as the nutrients of such fertilizers are slowly released into the water only as they are required. Indiscriminate feeding can cause considerable damage to the plants' roots.

Growing plants in clay granules, water and specially developed fertilizers is a much cleaner and more attractive way of presenting them, and it offers a new dimension in indoor plant growing. It is important that the directions for feeding plants and maintaining water

17

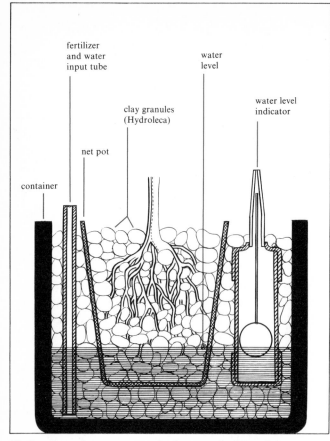

fertilizer
and water
input tube

water
level

clay granules
(Hydroleca)

water level
indicator

net pot

container

Hydroculture plants are grown in clay granules in special net pots which allow water to circulate around the roots. These pots are also embedded in the granules (Hydroleca) which fill the rest of the space in the outer container

levels are adhered to, otherwise they will require exactly the same consideration as more conventionally grown plants. Temperatures will have to be maintained as advised for individual needs of particular plants and they must be kept out of draughts and away from radiators. Pests and diseases will still have to be watched for and treated with the appropriate insecticide, or whatever. Plants with glossy leaves will have to be cleaned periodically. Aerial roots that grow from the stems of plants belonging to the aroid family should be directed into the Hydroleca when they are long enough.

In all probability, the accuracy with which water requirements can be gauged is the greatest benefit hydroculture gives to the average house-plant grower. For, provided the indicator operates satisfactorily, there should be no problem with regard to the amount of water required. Containers will usually go for some three weeks between each water-filling operation and this will clearly be a tremendous advantage when holidays are contemplated. No further need to cajole neighbours and friends to take on the onerous task of caring for one's treasures! However, it must be remembered that, although plants may not need water during such an absence, there will still be a need for the provision of

adequate temperatures should such absences occur during the colder parts of the year.

For the experimentally minded amateur the big question is almost sure to be 'What sort of plants can I hope to grow successfully in water'? And the answer, in relation to house plants, is that almost anything can be attempted and that many plants grow better than they do in the conventional potting compost. One paradox is the grape ivy, *Rhoicissus rhomboidea,* which does not seem to take kindly to water culture, yet grows like the proverbial weed in compost. Even sansevierias and many of the cacti appear to revel when introduced to hydroculture, and all the plants belonging to the *Araceae* family grow with obvious indications that they are content with the change.

Effective Display

The simple placement of a single dracaena or monstera can, in many situations, be much more impressive and eye catching than a clutter of smaller plants bundled together in no particular style. This is probably never more true than when a large plant of nephrolepis fern is seen in all its majesty on top of a pedestal support.

But this is not to say that all indoor plants are the better for standing in solitary splendour; far from it, the majority will look better and will very often fare much better when they have a few companions around them. In short, the proximity of other plants not only improves their overall appearance but also improves their performance. There is no shortage of suitable containers in which plants can be grouped, and should the economics of the situation be a problem then one of the most suitable of containers is an old baking tin. In this, half a dozen plants can be grouped together to achieve a very pleasing effect. The humble plant container can then be camouflaged by a piece of material or a timber surround.

It is an advantage when using containers of this type to place a 2-in (5-cm) layer of wet sand or gravel in the bottom on which the plant pots can rest. By keeping the sand or gravel moist it will be found that the plants will grow very much better and watering of the compost in the plant pot will be needed much less frequently. On the other hand, plant pots should never be allowed to stand in water for any length of time. A further word of warning on this subject is to recommend that no plant container, be it pot, trough or whatever, should be placed directly on the furniture – a cork mat put under it will prevent moisture damaging furniture.

With most plant arrangements it is very much better to leave plants in their individual pots as this will allow each one to be watered according to its individual requirements and will also offer the advantage of being able to rearrange the plants with much more ease.

Nevertheless I would hesitate to suggest that plants should be moved around too frequently, as they are usually better left in the same position once they have settled and are growing well.

If the unpotting and free planting in compost is an essential requirement of the plant arrangement then it is advisable that plants with similar needs should be put together; this will mean leaving the odd plant, sansevieria for example, in its pot for individual watering. Watering is an important consideration with these mixed plantings, especially so if the container used has no drainage holes in the base to allow surplus water to drain away. The best policy is to exercise restraint and to err on the dry side.

Propagation

To produce the millions of house plants that are offered for sale annually the grower employs many different methods of propagation – some of which require such a degree of skill that only specialist growers undertake the task. But, for every plant that requires the skill of the specialist, there are scores that can be raised with reasonable success in little more than average conditions.

Many of our indoor plants may be raised from seed (monsteras, bromeliads and saintpaulias for example), but the majority are increased vegetatively by taking leaf or stem cuttings, while a few are propagated by dividing the root system. Some of the dracaenas, *D. massangeana* in particular, can be increased from stout stems that would seem quite unsuitable for propagation purposes.

When growing plants from seed only the best quality seeds should be used. John Innes potting compost No. 1 is a good medium on which to sow the seed and since

most seed will germinate better in warm conditions a sheet of glass should be placed over the seedbox or pan to retain moisture. When a small number of plants are required only a very thin sowing of seed is needed and the seedlings should be evenly spaced in a seedbox as soon as they are large enough to handle without damaging them. Thereafter they are potted on into larger pots as required.

With any form of propagation that the indoor gardener may attempt, one of the prime requirements is that the compost, the pots, the boxes, the knife used for cutting and everything associated with the operation must be scrupulously clean. Furthermore, the plants used as a source of cuttings must be healthy and the pieces removed for use as cuttings must be the best pieces and not miserable little bits that will, in fact, have precious little chance of succeeding. Fresh sphagnum peat with a little sharp sand will provide a suitable compost for rooting the cuttings.

For the propagation of most plants excessive heat is not needed, but a steady temperature in the region of 18°C (65°F) will help considerably. In this respect a small propagating unit which has a heating element incorporated in the bottom to keep the compost warm will increase the chance of success. A small heated propagator of this kind can give a tremendous amount of pleasure and the close atmosphere of the unit will reduce transpiration to the minimum and help plants to root much more quickly. Good rooting is also aided by the use of a rooting powder or liquid. A makeshift propagator can be made simply by placing the plant pot and cuttings in a polythene bag and sealing it to prevent escape of air. Given the foregoing conditions it is possible to experiment with all sorts of plant propagation, and quite frequently the success achieved is surprising.

Air-layering, see page 44, is another method of propagation. An upward cut is made in the stem (left). After dusting with hormone rooting powder the cut is surrounded with damp sphagnum moss and wrapped in polythene

Abutilon hybrid

Achimenes hybrid

Easy Indoor Plants

The beginner to indoor-plant growing would be well advised to make his or her selection of starter plants from this section, rather than choose more delicate plants that may initially be more colourful but will, almost inevitably, be more disappointing in the end. Among the easier plants can be found a wealth of kinds with colourful and interesting foliage; even the humble tradescantia when properly grown can be much more appealing than the most delicate and beautiful plant that is suffering as a result of indifferent culture and inadequate temperature.

Generally speaking, the easier plants are the ones that will tolerate lower temperatures without suffering unduly. In this respect the ivies are ideal, as they remain fresher and crisper in moderate temperatures. Other plants that are especially suited to cool and airy conditions where adequate light prevails are the spring-flowering subjects such as azaleas, primulas and the winter-flowering *Jasminum polyanthum*. It is important, however, to avoid really cold and miserable situations that are totally devoid of feeling, so somewhere in the region of 10°C (50°F) should be the aim when setting minimum temperatures for indoor plants that are considered easy to manage.

For areas that offer poor light it is better to select plants with green foliage rather than those with colourful or variegated foliage. Aspidistras seem to thrive in poor light, as does the grape ivy, *Rhoicissus rhomboidea*.

Abutilon

Although it eludes me at present, there must be some very good reason why abutilons are not more popular as indoor plants. Some are most attractive on account of their maple-like variegated foliage and although often seen as centrepieces of garden summer bedding schemes are not too frequently found as indoor plants. Others produce masses of pendulous bell-shaped flowers that are not unlike miniature hollyhocks, and come in a wide range of colours. For the garden room and the larger room indoors, they will cover a trellis or similar framework quite quickly to provide an excellent backcloth of flowers and foliage for smaller plants placed in front.

Plants may be raised from seed or cuttings – both kinds of propagation being done in the spring. From seed it is possible to get plants with a wide range of colours, the best of which can be used as a source of cuttings in the following year.

Abutilons will flower over a long period and do not require a temperature of more than 10°C (50°F) in order to succeed. They should be kept moist and well fed during the growing season, on the dry side at other times, and will develop a more compact habit if the growing tips are pinched out to encourage them to branch. In September or October the stems may be shortened by half their length.

Abutilon megapotamicum has small red and yellow flowers and is one of the most popular kinds. Another favourite, with mottled variegated foliage and orange-yellow flowers, is *A. striatum thompsonii*.

Achimenes

If differing methods of propagation are anything to go by there is every reason for this plant being as popular as any. Not only can it be increased by leaf and stem cuttings taken in April but it can also be propagated from seed sown in February or March, or the scaly rhizomes may be teased apart in February and planted individually to form new plants. When starting plants from dormant rhizomes they will grow much more freely if the rhizomes are first plunged in hot water. This practice has, in fact, given achimenes its common name of hot-water plant.

Not at all difficult to care for, achimenes should have a light position by a window. While the plants are actively growing the compost must be kept moist and regular feeding with a weak liquid fertilizer will be beneficial. Although there are some compact kinds, most achimenes will need to have the growing points removed to improve the habit and, even so, plants will need staking. These are also good subjects for hanging baskets where they can be grown without staking. The attractive trumpet-shaped flowers come in a range of colours – pink, red to purple, mauve, blue, yellow, and white – according to variety.

The growth dies down naturally in the autumn and water should then be gradually withheld until the compost is quite dry. The rhizomes should be stored in a warm, dry place until they are started into growth again in the spring – in warm, agreeable conditions February is the best month.

Adiantum tenerum

Acorus gramineus

Acorus

Not all of us can accommodate, far less afford, the somewhat grand prospect of incorporating a water feature as part of the indoor-plant display, but for those who can it offers many fascinating possibilities. The soothing effect of moving or still water can add a new dimension to almost any display, and where the water is still there is the added pleasure of seeing the reflection of one's plants.

Alas, there are not many of our true house plants that can be put to use as water plants. One that can be utilized in this way is _Acorus gramineus_ which can be placed in the water in its pot, and will often be much happier in this situation than it would be if occupying a more conventional house-plant position on the windowsill.

Acorus form grassy clumps which reach a height of some 15 in (38 cm), and are not in the least difficult to care for provided the compost is kept permanently saturated – on the windowsill this can be achieved by standing the plant pot in a dish of water. Propagation is simply done by division of the clumps of roots at any time of the year. Divided pieces can be potted up into John Innes potting compost No. 2 immediately, there being no need to bother with peat mixes and proper propagating methods.

This acorus is hardy out of doors but plants may need to be hardened off before being planted outside – preferably in midsummer.

Adiantum

For the person interested in, or involved with, the business of displaying plants to good advantage there can be few plants that compare with adiantums, the maidenhair ferns. Colourwise they blend with almost anything that comes along and, being of full yet delicate appearance, they are most useful for concealing pots and other materials that may be used for creating a display.

The majority of ferns require conditions that are shaded, moist and reasonably warm if they are to succeed indoors. In view of this it is often an advantage if young plants can be encouraged to develop in the early stages in a glass plant case, in which they will be free from draughts, reasonably moist and just that little warmer than they would be if placed on the windowsill.

Most of the glossy leaved house plants will benefit from having their leaves cleaned periodically with a damp cloth or a proprietary leaf-cleaning chemical. However, it would be unwise to do more with the adiantum than mist the foliage over with a fine spray of water; this may be done daily in warmer conditions, less frequently if plants are in a cool room. Although it is not commonly accepted, few plants are harmed as a result of watering with water that comes direct from the domestic tap. But it will be no disadvantage to water adiantums with rain water, or water from a kettle which has been boiled and allowed to cool off before being given to the plants. Less water is required during the winter but the soil should never be allowed to dry out. The minimum acceptable temperature is in the region of 10°C (50°F).

Mature plants can be increased by using a sharp knife to divide the clumps into sections for planting individually into small pots of peaty compost. Alternatively, they may be increased in much greater number by sowing ripe spores on moist peat in very warm conditions.

When the plants seem too large in relation to the pots in which they are growing they should be potted on into slightly larger containers using a peaty compost. However, adiantums seldom require potting into containers that are larger than 8 in (20 cm) in size. Full, healthy plants in such containers can be particularly handsome when placed on a pedestal of some kind that allows them to be viewed from all angles, and also gives them ample space in which to develop.

A range of species and varieties is available, _Adiantum cuneatum_ (botanically _A. raddianum_) with its dark green fronds being one of the most popular. Another favourite with greyish-green, rather hairy fronds is _A. caudatum._ _A. tenerum_ with arching fronds and stalked leaflets is particularly good for pot culture, as are its various forms.

Allemanda cathartica

Alpinia sanderae

Amaryllis (Hippeastrum) hybrid

Allemanda

The majority of these are best suited to a greenhouse that can be maintained at temperatures in the region of 25°C (77°F), with a high degree of humidity. Needless to say, where these conditions are available, plants such as the climbing *Allemanda cathartica,* with yellow flowers some 5 in (13 cm) across, will provide a spectacular display. Trained up to the roof of the greenhouse they look fine but, being of climbing habit, few of the allemandas are suited to average home conditions.

However, in *A. neriifolia*, we have a plant that is much more compact in appearance and very much less demanding in its requirements. In warm conditions cuttings a few inches in length are not at all difficult to root; a fact which is worth remembering as most of these plants must be acquired as cuttings from friends, there being few allemandas offered for sale on the open market. Once rooted, cuttings should be transferred to 3-in (8-cm) pots filled with John Innes potting compost No. 3 as they are greedy plants that soon fill their pots with roots. Pinching out the early growing tips of the plant will induce it to become more compact and attractive. Established plants will require regular feeding, and potting on should not be neglected when pots have become filled with roots. It is also of particular importance to ensure that the compost does not at any time dry out – during the summer months more mature plants will need watering daily and, if this is done, 3-ft (1-m) high plants bearing rich yellow flowers in midsummer will be the reward.

Alpinia

For the experienced house-plant grower it is often more rewarding to have a measure of success with an unusual plant than it is to grow a more ordinary and easy plant to perfection. And in *Alpinia sanderae* there is just such a plant which, when well grown, has few peers in the world of purely foliage plants.

New plants are raised by dividing more mature plants and using the younger pieces on the outside of the plant for propagation. When removed it is important that the young plants, which will have some roots attached, are potted into 3-in (8-cm) pots filled with a peaty compost. Thereafter they will have to spend a few weeks in the agreeable conditions prevailing in a heated propagating case until roots have established in the pot.

In fact, in order to provide alpinias with an environment reasonably near the ideal, it would be wise to continue to grow them in a plant case or terrarium of some kind. When they become too large for the case young plants can be propagated to take their place. Keep the compost moist and feed with a weak liquid fertilizer once the plants have become established.

Amaryllis

Many plants masquerade under two names and the amaryllis or hippeastrum is no exception. In fact the latter is the correct one but I have given precedence to amaryllis as that is the name under which it is most generally known by the gardening public.

The amaryllis is one of the most spectacular of all flowering plants and, though costly to purchase at the outset, it is not a difficult plant to manage once it has been acquired. These days amaryllis are usually offered ready planted in the potting medium and in an attractive presentation pack with directions on how to proceed in order to obtain the best results.

Bulbs purchased without directions, however, should be planted in pots that are only a little larger in diameter than the actual bulb, and about two-thirds of the bulb should be above the surface. A rich compost containing a good proportion of leafmould and rotted cow manure (if it can be obtained) will suit them best. After potting, water very sparingly until the flower bud is evident then gradually increase the supply.

After flowering it is important that the plant should be kept moist and regularly fed in order to build the bulb up for flowering the following year. The plant may be placed out of doors in summer but should come in before frosts occur. In late summer the foliage should be allowed to die down naturally and the compost kept dry until new growth appears. Pot on every third or fourth year only.

Aralia sieboldii variegata

Araucaria excelsa

Asparagus plumosus

Aralia

The green form, *Aralia sieboldii*, possesses many excellent qualities that help to make it one of the most popular of the less expensive house plants. It is easily propagated from seed, can be grown in cool conditions, and is among the easiest of plants to care for indoors.

With careful culture mature plants may reach a height of some 8 ft (2·5 m) and still retain most of their lower leaves, but compact plants in smaller-size pots are by far the most effective indoors. *Aralia sieboldii*, or *Fatsia japonica* to use a synonym, has green, palmate leaves that are particularly well suited to plant grouping.

In milder areas this plant can be overwintered out of doors; a cool, shaded and moist situation being preferred. Indoors it will respond best to the location that offers similar conditions to those suggested for outdoor planting – cool and shaded – with a watering programme that keeps the compost moist without being too saturated for long periods. As they are somewhat vigorous plants regular feeding is essential, and plants should be potted on into slightly larger containers each year in the spring. Use a good quality John Innes potting compost No. 2 or 3 with the addition of just a little extra peat when potting.

New plants may be raised from root cuttings propagated in temperatures of about 25°C (77°F) but it will be much simpler to sow seed in agreeably warm conditions in the spring or, if only a few plants are wanted, to purchase tiny plants and grow them on.

The variegated form, *Aralia sieboldii variegata*, is slower growing and a little more demanding in its requirements.

Araucaria

For sheer elegance of form there can be few green foliage plants that match the beauty of *Araucaria excelsa,* or the Norfolk Island pine to give it its common name. The tiered leaves of this South Pacific native have an unmatched beauty that sets it apart from most other house plants. It is essentially an individual plant that is seen to best effect when set in splendid isolation rather than when arranged with other plants in a group.

New plants are raised from seed, but as this is very difficult for anyone outside the nursery trade to obtain it is usually better to acquire either established plants, or to purchase smaller plants and to grow them on. Cool, light conditions with some protection from strong sunlight will suit them best – in hot, dry rooms the needle leaves tend to brown and fall off at an alarming rate.

Potting on should only be necessary every second year, and once plants have become established in larger pots they can be sustained for many years simply by maintaining a regular feeding programme. The potting medium should contain a reasonable proportion of leafmould and sharp sand as it is important that the compost should be free draining – stodgy compost that holds water for too long will inevitably present problems.

In its natural habitat araucaria will attain a height of 100 ft (30 m) or more, but in the greenhouse and the home growth is, fortunately, much slower and it would take many years for plants to reach the 7-ft (2·5-m) mark.

Asparagus

A tough plant with cascading green leaves, *Asparagus sprengeri* seems to have an inbuilt capacity for withstanding all sorts of seemingly disagreeable indoor growing conditions. It is very much the beginner's plant, as it will put up with many variations in temperature, watering and light. However, though it has this wonderful capacity for toughness, this is no reason for making the plant suffer unnecessarily and, of course, the better the treatment the better it will be.

Ideally, the temperature should be in the region of 16°C (60°F) and the growing position should afford some protection from direct sunlight. Compost should be kept moist at all times, but care should be exercised in winter when it is better to keep the soil on the dry side. Feeding established plants with weak liquid fertilizer is important if they are to retain their bright green colouring. Small white flowers that are fragrant and followed by red berries are an added attraction.

Asparagus plumosus is a much more delicate and generally more graceful plant, and the more compact miniature forms are quite delightful when grouped with other foliage plants in mixed arrangements – they are also much used in the floristry trade.

Similar conditions and treatment are required by all the asparagus. They are also adaptable in that they may be used as trailing plants in baskets or hanging pots or, in the case of the stronger-growing ones, they may be encouraged to climb a trellis.

Propagate by means of spring-sown seed or, more simply, by division of the roots; water the compost and separate the roots at almost any time of the year.

Astilbe japonica rubens

Aspidistra lurida

Aucuba japonica

Aspidistra

The dear old cast iron plant, *Aspidistra lurida*, almost inevitably dominated the main window position in grandmother's parlour, and it seemed to go on for year after year with comparatively little treatment.

To succeed with this particular plant it should be remembered that it is tough and does not require too much attention with the watering can and with fertilizers and potting on into larger containers. It is important, however, that plants should enjoy a reasonable temperature, in the region of 16 to 20°C (60 to 68°F), and that they should not be exposed to direct sunlight. Even more important, it is absolutely essential that one should not resort to using chemically prepared concoctions when cleaning the leaves, as these are extremely sensitive to this sort of treatment in spite of their apparent toughness. Another interesting feature of this plant is the purplish bell-shaped flowers that appear at soil level.

Potting on need only be tackled when plants are very full and well established, and really old and mature plants in large pots can have the lower part of the root system cut away with a strong knife before resetting the plant in the same pot on a bed of John Innes potting compost No. 3. Harsh treatment perhaps, but no harm will be done to healthy plants – the alternative is to pot on into larger pots every four or five years. Can you then imagine the enormous sort of plant pot that a mature aspidistra some sixty years old would be in?

There is also a rather rare variegated form with dull white and green leaves.

Astilbe

In very wet outdoor situations the astilbe, or spiraea as it is sometimes incorrectly called, develops into a fine garden plant and produces large plumes of white, pink or red flowers. Being colourful and reasonably easy to manage it is also offered in limited numbers as a summer-flowering pot plant. The leaves are somewhat coarse in appearance, but when purchasing a plant the buyer should have in mind the dual advantage of the astilbe in that it will make a perfectly good garden plant when it has outlived its attraction for indoor decoration.

Far and away the most important cultural consideration is that the compost must remain moist at all times while the plant is in flower and leaf. Actually, moist is hardly the correct word: wet or saturated would be a very much better condition for the compost to be in. From the moment of purchase it will be important to ensure that plants are fed regularly as the pots are invariably very congested with roots.

Besides using them for indoor and garden decoration they are excellent plants for brightening up the garden room or the patio. Whatever the location it is better that they should have protection from bright sunlight as this tends to bleach the colour out of the flowers.

Plants may be propagated by means of seed or, to get plants of mature size more quickly, by division of the roots.

Aucuba

The spotted laurel, *Aucuba japonica,* is a garden plant that is also put to many uses as a pot plant. Indoors it will do perfectly in a light window position, with protection from direct sunshine, and a moderate temperature provided the compost in the pot is not allowed to become excessively wet for long periods. There are male and female plants, and the females produce attractive crops of red berries in winter provided there is a male plant in the vicinity when the plants are in blossom.

Although suitable for indoor use the aucuba is usually seen to best advantage when grown in a large tub on the terrace or patio, where it will develop into a plant of some 5 ft (1·5 m) in height with appropriate spread of leaves. If some shelter from the worst of the winter weather is given it will ensure that plants get an earlier start and grow away more freely in the spring.

Outdoors window boxes offer a further use for aucubas, which can be either individually planted or utilized in conjunction with other plants.

They are not particularly fussy in respect of compost, but John Innes potting compost No. 3 will obviously give better results than soil taken from the garden and given no preparation.

New plants may be raised from seed sown in cool conditions in the autumn. Alternatively, fresh plants can be propagated from cuttings a few inches in length inserted in cool conditions in the autumn – sophisticated equipment is not needed as they will root in the open if given a sheltered position.

Indian azalea

Bambusa angulata

Azalea

Usually available in winter and spring the florist's azalea, or Indian azalea, when it comes to propagation and early development of young plants, is very much the prerogative of the experienced nurseryman with the necessary skill and equipment at his disposal. Highly colourful in many shades of white, pink, orange and red they are, however, among the easiest of plants to care for indoors provided one follows a few simple rules.

Principal among these rules is the absolute necessity for keeping the compost in the pot wet, not moist, wet, and at all times. Any drying out will assuredly result in premature shrivelling of the flowers and subsequent loss of leaves. I am ever afraid of advising the house-plant grower to water his plants well as the tendency very often is to overdo it, but with the azalea this is not at all likely to happen. Submerging the plant pot in a bucket of water and leaving it there until all the air bubbles in the soil have been expelled is probably the most satisfactory method of watering where only a few plants are concerned. Use of rain water will also be of considerable benefit.

Following watering the next most important requirement is that the plant should enjoy cool temperatures indoors; the growing position should also be as light as possible without being too sunny. In centrally heated rooms where the temperature is frequently in excess of 20°C (68°F) azalea flowers will open much more rapidly than they will in a cool room, so one's pleasure from the plant will be over a much shorter period. However, it should be emphasized that when purchasing plants that are in very backward condition they must not be subjected to too low a temperature as there is the possibility that flowers will fail to open.

Ideally, an azalea plant should be purchased with a number of flowers fully open and lots of nice fat buds that are obviously about to open in a matter of a few days. The plants to avoid are those that have shrivelled or distorted flowers.

Having successfully flowered an azalea indoors the owner is then faced with the problem of what to do next in order to keep the plant going for subsequent years – albeit, more than a few decide that the dustbin is the best place for the plant once it has fulfilled its initial function of providing a colourful display in the home.

For those with an experimental turn of mind, and the time to care for their plants while they are out of doors during the summer months, the following is offered as a guide. As flowers die they should be pinched off, and when there is no longer the likelihood of a frost plants can go out of doors – in the shade in order to minimize watering. But if shade is impossible, then a sunny position will do no harm. At the time of putting them out it would be as well to pot plants on into slightly larger containers using a compost composed of peat and leaf-mould. Thereafter, keep them moist at the roots and sprayed over with water regularly. Bring them indoors before frosts occur.

There are a large number of named varieties of the evergreen Indian azalea, most of them are hybrids from *Rhododendron simsii* (syn. *Azalea indica*).

Bambusa

The majority of the bamboos are strong-growing plants that will attain a height of some 50 ft (15 m) in their natural habitat; however, do not anticipate them pushing the roof off when their roots are confined to pots, as their vigour will be considerably reduced when root development is restricted. But, where strong growth that will quickly fill a large space is needed, then the free-growing bamboos are fine. They are also very easy to manage and will withstand quite low temperatures in winter [7°C (45°F)] if the compost is not allowed to become excessively wet. Besides being well suited to large rooms, garden rooms or greenhouses bamboos will do perfectly well in sheltered positions in less exposed gardens.

Originating from China, *Bambusa angulata* is quite dwarf in comparison with many of the other bamboos, attaining a height of some 3 ft (1 m) only, and is, therefore, much more suitable for the average home. Not difficult to care for, the bamboos require reasonable light and warmth and should be well watered during the summer months, less so at other times, and fed regularly when they are growing.

The simplest method of increasing plants is to divide them in the spring and to pot up the divided pieces in John Innes potting compost No. 3 making sure that the pot is well drained. New plants can also be raised from seed or by cuttings of rhizomes taken in the spring; a heated propagating frame will be an advantage when using the latter method.

25

Begonia masoniana

Begonia lucerna

Begonia Roy Hartley

Begonia

Among the begonias there would seem to be plants to suit everyone's taste – exotic flowers, colourful foliage, easy and difficult kinds, even some that can be grown in the garden at milder times of the year. With such a diverse group it is difficult to generalize in respect of care and attention; however, one can say that temperatures should be in the 10 to 20°C (50 to 68°F) range, with the more tender and difficult plants needing temperatures at the higher end of the scale. For plants in smaller and intermediate size pots a compost of equal parts of John Innes potting compost No. 2 and clean sphagnum peat is advised. It is also advisable to provide some protection from direct sunlight for those growing under glass, or in light window positions indoors.

The large-flowered tuberous begonias may be grown from seed but are much better bought as established tubers in February. Acquired in this way the tubers should be planted concave side uppermost, in shallow boxes filled with clean moist peat. These should then be placed in warm conditions in order to start the tubers into growth. When a reasonable number of leaves have been produced the tubers must be lifted carefully and planted into small pots to begin with, the plants later being transferred to larger pots as they increase in size. Regular feeding is essential. Roy Hartley, pink, Gold Plate, yellow and Crown Prince, crimson, are some of the many superb varieties which are available.

The pendulous begonias (varieties of *B. pendula*) are treated in exactly the same way, except that they will do infinitely better if they are planted in hanging baskets instead of conventional pots when the final planting is undertaken. It is also important that the basket chosen should provide a reasonable body of soil so that plants may develop to their full potential; grown in this way pendulous begonias are among the most spectacular of all flowering pot plants.

Begonia rex can have few competitors when it comes to sheer variety of leaf pattern and a quite astonishing range of colours. Exceptional plants of the larger leaved types that have been grown in perfect conditions may be encouraged to develop into specimens measuring as much as 3 ft (1 m) in diameter. Plants reaching this size would be in the region of three years old and should be growing in pots of some 10 in (25 cm) in diameter. However, when they are required for indoor decoration it is much better to choose the varieties that have smaller leaves as they are very much easier to manage and will make fewer demands on available space. In room conditions, most plants tend to lose many of their lower leaves as they age, and as they do so a stout rhizomatous stem develops and the plant loses much of its attraction and may have to be discarded. Though it is not easy, new plants may be made by cutting mature firm leaves into postage-stamp-size pieces which should then be placed on moist peat in a warm propagating case. Alternatively, the leaf stalk should be removed and the leaf pegged down on moist peat after the veins on the undersides have been cut with a sharp knife. New plants will eventually form from the cut veins. In conditions that are damp and cold, mildew on the leaves may prove to be a problem and should be treated with a proprietary fungicide.

Unless it is during the winter months, plants that are of reasonable size when purchased are often better for being potted on into slightly larger pots without too much delay.

Another rhizomatous-rooted begonia which is useful in plant groupings is *B. masoniana*. This is commonly named *B.* Iron Cross on account of the dark green pattern in the centre of the leaf which resembles an iron cross. It needs similar conditions to those suggested for *B. rex*, although it prefers a more shaded position during the brighter months of the year. It is, however, more difficult to raise from cuttings; more time and great care with watering being needed while the rooting process is taking place.

In the larger rooms where space is not a problem there are many fibrous-rooted cane-type begonias that are reasonably easy to care for and also offer a spectacular display for many months of the year. One of the most reliable that is also fairly easy to acquire is *B. lucerna* which, in fair conditions, may attain a height of 5 to 6 ft (1·5 to 2 m). It has dark green, silver-spotted leaves and pink flowers in spring and summer. Other kinds growing to a similar height are *B. fuchsioides*, with small leaves and pinkish-red flowers throughout the summer months, and *B. maculata*, with silver-spotted leaves and pink flowers. The main feature of these cane-type begonias is

Beloperone guttata

Begonia rex varieties

Beloperone

heavy trusses of pendulous flowers. There are many more species and varieties of this type of begonia that will be well worth trying, both indoors and in the greenhouse. Larger plants should be grown in pots of 10 in (25 cm) in size and the compost should be a little heavier than for smaller plants – two parts of John Innes potting compost No. 3 to one part of sphagnum peat. It is also wise to use the heavier clay pots to prevent tall plants from overbalancing. For growing in hanging baskets I would recommend *B. glaucophylla*. The main attraction of this fibrous-rooted begonia is the mass of pendulous flowers that appears early in the year and varies in colour from rose-pink to brick red.

Cuttings of the cane-type begonias will, on the whole, root very readily in modest conditions, there being little need for creating a special environment to encourage them.

Native to Mexico, the most important of these attractive plants is *Beloperone guttata*, which is commonly named the shrimp plant. The common name is derived from the heads of petal-like bracts that are shrimp like in appearance and vary in colour from deep pink to shades of light autumnal brown. The variation in colour is dependent on the amount of light that is available. The tubular flowers which grow out from the bracts are not in themselves particularly attractive but they add to the generally pleasing appearance of the plant. Again depending on the growing position, the leaves will vary in colour from pale to dark green.

The growing position should be light but not too sunny, and the best growing temperature is in the region of 18°C (65°F); in very hot rooms plants tend to become thin and drawn. Although the plants should not remain saturated for long periods it is, nevertheless, essential that the compost should not at any time dry out excessively, a moist compost that drains freely is the most suitable.

New plants may be raised from cuttings, about 3 in (8 cm) in length, inserted in peat and placed in a warm propagating case until they have rooted: the temperature should be in the region of 20°C (68°F) with a high humidity level. Non-flowering shoots are the best material for making cuttings, but as it is often difficult to find any new growth that does not have flowering heads of bracts it is usually necessary to remove these before inserting the cutting. In order to produce plants that are a reason-

able size it is advisable to insert four or five cuttings in each small pot. Also, to promote more bushy growth, the growing tip of each shoot should be removed once the cuttings are well rooted and have started to grow away.

Healthy plants of beloperone produce an abundance of heads of bracts which often weaken the plant, so it is wise to remove the first bracts that are produced in order to encourage the plant to develop more leaves and become sturdier and capable of producing a much greater number of bracts in time. John Innes potting compost No. 2 with a little peat added will suit them best, and it is important that plants should be potted on into larger pots once each year until they have become established in pots of the 7-in (18-cm) size, thereafter they may be sustained by regular feeding. Regular feeding of established younger plants is also essential if they are to remain attractive.

Pruning is only necessary when the plants become untidy in appearance, or when older plants become overgrown, and should be done in the autumn when there are usually fewer heads of bracts present.

Another interesting species is *B. lutea*, which has lime-green bracts that are particularly attractive in larger plants; these are seen at their best when growing in 7-in (18-cm) pots. To encourage plants to grow to a more mature size it is wise to remove all bracts as the plant is developing, so getting maximum-size plants in the minimum time.

Aechmea rhodocyanea

Bromeliads *(Aechmea to Vriesea)*

It seems that, like cacti, either you like bromeliads or you do not – it may have something to do with the fact that many of them have edges to their leaves that are not unlike the teeth of a saw. Almost all the members of the fascinating *Bromeliaceae* family are indigenous to tropical South America where they grow in trees, on the forest floor, and almost anywhere else that offers a foothold. Some develop into large specimens, while others seem to be little more than wispy strands of growth that would hardly seem worthy of classification as plants. *Tillandsia usneoides,* Spanish moss, is just such a plant producing a matted growth of silver-grey strands that require nothing more than the moisture in the atmosphere to keep them not only alive but growing rampantly. So much so that it is one of the most troublesome of tropical weeds.

In spite of their tropical origin bromeliads are amongst the easiest of plants to care for, and most of them are perfectly suited to room conditions. Besides their exotic rosette shapes, many of them have brilliantly coloured foliage and others have flowering bracts that are a match for any flower in both colour and shape. Some flowering bracts are carried on stems several feet long while other plants in the family have flowers that barely emerge from the water reservoir in the centre of the rosette of leaves. An important need with all the rosette-forming species is that of keeping the water reservoir topped up. In room conditions all the bromeliads are slow to mature and take many years to produce their flowers.

Aechmea

Among the aechmeas there are a number of plants that the keen house-plant grower may be tempted to purchase in order to improve his collection, but it must be said that some of them, such as *Aechmea mariae-reginae,* will become much too large for most households. This species also takes somewhere in the region of twelve years before it produces flowers, so it is really best suited to the plant collector with a large greenhouse at his disposal.

Doubtless the best known is *A. rhodo-cyanea* (*A. fasciata*), the culture of which has been developed to a very fine pitch by one or two specialist nurserymen on the Continent. For commercial purposes new plants are raised from seed and, as they take a number of years before they get to flowering stage, they tend to be expensive to buy.

The leaves are predominantly grey in colour and have a natural downy covering which should not be wiped or cleaned as this will mar their appearance. They are broad and strap like and are formed in the shape of a rosette which, in fact, provides a natural watertight vase. Keeping the centre of the rosette permanently filled with water is essential to the well-being of the plant; the compost in which the plant is growing should be kept just moist.

The head of pink bracts and small blue flowers is very exciting in appearance and will remain colourful for six to ten months from the time of its appearance in the bottom of the vase of water. I am asked many questions about what should be done when the plant has finished flowering. The best procedure is to remove the head of bracts and its stem when it is no longer attractive and to remove the rosette of leaves when this dies down naturally. By then new young growths (offsets) should have developed at the base of the plant and care should be exercised not to damage these as they will be the rosettes that will bear flowers when they have developed to sufficient size – usually in three years. Alternatively, the small rosettes can be removed and planted up individually when they have produced several leaves of their own.

This advice applies to all the rosette-forming bromeliads.

Ananas bracteatus striatus

Billbergia nutans

Ananas

The principal distinction of *Ananas commosus* is that it is the only member of the truly exotic and fascinating bromeliad family that is of any value to commerce – to those with a taste for exotic fruits it is better known as the pineapple. The dull green leaves with vicious spines along their margins cannot be described as beautiful by any stretch of the imagination, but the plant has the distinction of being able to produce small pineapples on the ends of long stems when grown in pots as small as 5 in (13 cm) in diameter. Even when in fruit it cannot be described as beautiful, but it has a fascination for many people who feel there is something special in having a pineapple plant in fruit on the kitchen windowsill!

Raising new plants in quantity is a task for the skilled plantsman, but there is no reason why anyone with an experimental turn of mind should not attempt to grow the odd plant from a pineapple fruit. The tufted top of the fruit should be removed with an inch or so section of the fruit itself. Follow this by removing the sappy part of the fruit from inside the skin, which should be dusted with a hormone rooting powder. A potful of peat covered with a generous layer of sand is prepared and the pineapple is pressed, tufted section uppermost, into the sand. The pot should then be kept in a closed case or propagator in a heated greenhouse until roots have formed and the tuft starts to grow. It may surprise you to discover that it is not so difficult as might be imagined.

Where the foregoing plant may be at the end of the scale as far as beautiful brome-liads are concerned, there can be no doubt that the variegated *A. bracteatus striatus* when bearing fruit must rank as one of the most beautiful of all the plants that is likely to be purchased in a pot. The leaves tend to be very much longer and broader with rich cream and green colouring. When about to produce fruit (on plants some four years old) there is an added bonus when the central leaves of the rosette change to a rich reddish pink, and one may also have the good fortune of seeing the larger outside leaves suffused with the same rich colouring. The fruits are also much more spectacular being carried on stems that may reach a length of 18 to 24 in (45 to 60 cm) and are again reddish pink in colour with short-lived flowers of the most intense blue.

As the fruits develop it is usual for the plants to produce strong side growths from amongst the overlapping leaves. These should be removed in their entirety and used for propagating new plants; for this operation a heated greenhouse will be required. Side growths should be allowed to develop to a reasonable size before detaching them, by which time they will, in fact, resemble young plants rather than a conventional cutting.

Good light and reasonable warmth are the principal needs of all pineapples. The compost should be on the dry side for the best results and feeding should not be necessary. When potting, an open free-draining potting mixture is important, so I would recommend a peat and leafmould mixture rather than heavier loam-based compost.

Billbergia

Given reasonable growing conditions the more common of the billbergias, *B. nutans*, is one of the easiest of indoor plants to care for, in fact it often seems to thrive with the minimum of attention. The foliage is typically that of the bromeliads, but clusters of plants increase much more rapidly than those of the majority of plants in this family. Consequently it is necessary to split up the clumps much more frequently than would be expected of most bromeliads.

Clumps may be divided at almost any time when the plant is not actually in flower. When division is deemed necessary the compost in the pot should be well watered in advance, and the plant must be knocked from its pot before being divided into either individual plantlets or more manageable smaller clumps that may be potted up individually. Individual plants should go into 3½-in (9-cm) pots, while the small clumps will do better if potted immediately into 5-in (13-cm) pots. For a few weeks after potting in this way the compost must be kept on the dry side until the plant makes a reasonable amount of new roots. In any event, the compost should at no time remain saturated for long periods.

Alternatively, a number of young plants may be planted up in hanging baskets of reasonable size to give a grand display when they produce their multi-coloured flowers with exotic pink bracts. Individual flowers last for little more than a few days, but a large clump in a hanging basket will provide a succession of bracts over two or three weeks.

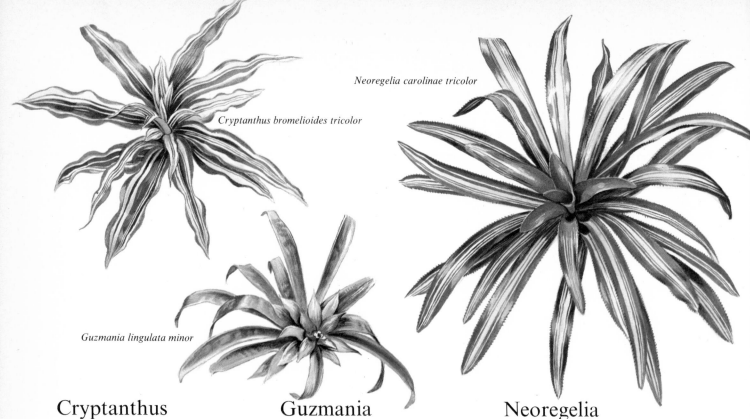

Neoregelia carolinae tricolor

Cryptanthus bromelioides tricolor

Guzmania lingulata minor

Cryptanthus

Although much smaller than the other members of the fascinating bromeliad family, cryptanthus, or earth stars as they are commonly known, are no less attractive in their way. Few of them have flowers that can be described as anything other than insignificant, but their shape, colouring and, in particular, their usefulness make them firm favourites with the plant enthusiast.

Being small plants that seldom produce individual rosettes of more than a few inches in diameter they are ideal for the keen collector who does not have a great deal of space at his disposal. They are also particularly useful when it comes to planting up small dish gardens and bottle gardens, as they are never invasive and can be especially attractive in a naturalistic setting that incorporates small rocks or cork bark.

Many of the more choice kinds, such as *Cryptanthus fosterianus*, are almost museum pieces and are keenly sought after by the enthusiast, but there are more common types, such as *C. bromelioides tricolor* and *C. bivittatus*, that are reasonably easy to obtain. New plants are raised from offsets, so increasing one's stock of cryptanthus is inevitably a slow business.

Another excellent use for cryptanthus is in the making of bromeliad trees, as they fit perfectly in the many smaller recesses that will be formed naturally by smaller branches of the tree. Though naturally more terrestrial in their habit, the cryptanthus will adapt very readily to tree dwelling where they often grow very much better, and almost invariably produce rosettes with very much brighter colouring if the moss surrounding the roots is kept moist.

Guzmania

Of all the many interesting plants in the bromeliad family, *Guzmania musaica* must surely rate as one of the most striking with its mottled foliage and colourful yellow-orange flowering bracts. Alas, these are slow-growing plants and so are not often offered for sale by the commercial grower. Besides being slow growing they also require a slightly higher temperature than the average run of bromeliads in order to do well, a minimum of 18°C (65°F) should be the aim. As they produce a lot of leaves they become rather heavy and so are not particularly suited to being grown on trees as epiphytes – clay pots that offer a good anchorage are the best type of container for them.

Less demanding and more easily obtained is *G. zahnii*, but it is equally impressive with long strap-like crimson-coloured leaves and conspicuous yellow bracts that will remain colourful for some two months. Guzmanias are larger plants and more space is required for their development, but otherwise they need similar treatment to other bromeliads. *Guzmania lingulata minor* is another interesting species which enjoys being grown as an epiphyte on a bromeliad tree. It has bright orange-red bracts and the typical rosette arrangement of leaves.

Neoregelia

Here there are a number of plants that are much favoured by the professional plant decorator who is interested in their clean lines and exotic appearance. *Neoregelia carolinae tricolor* is possibly the most exciting with its rather flat rosette that may be 24 in (60 cm) or more in diameter. The leaves are cream and pink variegated, and as the insignificant blue flowers appear the short leaves in the centre of the plant turn a brilliant red in colour. Although the flowers are short lived the leaves retain their brilliant colouring for many weeks. Eventually the parent rosette will die, but before it does so up to five young plants will be produced around the base of the original rosette. When these young plants have produced some five or six leaves of their own they may be removed with a sharp knife and potted up individually in small pots filled with a peaty compost. When no longer attractive the old plant should be discarded. As an alternative to removing the young plants they may be left attached to the old stump of plant and allowed to form an attractive cluster of new growth.

Neoregelia spectabilis is commonly known as lady's fingernail because of the crimson tip at the end of each green leaf which resembles a painted fingernail. When the flowers appear the short leaves surrounding the water reservoir change to an incredible purple colour which does give the plant a spectacular appearance.

30

Pot chrysanthemums

Cineraria *(Senecio cruentus)*

Chrysanthemum

The chance discovery that the chrysanthemum, in common with the poinsettia, initiates its flower buds according to the amount of available daylight (whereas• many other plants can be encouraged to develop flower buds earlier than normal simply by subjecting them to higher temperatures – spring bulbs being a good example) has led to a small revolution in the pot-plant industry. Instead of having these plants in flower at their normal time in the autumn, the nurseryman can now control the amount of daylight available to the plant by using black polythene to blackout completely areas in which chrysanthemums are growing, so simulating autumn day length conditions when there is twelve hours or less of daylight. This encourages plants to flower more or less as and when required. This method is used for both cut flowers and pot-grown plants.

A further advantage for the grower of potted chrysanthemums has been the development of chemicals that will restrict the growth of plants such as the poinsettia and the chrysanthemum. By using such chemicals the chrysanthemum, which would normally grow to a height of some 3 ft (1 m) can now be evenly controlled and restricted to a height of some 15 in (38 cm). Such plants have got many obvious advantages over the taller, less manageable natural plants. In the normal course of events five to six cuttings are potted into 5-in (13-cm) half pots, and each cutting has its growing tip pinched out so that it will branch and produce a greater number of buds. The finished plant will then have somewhere in the region of twenty flowers by the time it is marketed.

The art of all-the-year-round chrysanthemum production has been developed to such a fine skill that the nurseryman can plant up his rooted cuttings and tell almost to the hour when they will be marketed, usually some ten weeks after insertion.

When pot chrysanthemums are bought in the shop they should not be accepted if they are in a too-backward condition, neither should they be accepted if they are too far advanced – the happy medium should be the aim. Once indoors a light windowsill in a cool room will suit them, and with moderate watering they will last a full six to eight weeks. When obviously past their best they can be planted out in the garden where they will grow like ordinary garden chrysanthemums as they very soon lose the dwarfing effects of the growth-restricting chemical.

Cineraria

This is a perennial that is best treated as an annual by sowing seed each year – if sowing is staggered in April, May and June the actual flowering time of the plants can be spread from December onwards. The seed should be sown in John Innes potting compost No. 1 and the seedlings potted on into small pots filled with John Innes potting compost No. 2 when they are large enough to handle. When growing them on a temperature in the region of 10°C (50°F) is required, and the location should be airy and lightly shaded. Although it is important that the compost should at no time dry out, it is equally important that it should at no time become permanently soggy, so good drainage must be provided in the pot. Plants should be potted on as they fill their pots with roots until they are in their final 5- or 6-in (13-cm) pots, thereafter regular feeding will be needed. Cinerarias are hybrids from *Senecio cruentus* and for anyone with limited space who wishes to have as many different coloured plants as possible the *nana* strain should be chosen. The *multiflora* strain will suit the person who wishes to grow the biggest and best plant in the neighbourhood, and these do develop into quite magnificent plants if feeding and potting is regularly attended to.

When purchased as mature plants for room decoration it is important that, to some extent, the conditions prevailing on the nursery where plants were grown are maintained. That is to say cinerarias should enjoy the benefits of a light windowsill position in a room that is airy and cool. After flowering they should be discarded.

35

Cissus antarctica

Citrus mitis

Cissus

As the common name kangaroo vine suggests, *Cissus antarctica* is an Australian native that has long been a popular house plant. It is a natural climber and being quite quick growing it will soon cover a wall or trellis and, indeed, is seen at its best trained in this way.

As the plants increase in height and become older it is almost inevitable that the lower leaves will lose their colour and become crisp and dry before falling off. Actually it is very much more sensible that such leaves should be removed before they become too much of an eyesore, as dead leaves hanging limply from a plant do nothing for it whatsoever. When faced with the problem of taller plants that have lost their lower leaves it is wise to cheat a bit by placing a smaller plant in front to cover up the defects. This is another reason for grouping plants together in a larger container – they complement one another and many a bare-stemmed taller plant can be camouflaged in this way.

Indoors *C. antarctica* should have a lightly shaded, cool position, as very hot rooms, particularly if plants are close to radiators, can be harmful. Keep the compost moist but not saturated and feed regularly with weak liquid fertilizer. Cuttings are easily rooted and bushier plants result if at least four cuttings are placed in each pot.

Citrus

There is ever a degree of fascination associated with growing exotic fruits in a pot, either in the greenhouse or indoors, hence the interest in lemon, orange, and similar trees. A start can be made by raising plants from pips, which will germinate fairly readily in moist compost in a high temperature. The seedlings can then be gradually potted on into larger pots. However, it must be said that this is not necessarily going to be a very rewarding exercise, as it takes many years for plants grown from pips to produce fruit. And by the time they do the plants are usually 5 or 6 ft (1·5 to 2 m) tall and have become very leggy and unattractive; certainly not the sort of plants that could be used to decorate anything other than a very large room. Another disadvantage is that these larger citrus have vicious barbs that make them difficult to handle. But, if time is on your side it might be worth trying.

A much superior plant for indoor decoration is *Citrus mitis,* the dwarf Calamondin orange, which is compact, spineless and often bears an astonishing amount of fruit in comparison to the size of the plant – incidences of plants little more than 3 ft (1 m) in height bearing over 200 fruits have been known. Most of these are imported into Europe as mature plants from the sunnier parts of the United States.

A clue to their indoor care may be found in the use of the word sunnier in the previous paragraph – it is absolutely essential that citrus plants of this kind should have the maximum sunlight that is available. This will mean placing them out of doors in full sun during the summer months of the year and having them on the lightest possible windowsill at other times. It is also important that the compost should be free draining and that it should at no time be allowed to dry out, as this will result in the leaves curling up and eventually dropping off.

Larger plants are inclined to be top heavy, and so, when potting them on, the heavier clay pots should be used as these will provide a better anchorage. The emphasis when using clay pots for plants that need free drainage must be on ensuring that a good layer of broken pots is placed in the bottom of the pot before any compost is introduced, this will prevent the hole in the bottom of the pot becoming blocked. *C. mitis* does not have a very strong root system, so it is wise to use a compost that is not too heavy. A half and half mix of John Innes potting compost No. 3 and sphagnum peat is recommended. When established in the new compost, or when plants are still in their original pots, they should be fed with a weak liquid fertilizer, but never in strong doses. Pruning is seldom necessary, but untidy growths can be removed at any time while the plant is not in flower or fruit.

Scale insects and, to some extent, caterpillars, can be troublesome and should be dealt with as soon as they are seen. Leaves that are stuck together unnaturally are an indication that caterpillars are present, and the surest method of killing them is to squeeze the leaves between finger and thumb! A sponge soaked in malathion solution should be used to wipe scale insects from leaves and stems.

Cobaea scandens

Cocos weddelliana

Clivia miniata

Clivia

Clivia miniata is a handsome plant with strong, green, strap-like leaves that should be wiped over with a damp cloth occasionally with a view to keeping up appearances, if nothing else. Besides having attractive leaves the Kaffir lily, to give clivia its common name, also obliges with clusters of orange lily-like flowers in early summer. One slight drawback is that to have a reasonable show of flowers the plants should be in pots of some 10 in (25 cm) in diameter, but as they flower very much more freely when the pots are well filled with roots, one should not be too disappointed if during the early potting-on stages plants do not respond too well in the matter of producing flowers. When clivias are transferred to their final pots it is usual to include in the compost a proportion of dry cow manure – not a very fashionable commodity in these modern times but it does help to sustain the plants.

Older plants that are not flowering so well, because they have completely exhausted the compost in which they are growing, can be divided early in the year and ˙potted up into several smaller containers using John Innes potting compost No. 2.

Clivias require protection from direct sunlight and may be placed out of doors during the summer months; in decorative pots they are excellent for adding interest to the patio area between house and garden. In winter they will get by with temperatures in the region of 10°C (50°F) if the compost is kept on the dry side, at other times 16°C (60°F) will suffice.

Cobaea

Cobaea scandens is a real space filler that can be raised with little difficulty from seed sown in the spring. Once seedlings are large enough to handle they should be potted gradually into larger pots until the 10- or 12-in (25- or 30-cm) size is reached. Thereafter they will require regular heavy doses of liquid fertilizer to keep them going, at least double the strength advised by the manufacturer.

Commonly named cups and saucers, this plant will climb vigorously and ramble all over the place if it gets a chance and is, therefore, better suited to the garden room or patio, but should not be put out of doors until all possibility of a frost has passed. Alternatively, it may be planted out in the garden – as a summer resident only. Although perennial it is much more satisfactory to raise new plants from seed each year and to discard the older overgrown plants.

As a temporary plant for covering a trellis or wall during the summer months the rapid-growing cobaea can scarcely be improved upon. To get the plant started it will be necessary to tie the initial growth to the support, thereafter natural tendrils of this climber will twine around any convenient framework. The violet-coloured flowers tend to deepen in colour as they age.

Cocos

Anything that qualifies as being unusual is worth trying as an indoor plant and recently the coconut palm, *Cocos nucifera,* has been offered as a pot plant. The principal attraction is the large coconut encased in a fibrous husk which lies on its side half buried in the compost and from the end of which the palm growth emerges. As a novelty it is amusing, but it does not seem likely that this plant will supersede the more elegant kentia palm. When well developed the coconut palm has a large bulge at the base of its trunk and in the tropics it reaches a height of 80 ft (25 m).

Much more manageable indoors and infinitely more elegant in appearance is *C. weddelliana* which rarely grows to more than a few feet (1 m) in height.

As they are slow growing cocos are inclined to be expensive and somewhat scarce. Indoors they will require a minimum temperature of at least 16°C (60°F) and a position that offers good light with some protection from direct sunlight. Plants should not be potted too frequently, but when this is undertaken it should be done in the spring of the year and the compost should be composed of something akin to two parts of John Innes potting compost No. 3 and one part of sphagnum peat.

Coleus blumei varieties

Coffea arabica

Coffea

Coffee beans growing in the parlour, maybe and maybe not, but *Coffea arabica* is surely one of the interest plants that may well add something to a collection. Anyway, even though production of beans may not be easy, the clean glossy leaves are attractive, and, as it adds to the general appearance of the plant, occasional cleaning of the leaves should not be neglected.

Coffea may be propagated from seed sown in boxes or pots of good seed compost in reasonable heat, or they may be raised more easily by taking cuttings, 4 or 5 in (10 to 13 cm) in length, and inserting them in early summer in a warm temperature. For producing small quantities of a few plants use a small propagating case.

A word of warning should be given here to say that plants of *C. arabica* will attain a height of some 6 ft (2 m) and, as they are full in appearance when well grown, they are not suitable for homes with limited space. The potting-on sequence should be gradual, and once plants are in pots of 10-in (25-cm) diameter there they should remain to be kept going by regular feeding while they are putting on new growth.

Indoors the coffee plant will require good light, while in the greenhouse it should enjoy light shade. Temperatures in the region of 18°C (65°F) will suit them best, and fluctuating high and low temperatures should be avoided. Compost in the pot should drain freely, and given this there will be a need for regular watering of plants during the spring and summer months, with rather less water being given during the winter.

Coleus

At some time or other I would imagine that just about everyone with an interest in plants has grown coleus, either as pot plants or as part of the summer bedding scheme in the garden. Some reasons for this are that they are easy to grow, they are always plentiful, and there is little difficulty in raising one's own from seed. Albeit, seed-raised plants are seldom the best of the many fine plants that are available, but they do offer a very wide range of brightly coloured foliage at very little cost. However, it must be said that in recent years there has been a vast improvement in the colour range that is available from plants raised from seed. Coleus are grown purely for their leaf colouring and it is advisable to remove the insignificant flowers as they appear. Seed should be sown in February in John Innes potting compost No. 1 in a temperature of around 18°C (65°F), and the young plants gradually potted on into slightly larger containers as they fill their existing pots with roots. Once in 5-in (13-cm) pots plants can be kept in good condition simply by feeding.

It is also possible to obtain named varieties of coleus, most of which make very fine pot plants. In order to keep these named varieties going it is usually advisable to have a few small plants coming on from cuttings so that the older ones can be disposed of when they become overgrown. Cuttings may also be taken from plants raised from seed if there are any colours of which one is especially fond. Cuttings may be taken at almost any time during the spring and throughout the summer months.

Once established, the growing tips of young plants should be removed to encourage them to branch and so acquire a more attractive, bushy habit.

When growing coleus indoors as opposed to the greenhouse it is most essential that they should enjoy the lightest possible position in the sunniest window. Growing them in poor light will be a complete waste of time as they need brighter locations if they are to retain their attractive colouring. For best results the growing temperature should not fall below 10°C (50°F) and the compost must be kept moist and the plants fed. Where space is limited it is best to keep only a few small plants over the winter for growing on in the spring, thus saving the space demanded by older specimens.

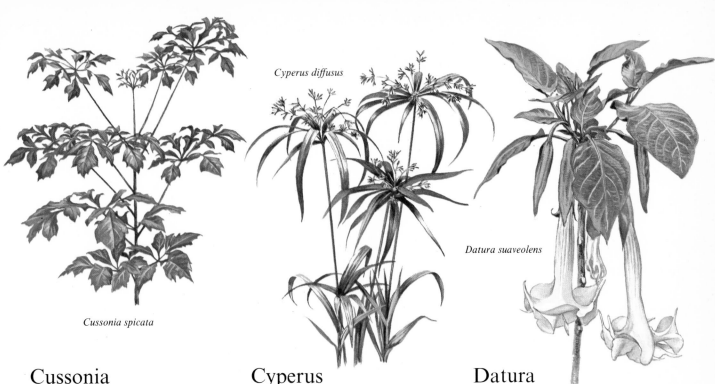

Cyperus diffusus

Cussonia spicata

Datura suaveolens

Cussonia

Some newcomers to the hobby of growing plants indoors are discouraged by the slow growth which is a characteristic of so many. *Cussonia spicata*, however, is a notable exception in that it grows almost too quickly – in fact it can almost be seen to grow when it is in agreeably warm and moist conditions, and will become a small tree in little more than two or three years from the time seed is sown. This is the ideal plant, then, for someone who has a tall empty staircase, entrance hall, or whatever, that is simply crying out for something to provide almost instant height to fill the upper reaches!

Cussonia is very easy to grow in warm, light conditions provided the compost in the pot and the surrounding area can be kept moist, and that the plants are fed and fed and fed. They should also be potted into fairly large pots as soon as the root development demands it. Use John Innes potting compost No. 3 and the elegant leaves will begin to make their way to the ceiling. The main stem and leaf stalks have an attractive grape-like bloom and the general appearance of the plant resembles that of its relatives the schefflera and heptapleurum.

For such large, seemingly robust plants, cussonias have very fragile stems that will snap off simply by leaning the plant over from its upright position, so care must be exercised when the plant is being moved.

Seed of cussonia can be sown in warm conditions as soon as it becomes available, and from the time they can be handled it is wise to keep plants on the move by potting into larger containers as soon as it becomes necessary.

Cyperus

The principal reason for most of the average indoor plants shedding leaves and taking on a generally dejected appearance is over-watering on the part of the owner, who simply cannot leave his plants alone for more than a day without thinking that the poor things must need something done to them. In fact, the majority of plants growing in pots are far happier if the compost is allowed to dry out a little between waterings.

However, in the case of the cyperus, I can quite categorically say that you can never give it too much, no matter how heavy handed you may be with the watering can. The cyperus will be perfectly happy if the pot in which it is growing is standing in water all the time.

The most common species is *Cyperus diffusus*, which normally has umbrella-like rosettes of leaves and small greenish flowers to a height of about 2 ft (60 cm), but this can be increased by potting plants in larger pots. It is a very easy plant to care for, needing little more than warm, shaded conditions in order to succeed.

Much more majestic is *C. alternifolius*, which develops the umbrella-like rosettes of leaves and flowers on very stout stems to a height of 7 ft (2·25 cm) when the roots are confined to a pot. Not a very satisfactory plant for the average home, but a superb plant at the border of a water feature in more spacious premises. Both species can be propagated by dividing the clumps, and in the case of *C. alternifolius* the leaf rosette will root if placed in a glass of water. Umbrella plant is the rather apt common name given to both kinds.

Datura

Tubs, troughs and other containers for brightening up an area of patio and terrace may be filled with all manner of plants from a wide range of colourful annuals, and garden shrubs such as hydrangeas, to something unusual and interesting such as *Datura suaveolens*. This is a tender South American shrub that reaches a height of some 6 ft (2 m) and bears exotic, pendulous, heavily scented, white trumpet-shaped flowers during the summer months. During the winter months of the year this plant will need the protection of a warm greenhouse or garden room, and should only be placed out of doors when there is no further chance of frost; needless to say, it should be taken inside again before colder weather sets in.

New plants may be propagated from cuttings taken during the spring or summer and placed in a warm propagating case. Once rooted they should be potted up in John Innes potting compost No. 2, and thereafter gradually potted into larger containers as they fill their existing pots with roots. These plants never look their best until they are in fairly large pots. Before bringing them in for the winter much of the old growth can be trimmed away so that they do not occupy too much valuable heated indoor space. Indoors they require a light position in a cool room, and need ample water in summer but should be kept on the dry side in winter. Feed while actively growing once the plants have filled their pots with roots.

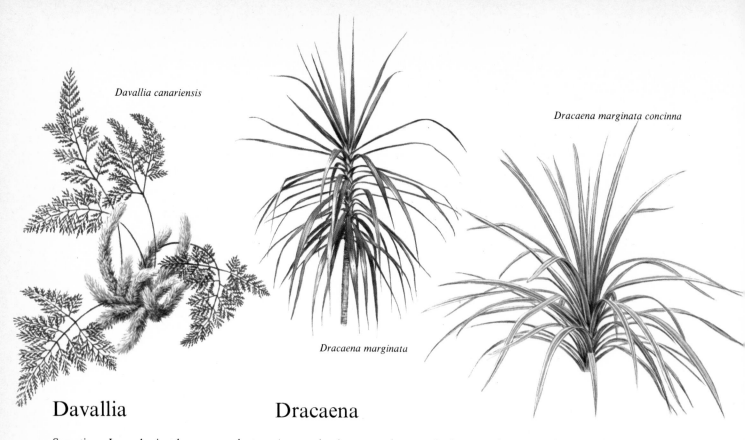

Davallia canariensis

Dracaena marginata concinna

Dracaena marginata

Davallia

Sometimes I wonder just how many plants there are on the windowsills around the world that have no commercial value whatsoever, and just how many there are that would seem to have little attraction for all but the owner of the plant. My plant of the hare's-foot fern, *Davallia canariensis*, is probably just such a plant, in that very few visitors come in and say the expected nice things that are normally said about the remainder of the plants. Why do we keep them? Why do I keep my comparatively unattractive davallia? It is sentiment, no less, someone gave it to me and much as the lady of the house wishes to put it in the dustbin it is hung on to as a reminder of that person.

However, davallia is a curiosity and very easy to manage in almost any conditions that offer a cool shady position. It has rather coarse fern foliage and the principal interest lies in the amusing rhizomatous growths that protrude from around the centre of the plant at soil level and look like fur-covered feet, hence the unusual common name. It is probably better grown as part of a collection of other plants, and will be perfectly happy on a windowsill out of doors during the summer months. Water and regular feeding will be appreciated during the summer but the plant should be kept on the dry side in winter.

Davallia is easily increased by division of the rhizomes early in the year.

Dracaena

Among the dracaenas there are both easy and difficult plants; most are tall and stately and will add that exotic touch to almost any plant collection.

Possibly the easiest to manage is *Dracaena marginata*, which has narrow pointed leaves that are green in colour with dull red margins – hence the name. These will happily survive at a temperature as low as 10°C (50°F) if the compost in the pot is kept on the dry side. Wet conditions at any time, but especially when it is cold, will be harmful to almost all the dracaenas. With *D. marginata* and all the taller growing dracaenas there is a natural tendency for them to shed their lower leaves as they increase in height, but this can often enhance rather than mar their appearance. Plants of differing height grouped together have a particular appeal.

One of the best foliage-plant introductions of recent years has been *D. m. concinna*, which is a beautiful variegated form of *D. marginata*. A little more difficult to care for it is still in short supply, but it is a plant that will add considerably to any collection. The colour of the foliage – cream and green striped with pinkish-red margins to the leaves – will vary according to the amount of light that the plant is subjected to. Very strong direct sunlight should be avoided, but good light is important if plants are to retain their rich colouring. If plants are constantly overwatered they will also lose much of their sparkle, so watering requires to be done with care, and the tendency should be towards rather too little than too much. Feeding is not desperately important, but established plants will obviously respond to regular feeding with a weak fertilizer, but it should not be overdone.

Almost all the dracaenas will be the better for potting in John Innes potting compost No. 2 or 3 rather than the very peaty composts that seem to be the vogue today. Most of the ones with thicker stems can be rooted by cutting the stems up into sections a few inches in length and pressing them into boxes or pans filled with moist peat. Even the oldest most unlikely pieces will root if the temperature is reasonable and general conditions satisfactory. Those which produce thicker, more fleshy roots may also be propagated by cutting the roots up into small sections and burying them in peat.

Other dracaenas with narrow green leaves that can be relied upon to do well in moderate conditions are *D. indivisia*, *D. parrii* and *D. volckaertii*. However, not all of these will be as easily obtainable as those first mentioned.

Some of the more difficult kinds of dracaena are dealt with on page 88, and a related plant – *Pleomele reflexa* – on page 81.

Episcia cupreata Silver Queen

Erica hyemalis

Eucalyptus gunnii

Episcia

Useful plants with attractive foliage and colourful flowers which are not too demanding in respect of space, although they do require a temperature in the region of 16°C (60°F) and a moist atmosphere if they are to do well. In these conditions cuttings of episcia root like weeds and can be grown on as ground-cover plants between other pots (in planted troughs for example), as potted plants for display on their own, or they make superb plants for hanging baskets.

There are a number of striking hybrids of *Episcia cupreata*. Most have dark, slightly quilted leaves with metallic silver or pink variegations and bell-shaped flowers in shades of scarlet and orange which appear mainly in spring and summer but can be carried at any time of the year.

The plants should be kept on the dry side in winter, and fed in the summer. As the young plants are more attractive it is a good idea to keep some cuttings coming along to replace older plants.

Another interesting plant in this genus is *E. dianthiflora,* which has soft green, naturally trailing leaves that are arranged in small clusters at intervals on the slender stems. These clusters can be snipped off at any time and used to propagate new plants. White flowers which are deeply fringed along the margins of the petals nestle amongst the foliage. This is a homely little plant that is very easily managed if kept moist, shaded and reasonably warm.

Erica

Fashions change with plants in very much the same way as they do with clothes, furniture, and almost everything else, and as a result many plants fall out of favour. The Cape heath is one of the plants that we seem to see less and less of as the winters go by, and much of the reason for this, one presumes, can be laid at the door of the poinsettia which has become so important as a Christmas-flowering plant.

Cape heath is the collective name for the South African species *Erica gracilis, E. hyemalis* and *E. nivalis*, all of which produce white or pink flowers during late autumn and winter. They are normally purchased as mature plants in flower and are not especially easy to care for once they have been introduced to dry and hot indoor conditions; it is often a problem to retain the leaves long enough for all the flowers to develop. Indoors the ideal to aim for is cool, light and moist conditions. In fact, while there is little chance of frost, plants will fare very much better out of doors on a window-sill. Care is needed with the watering and it is better to use rain water than hard tap water. Ericas are at their most attractive when a group of them are placed together in a larger container filled with moist peat.

Inch-long cuttings can be rooted in the spring in a propagating case at a temperature in the region of 20°C (68°F), using a peat and sand mixture.

Eucalyptus

Here we have another plant that is suitable for many purposes: as an indoor or greenhouse plant, for decorating the patio in an ornamental pot or, in milder climates, for planting out in the garden in a sheltered position. When eucalyptus is grown in pots the cool grey leaves of this elegant Australian gum tree present a beautiful picture, and there is the added bonus of the aromatic eucalyptus scent when a leaf is broken or crushed. *Eucalyptus gunnii* and *E. globulus* are the kinds usually offered as indoor plants.

Young plants may be raised from seeds sown in a warm propagator in the spring and potted on into small pots as soon as they are easily handled, certainly before they have made too much root in the seed pan or box. Thereafter plants should be potted on as they fill their pots with roots; it is especially important that they should not suffer any root damage in the process. Damage to stronger roots of larger plants can quite frequently be fatal.

The dark corner is most certainly not the place for this plant, as it must have good light to do well, and to show off its lovely foliage to full advantage. So, grow them in a light, cool position and keep the compost moist, while ensuring that it is well drained. Feeding is not particularly important if potting on is attended to, and when plants have become old and woody it is usually best to start again with a fresh one and to put the old friend out to grass in a sheltered spot in the garden! Plant them out in the summer so that they have a chance to become established before the winter.

Eucharis grandiflora

Euphorbia pulcherrima

Euonymus medio-pictus

Eucharis

At the mention of bulbs there are all manner of garden sorts that come to mind, but there is also a range of more tender kinds that need something much more than the average cold-garden conditions in order to survive.

The added bonus of scent is a considerable advantage where flowers are concerned and many of these tender and exotic bulbous plants are well endowed in this respect. The Amazon lily, *Eucharis grandiflora* (syn. *E. amazonica*) – what a grand selection of names – has attractive, naturally glossy leaves and heavily scented white flowers that are borne in late winter and spring on stems some 18 in (45 cm) in length. These are much coveted by the florist seeking that extra special centrepiece for the bride's bouquet.

When the flowers die down naturally the compost should be kept dry until midsummer when the bulbs are planted up again in fresh John Innes potting compost No. 3; several bulbs should be placed in a 7-in (18-cm) pot in order to conserve space and to get a good show of flowers. Once they are in growth the compost should be kept moist, and warm shaded conditions provided. Although older books on the subject mention the need for temperatures in the eighties on the Fahrenheit scale, most of these tropical bulbs will do perfectly well at around 16°C (60°F). Increase from offsets at potting time.

Euonymus

Euonymus japonicus is another of the garden plants that is acquiring a further use as an indoor plant and *E. j. aureo-variegatus*, as the name suggests, adds a warm golden colouring to the collection. In fact, considering the success of this very simple old-fashioned garden plant in the house-plant world, I wonder how long it will be before many similar plants are being adapted for the dual purpose.

Other good forms are the silver-variegated *E. j. argenteo-variegatus* and the strikingly yellow-variegated *E. j. medio-pictus*. All these can be rooted very easily by inserting several cuttings in pots of John Innes potting compost No. 1 and placing them in a warm propagating case. When potting them on into John Innes potting compost No. 2 in slightly larger pots they should all have their growing tips removed to encourage the formation of bushier plants. Pinching out the growing tips in this way is something that should be repeated at intervals as the plants are establishing themselves. In time they make superb specimens in larger pots up to the 10-in (25-cm) size, and can well form part of the plant decoration on the patio.

If they do grow too large they can then, with advantage, be planted out in the garden. Indoors, provided they have good light and the compost is kept moist they will present few problems. It will do no harm to give established plants regular applications of weak liquid fertilizer.

Euphorbia

There are many plants in the spurge family (*Euphorbiaceae*) and far and away the most important as far as potted plants are concerned is *Euphorbia pulcherrima*, the Christmas flower that is much better known as the poinsettia. The improved strains of recent years have firmly established these as the most popular of Christmas-flowering plants, and their lasting value indoors ensures that they are in ever greater demand.

Red is the most popular colour, but there are white and pink kinds that offer a pleasing change. When purchasing a plant it is best to seek out a good supplier with agreeably warm premises, as cold conditions existing for even a temporary period can have a detrimental effect on the plants at a later date. Thereafter, in the home, they require a temperature in the region of 16 to 20°C (60 to 68°F) and a position that affords maximum light. Too much water can be harmful, and it is suggested that the compost should be allowed to dry out a little between each application. Feeding should not be necessary while the plants are in flower, but a little weak fertilizer occasionally will do no harm.

Plants may last for anything from six weeks to six months, and die back naturally after flowering. When this happens the main stem must be cut back to about 4 in (10 cm) from the oldest growth and the compost must be allowed to dry out and should then be left almost completely dry for several weeks; until such time, in fact, as new growth is evident where the leaves were previously. When growth starts the compost is watered and the plant is potted into

Exacum affine

Fatshedera lizei

Exacum

Fatshedera

fresh John Innes potting compost No. 2 or 3 depending on its size. When the plant has produced several new leaves the growing tip of each new shoot should be removed.

Good light is always an essential requirement, but from mid-September onwards poinsettias should only be subjected to natural daylight, as additional artificial light in the evening will prevent the formation of flower buds by encouraging the plants to continue growing. However, it must be added that plants seldom do as well in subsequent years indoors as they do during their first year while growing on the nursery, but there is a decided sense of achievement in being able to encourage them to produce their red bracts for a second time.

Cuttings of the poinsettia root with little difficulty during the summer months. These should be 4 to 6 in (10 to 15 cm) in length and allowed to dry at the point of cutting before being inserted in peaty compost.

There is one other euphorbia that the house-plant grower is likely to come across and that is the crown of thorns, *E. milii*, which is a much less pleasant spurge, having a succulent stem from which vicious barbs protrude. It is also somewhat sparsely furnished with small green leaves and produces small, but attractive, reddish-pink bracts during the summer months. Plants should be kept light, warm and on the dry side most of the time. Cuttings a few inches in length should be removed and left for a day or two to dry before being inserted in small pots of John Innes potting compost No. 1. See also page 169.

Exacum affine is an attractive bushy little plant with glossy green foliage and lots of pale blue, fragrant flowers that are carried for a long period from June onwards. It can be raised from seed with little difficulty, this being sown in the spring and the seedlings gradually potted on until they are in 4-in (10-cm) pots.

Strictly speaking exacum is a perennial and, therefore, may also be propagated from cuttings but more satisfactory results are obtained if fresh plants are raised from seed annually. Caring for plants indoors presents few problems if cool, light conditions can be provided.

In keeping with many of the smaller and cheaper flowering plants, the exacums are much used by florists for planting in containers filled with a mixed selection of plants. The majority of the plants in the containers are usually foliage ones that will continue to grow in the same container for a surprisingly long period, while the flowering plant is included to colour the scene for a more temporary length of time. Having been given, or having purchased a planted bowl of this kind it is necessary to water it sparingly as these ornamental bowls seldom have drainage holes to get rid of surplus water. Also, when small flowering plants have gone past their best they should be replaced with a similar fresh plant or with a small foliage plant.

These are tall, elegant foliage plants with dark green leaves that are not at all difficult to look after, though they have a tendency to develop brown leaves which are eventually shed as plants age. They are not natural climbers, and if a tall plant is required then it must be provided with a stake to which it can be secured as it increases in height. In the greenhouse fatshedera, if not staked, seems quite content to grow along the floor, winding around and about any objects that may get in the way. Providing adequate and secure stakes for larger plants is a task that is frequently neglected, which is a pity as the plants look so much better for having them.

Fatshedera lizei is the proper name, and there is a variegated type (*F. l. variegata*) which, unfortunately, is a little less easy to care for. The plant has resulted from a cross between *Fatsia japonica* and *Hedera helix hibernica*, and from the two parents we get the name fatshedera; fatsia and hedera belonging to the same family *Araliaceae*. This is also the reason why it is possible to graft small cuttings of hedera (ivy) to the stems of the more stately fatshederas. Once the grafts have taken the leaves of the fatshedera can be removed so that in time one has a small tree with showers of ivy leaves coming away from it.

Indoors, provide good light with protection from the sun and a reasonable temperature, and water and feed moderately. New plants are not difficult to raise from cuttings either of a single leaf with a piece of stem attached or of firm tips.

Ficus elastica robusta

Ficus lyrata

Ficus elastica schryveriana

Ficus

Ficus is a large genus which encompasses a tremendous assortment of plants from the edible figs to the well-known rubber plants of house-plant fame. And when it comes to house plants there is something here for everyone with an interest in foliage plants. There are large plants, little plants, green ones and variegated ones. Some of them are very easy to care for, while others will tax the skill of the most accomplished plantsman. We hear it said that in order to be successful as a foliage plant there is a considerable advantage if the plant has naturally glossy leaves, and in the ficus family there are many such plants. Although naturally glossy leaves are, indeed, an advantage, they quickly lose their lustre when growing in dusty surroundings, and in order to keep them up to standard it is necessary to clean the leaves periodically. A regular light dusting does glossy leaved plants no harm, but the frequent use of chemical leaf-cleaning agents should be avoided, and at no time should the soft new leaves of any plants be cleaned as these are very easily damaged. A damp sponge is all that is needed to maintain a reasonably clean appearance, with an occasional application of a proprietary leaf cleaner for that extra special lustre.

Our old friend *Ficus elastica*, the rubber plant, has had a number of important changes since the first narrow, droopy leaved ones became popular as house plants. Following *F. elastica* there was *F. e. decora* with stiffer and more rounded leaves. Currently *F. e. robusta* rules the roost and it is a vastly superior plant both in appear-

ance and lasting quality. However, nothing seems to stand still in horticulture and we now have *F. e.* Abidjan (Black Prince), with very dark, almost black leaves, trying to make the running. No matter how successful the latter may be, like its predecessors it will in the minds of most purchasers still be a simple rubber plant. And to do well the simple rubber plant needs coolish conditions [10 to 16°C (50 to 60°F)] and reasonable light and, above all, it hates to have its root system permanently saturated. Allow the compost to dry a little between each watering and in winter, when growth is less active, water should be given very much more sparingly. Feed with a weak liquid fertilizer while the plant is producing new leaves.

Similar treatment is also applicable to the easiest of the variegated rubber plants, *F. e. schryveriana*. On account of the added colour they offer variegated plants are, on the whole, more popular than their green counterparts. However, this is not so in respect of *F. e. schryveriana* which is green and dull mustard in colour, although the colour varies considerably from plant to plant depending on the light conditions in which they have been grown. The problem with this plant is that, where variegated plants generally are the result of a virus of some kind, this variegated ficus often looks as if it is suffering from a virus attack. So it is not so popular, which is unfortunate as well grown plants can be particularly impressive, especially when three or more stems are potted in the same large pot. As with all the ficus with larger leaves propa-

gation of new plants is effected by cutting the plant up into individual leaves with a piece of stem attached and inserting them in a peat and sand mixture in very warm beds that do not fall below 20°C (68°F).

For rubber plants potting on is only necessary every second year as a rule, and once plants are in pots of about 10 in (25 cm) in size they can be kept going simply by regular feeding. Plants that have become too tall for their head room can be reduced in height by having the top section removed with a pair of secateurs; this will encourage the bottom half to branch. Alternatively, the plant can be air-layered, an operation that is simpler than it sounds. As the top of the existing plant will form the new one, begin by removing a leaf at a point on the stem which will give a suitably sized new plant. Then make an upward cut about halfway through the stem at the point where the leaf joined it; insert a matchstick to keep the cut open and dust the area with rooting powder to encourage root development. The area surrounding the cut should then be bound with wet sphagnum moss which should be tied in position with clear polythene. Make sure that the moss is completely enclosed by the polythene and that this is sealed around the stem above and below the wounded area. After about two months, when the moss is well filled with roots, the main stem should be cut just below the moss and the severed end allowed to dry before being potted in the conventional manner. There are a number of other ways of going about this interesting operation, but I do know that this one works!

44

Ficus diversifolia

Ficus benjamina

Ficus pumila

The section of plant that is left will begin to grow again to give a rubber plant with a standard effect that can be quite attractive.

Ficus lyrata, the fiddle-leaf fig, is probably the most stately of all the ficus plants that are used for decorative purposes, and when well grown it has few rivals among the larger indoor plants. However, getting it to grow well is not the easiest of tasks, as it requires a minimum temperature of at least 18°C (65°F) and spacious surroundings that are able to cope with its majestic size. Potting on regularly is essential and really large plants may eventually be in pots that resemble dustbins. These are necessary to accommodate the very vigorous root system. Keeping the plants in smaller containers will restrict their growth, but they seldom do as well and have a tendency to lose their lower leaves. The common name of fiddle-leaf fig is derived from the shape of the leaf which resembles a violin body. The leaves have a superb natural gloss and the veins are faintly yellow in colour. Much water and feeding are needed by vigorous plants.

Berried plants are interesting and there is a limited number, no more than a trickle, of *F. diversifolia* offered for sale. These are much more compact plants with small leaves and masses of berries that are ever present on the plant and develop at a very early age. They may reach a height of 6 ft (2 m), but it is much more usual to see plants several years old that are no more than 2 ft (60 cm) tall. They are reasonably easy to look after, needing slightly more warmth – 16°C (60°F) – than the ordinary

rubber plant but otherwise similar care.

Another plant which needs a minimum temperature of 16°C (60°F) is *F. benjamina*, the weeping fig. Although growth may be restricted by growing plants in smaller pots, this is a plant that will reach tree-like proportions in about ten years when growing conditions are ideal. The average home owner should not, however, live in fear of the roof being lifted off the homestead as room conditions are seldom ideal and growth is usually very much slower. Almost all the ficus may be purchased as small plants to be grown on indoors, and if they get out of hand their growing stems can be quite severely cut back to a more manageable size. Loss of some leaves lower down on the plant may result, but healthy plants get over the setback surprisingly quickly. When moved to a new environment, either when it is first acquired or its position is changed in the home, the weeping fig has a tendency to produce yellow leaves which are eventually shed. However, provided conditions are suitable it should soon settle down and grow away.

Of all the ficus plants, *F. benghalensis* (not illustrated) is one of the most vigorous growing and really does need some space in which to expand as it branches freely and attractively in all directions. Alas, dull, down-covered leaves reduce the appeal of this very fine plant – glossy green leaves are ever popular.

Lovely pale green leaves on wiry creeping stems do not conjure up the usual picture of a ficus plant, but that is the appearance and habit of the delightful creeping fig,

F. pumila. This is mostly sold in small pots and is ideal for mixing with other plants in troughs and similar containers. In containers that are filled with peat in which plant pots are plunged, the creeping fig does well if a few plants are spaced out at intervals in the container and the creeping strands of growth are allowed to wander over the surface of the peat to provide an attractive green carpet. A shaded, warm and moist location is ideal as it abhors direct sunlight and being allowed to dry out.

Fortunately ficus plants are not troubled too much by pests – their main difficulty arises when the compost in the pot becomes waterlogged from too frequent watering and the roots rot and die as a result. Once roots have become inactive and the compost waterlogged it takes a considerable time for the compost to dry out but this can be speeded up by removing the plant from its pot and standing the rootball on top of the upturned pot. This method of drying the soil in the pot applies to any plant that has sufficient root to hold the compost together.

When potting plants into larger containers use John Innes potting compost No. 2 for smaller plants and John Innes potting compost No. 3 for larger plants – the addition of a small amount of sphagnum peat will usually encourage quicker rooting.

Some of the more difficult ficus will be found on page 89.

45

Fuchsia hybrids

Furcraea foetida

Fuchsia

The possession of a small greenhouse or garden room means that the indoor gardener gains a considerable advantage when growing indoor plants over the householder whose only assets are the walls surrounding him. There is the benefit of having somewhere to put plants that have lost their lustre out of sight until they recover, and with a greenhouse it is possible to grow a much wider variety of plants which can be brought into the home as they mature. One of these is the fuchsia. This is, perhaps, the best flowering pot plant of them all, in that it is easy to care for and quite simply flowers for months on end. With a small mixed collection and a greenhouse that is kept warm in spring, these plants can be in flower from March to October and there is no need to heat the greenhouse from about the end of May. But a minimum temperature of about 5°C (41°F) will be needed to see plants through the winter months and get them off to a good start in the spring.

There are so many different sorts to choose from it would seem futile to offer a list here; far better to browse through the catalogue of a specialist fuchsia grower. It would also help to inspect a collection growing in someone else's greenhouse, and perhaps get some first-hand advice at the same time.

Propagation is by cuttings which will root at any time of the year in very average conditions. Cuttings 3 to 4 in (8 to 10 cm) in length are the best; these should have one or two of the lower leaves removed and any flowers or flower buds that may be present before being inserted in pots. Once rooted they can be gradually potted on as required using John Innes potting compost No. 2. They do respond well to regular feeding once in their final pots, but be careful not to feed plants until they are well rooted. During the winter months plants will need to be rested when they will require much less water and no fertilizer and should be kept in cooler temperatures although free from frost.

Fuchsias may be grown as conventional pot plants by removing early tip growth to make a shapely plant; more vigorous varieties can be trained to climb the greenhouse wall and along the roof to give a breathtaking display. Stems of bolder types can be run up on one leader to a height of 3 to 4 ft (1 to 1·25 m) before removing the growing point and allowing the plant to branch. Thereafter frequent removal of growing tips will produce mop-headed standard plants. And there are superb varieties such as Cascade and Marinka that trail down and give a wonderful show in hanging baskets.

In the spring older plants should be trimmed back to a few inches from the main stem, and at the same time much of the old soil is removed and the plant repotted in the same container using fresh compost. It is then possible to have a succession of them indoors where they should occupy the lightest possible window in a cool room, but do not expect them to last too long before they begin to drop their flowers.

Furcraea

There are a number of these succulent-type plants that produce large basal rosettes of growth and are not unlike overgrown agaves in appearance. However, it is unlikely that one will be offered any plant other than *Furcraea selloa marginata* or, on the very rare occasion, *F. foetida*. The latter is a more delicate plant and has the advantage of smooth-edged leaves as opposed to the spiny fleshy leaves of the first mentioned. Both have attractive cream and green variegation.

Their spreading habit demands that furcraeas should have reasonable space in which to grow and, for those with spines, they should be out of harm's way – certainly not in the flow of traffic in a busy home or office. As they have succulent leaves that retain a great deal of moisture it is not necessary to water the compost too frequently, and over the winter months they will get along with very little water. In winter a minimum temperature of 10°C (50°F) is advised, and during the summer months a little bit of what may seem like neglect in respect of watering will not go amiss. During the summer they are ideal as decorative plants with that exotic touch for enhancing the appearance of the patio.

Propagation is simply done by removing small offsets from the side of older plants and potting them up individually in small pots filled with a free-draining compost. A compost of this sort is essential for plants at all stages of growth, and extra sand or mortar rubble should be added to established composts such as John Innes potting compost No. 2.

Gloxinia (*Sinningia speciosa*)

Grevillea robusta

Gynura sarmentosa

Gloxinia

Gloxinia (syn. *Sinningia*) is another of the plants that is interesting to raise from seed sown early in the year. The seed is sown very thinly on the surface of seed-sowing compost in a temperature of some 16°C (60°F), but remember not to sow too much seed as the plants when mature take up a considerable amount of space.

When large enough to handle the seedlings should be potted into small pots filled with a mixture of equal parts of John Innes potting compost No. 2 and sphagnum peat; a mix of this sort should be used at all potting stages as gloxinias seldom do well in heavy composts. The flowers, which are mostly produced in late summer, have a velvet texture and are available in many bright and attractive colours and in double as well, as single forms. All have been developed by hybridization from *Sinningia speciosa*. After flowering, plants may be stood out of doors in a sheltered place and kept moist until the leaves die down when they should be brought in and kept dry until the turn of the year. The corms, which will have formed in the centre of the pot, can then be repotted in fresh compost to grow on for a further year. Plants of particular merit may be increased by means of leaf cuttings inserted in a propagating case in early summer, mature leaves with a piece of stalk attached are not difficult to root.

For the less adventurous, plants in flower may be purchased throughout the summer and are best placed on a light windowsill and watered regularly without allowing the compost to become totally saturated for very long periods.

Grevillea

Grevillea robusta, an Australian native, is one of those very ordinary plants that tends to be a little despised when mentioned in association with other house plants, and I wonder why. It may be raised without difficulty from seed and is very easy to grow, needing no special care other than the standard requirement of reasonable warmth, good light and moderate attention in respect of watering and feeding. It may even be planted out in the garden to enhance the other features during the summer months and, provided it is taken indoors before frosts occur, it will come to no harm.

Another name commonly given to the grevillea is silk oak, which must relate to the silky appearance of the foliage, particularly when it is disturbed by a gentle breeze. Being of vigorous growing habit it is essential that feeding is not neglected and that plants are potted into slightly larger containers as soon as the pots have become filled with roots. Rather than put plants into very large unwieldy pots it is usually better to have a few younger plants coming along that can take the place of the older one. The latter can then be disposed of or donated to a friend with more space to accommodate the monster!

Gynura

The purple, hair-covered leaves of this plant have an immediate attraction that makes it an instant seller, and it can be most decorative when placed in a light sunny window position. Besides being attractive as a conventional pot plant it is also effective when planted up in a group in a larger, shallow container, or when a number are grouped together to form a well-filled hanging basket. Gynura should be fed occasionally and watered moderately at all times.

Having said all these nice things it must be stated now that it is not my idea of a nice indoor plant (but that statement won't deter purchasers), as the orange-yellow flowers, produced in some quantity during the summer months, have a very unpleasant smell that can be most disagreeable. There are two varieties commonly available, *Gynura aurantiaca* and *G. sarmentosa*. The latter is an attractive trailing plant and is the one to go for if you have a choice.

Gynura grow vigorously and make lots of roots, so very soon become pot bound and in need of potting on, and this is one reason why plants should not be retained for a second year. It is very much better to raise new ones from cuttings each year and to have a few on hand to fill the gaps made by departing older specimens. Incidentally, removing the flowers as soon as they open, or at the bud stage, will help to make the sitting room a sweeter place to live in!

Hedera helix Gold Heart

Hedera helix Adam

Hedera helix Lutzii

Hedera

At first sight the ivies (the common name for hedera) may seem ideal trailing plants to have in a room, but this is not necessarily the case as they are plants that must have cool conditions indoors if they are to do anything at all. In hot conditions the foliage tends to shrivel up and turn brown before falling off, so they will only be satisfactory where the temperature centres around 10°C (50°F).

Ivies are dual-purpose plants in that they can be planted out in the garden when they have outlived their life as indoor plants. Out of doors they make ground cover for planting under shrubs to keep down weeds, or they will make excellent wall plants that require little attention, and as foliage for use in flower arrangements outdoor ivies will provide an almost endless supply of material.

Besides these uses ivies are particularly attractive when seen in hanging baskets, either combined with other plants or planted on their own and allowed to trail down from all sides. And at this point it may be wise to consider the use and value of wall brackets for displaying trailing plants. One thing for sure is that the position the brackets are to occupy on the wall should be given some thought before any nails are driven in. They must be located where the plants will get a reasonable amount of light in which to grow, and they should not be too high on the wall as this will make subsequent maintenance difficult. Also, it is important that there should be some sort of drip tray or saucer for the plant pot to stand in to prevent drips falling

on furniture and carpets. But the most essential factor of all when positioning wall plants is to make sure that they are not directly over radiators or similar heating appliances, as the hot air from such heaters will quickly put paid to almost all plant life.

All the hederas are started from cuttings inserted directly into the pots in which they are intended to grow. Smaller-leaved sorts are prepared from strands that are cut up into sections each with two leaves attached – the soft growth at the tip of the strand seldom does as well as the leaf cuttings. Prepared pieces are inserted in 3½-in (9-cm) pots filled with a reasonably peaty potting compost – John Innes potting compost No. 1 – at least five pieces going into each pot. If available a propagating case may be used, but equally good results will ensue simply by placing a sheet of thin clear polythene directly on top of the cuttings. The covering can remain there until the cuttings have rooted, but regular inspection should be made to ensure that everything is in order under the polythene. Once a few new leaves have been produced the tips of all the cuttings should be removed and the plants spaced out to allow a little air between the pots and foliage. When plants of ivy stand close together for too long there is a tendency for them to rot.

Though ivies are very good as garden-wall plants and equally fine as house plants in cool conditions, they can be a problem in temperatures that are in excess of 16°C (60°F). The principal problem is that they are very susceptible to attack from red spider mite and are especially vulnerable in

the hot, dry conditions which are particularly suited to the well-being of the minute red spider. Regular spraying of the undersides of the leaves with an appropriate insecticide will help to keep red spider in check, but it is a very difficult pest to stamp out completely. On ivies their presence is indicated when the outer edges of the leaves become dry and brown and show a tendency to curl, there will also be very small pinprick holes on the undersides of the leaves. The mites can be detected with a magnifying glass but are difficult to see with the naked eye.

There are some three ivies with larger leaves that are sold as house plants; *Hedera canariensis* (syn. *H.* Gloire de Marengo), with cream, grey and yellow foliage, *H.* Goldleaf, with a small amount of dull yellow colouring in the centre of the dark green leaves, and *H. maculata*, with green and cream mottled foliage.

Hedera helix, a British native plant, is a smaller-leaved type of ivy which has a large number of named varieties in a range of leaf colours and shapes. *H. h.* Chicago, *H. h.* Minigreen, *H. h. cristata* and *H. h.* Pittsburgh have green foliage, while selected plants of Chicago have lovely cream and green foliage. One of the best of the *helix* ivies for growing indoors is Adam, which has grey and green variegations. Others with slightly larger leaves and similar colouring are *H. h.* Heisse, *H. h.* Glacier and *H. h.* Little Diamond.

H. h. Jubilee is also known as *H. h.* Gold Heart, and it makes one of the finest purely foliage wall plants ever likely to be seen

48

Hedera canariensis

Heliotropium peruvianum

Helxine soleirolii

Heliotropium

Helxine

growing out of doors. The adventitious roots which form along the stem keep the growth hugged tightly to the wall of the garden or of the sun room, and in this situation the leaves will become very much larger and more colourful. When growing this variety as a pot plant it is essential that the pot is well filled with cuttings if a plant of full appearance is required, as it is not as free branching as most other ivies. When the growing tip is removed the plant simply produces one more shoot at the next leaf axil down the stem.

With mustard and green foliage *H. h.* Lutzii is the very opposite and branches with the utmost freedom when tip growth is pinched out. Like most of the *Hedera helix* varieties it is little trouble to care for provided its temperature requirements can be met.

The fragrance of the purple flowers is the principal attraction of the heliotrope, *Heliotropium peruvianum*. They are usually seen as pyramid or standard-grown plants forming the centrepiece of the local parks department's summer display, or they may be seen trained against the wall inside a greenhouse. But there is another somewhat neglected use to which they can be put and that is as pot plants on the sunny windowsill.

For this purpose, cuttings should be taken in June or July instead of in the spring and grown on, any flowers that may appear up until the end of September being pinched out. Grown in this way it is possible to enjoy the fragrance of the flowers indoors in early winter. It is better to raise fresh plants from cuttings each summer and to either discard the old plants or keep them for stock. New plants may also be raised from seed but this may not be such a satisfactory way of obtaining good specimens.

Standard plants can be made by allowing a single shoot to grow upwards, supported by a cane, while gradually removing the lower growth until such time as there is a stem 3 to 4 ft (1 to 1·25 m) in height with about 6 in (15 cm) of growth at the top. The top growth should have the growing points removed from all sideshoots to give a bushy and compact appearance.

Given reasonable treatment – watering freely in spring and summer, moderately in autumn and sparingly in winter – heliotrope grown in pots are not difficult to care for. When potting, John Innes potting compost No. 3 with a little extra peat is the best compost to use.

To make life easier for the people who wish to have a few plants indoors without necessarily wanting to delve too deeply into their nomenclature, many plants have common names as well as their official ones. *Helxine soleirolii* is fortunate in that it has two such names; mind-your-own-business and baby's tears. Most common names come about for descriptive reasons, so why mind-your-own-business? It is said that this is one of the plants that you cannot meddle with by pushing your fingers into the foliage without being discovered, as the indentation made will be left there for some time afterwards – so beware!

The dense mass of tiny green leaves is excellent for smothering other weeds under the greenhouse staging, and also makes attractive mounds of colour when plants are grown in pots. Very easy to care for, all helxines seem to require is moisture and an agreeable windowsill on which to grow. When they become overgrown new plants are simply produced by preparing a fresh pot of compost and pushing a few pieces of the old plant into it. In fact, the ease with which new plants of helxine can be produced may well appeal to children and arouse their interest in growing things.

Hibiscus rosa-sinensis hybrid

Heptapleurum arboricola

Hosta sieboldiana

Heptapleurum

In reasonable conditions *Heptapleurum arboricola*, commonly named the parasol plant, grows at a fairly prodigious rate and is not difficult to care for. Even so, the occasional apparently quite healthy plant will collapse and die for no good reason. The leaves are a pleasant green and radiate from the leaf stalk like the fingers of a hand. In appearance the plant is not unlike a miniature schefflera, and has the same graceful open habit of growth. A main difference, however, is that the parasol plant can be induced to branch freely from lower leaf axils by removing its growing tip, whereas the schefflera if similarly treated simply produces a single shoot at the topmost remaining leaf bud.

In reasonable growing conditions heptapleurums will quickly fill their pots with roots, so potting on of young plants should be undertaken annually, while older plants may go for two years between pottings until they are in 10-in (25-cm) pots, when regular feeding will sustain them. Pruning presents no problems as the stems can be cut back to more manageable size at any time, but early summer is probably best as plants will then make new growth fairly quickly. Trimmings can be used for propagation; pieces of stem with one leaf attached should be inserted in a peat and sand mixture in reasonable warmth.

Indoors the principal needs for successful growing are good light (with protection from sun), moist and warm surroundings and regular feeding once established.

Hibiscus

These hard, woody, tropical shrubs that are hybrids of *Hibiscus rosa-sinensis* become more and more popular as it is realized that they are not nearly so difficult to care for as they might seem to be at first appearance. The green leaves are nothing to sing about, but the exotic single or double flowers in red, pink, yellow or lemon more than make up for this. The one drawback is that individual flowers last for little more than 24 hours, but there is a continual succession of them throughout summer into autumn.

The plants may be kept short by pruning after flowering or they may be allowed to grow into large bushes. Even standards can be made by allowing a strong central stem to grow upwards to 3 or 4 ft (1 to 1·25 m) before the growing tip is removed.

To do well they need good light, plenty of water during the growing season, and applications of feed. The room temperature should be in the region of 16°C (60°F). Hibiscus will retain most of their leaves in winter if the compost is kept moist, or it can be dried out so that the plants lose all their foliage and rest for the winter. They can then be started into growth in February simply by adding water to the dry compost. Potting may be undertaken in the spring and the compost should have some body to it, John Innes potting compost No. 3 is suggested. Propagate from cuttings of new growth in spring. Greenfly is sometimes a problem and should be treated as soon as noticed on the new young growth. In locations where there is poor light, or wide fluctuations in temperature or the amount of water given bud dropping may occur.

Hosta

Earlier mention was made of the advantage of having a greenhouse to provide a succession of plants for brightening up the indoor scene. Hostas can also be used for the purpose of providing that additional spot of colour in the spring, and for this a greenhouse is not required as plants can be taken in from the garden. The many beautiful hostas with their most attractive leaves are seen at their best when growing in moist, shaded places.

For indoor decoration select the more compact plants with the most pleasing colour. When dividing clumps of hosta in the autumn some of the divided sections should be put in 5- or 7-in (13- or 18-cm) pots which are subsequently buried in the garden. In the spring, with their fresh new growth, these pots can be lifted and taken indoors where they should have a cool, light position. Feed regularly while the plants are in active growth and water fairly freely. Their indoor life is very much of a temporary nature and the plants should be replaced in the garden when they have gone past their best in the home – remove the pot before planting!

The pastime of flower arranging has attracted a tremendous following and there is a never-ending search for unusual foliage that is colourful and lasts well when cut from the plant. Here the hosta is very much favoured and as a result has become a very popular garden plant in recent years.

Hoya carnosa variegata

Hydrangea macrophylla
Hortensia variety

Hoya

In the greenhouse *Hoya carnosa* is one of those plants that is sometimes seen free planted in the ground with its growth trained up the wall and along the ridge. In such warm and agreeable locations the growth of hoya can be positively rampant. However, when growing strongly in this way it will often flower less freely than when the roots are confined to a pot, so there is little to be gained, and a great deal more work in keeping the thing under control.

The same lesson applies indoors – do not be tempted to put plants into pots that are too large unless, of course, getting the maximum amount of growth is preferable to flowers. Indoors, plants should be fanned out on a trellis with the growth twisting about to fill in the framework. The clustered, star-shaped flowers of the hoya have an almost unnatural waxy texture that is most attractive and has earned for the plant the common name of wax plant. Hoyas need good light indoors, moist compost and a moderate temperature; established plants benefit from feeding while actively growing.

There is also a variegated form, *H. c. variegata,* with cream and green leaves, that is rather shy of flowering, but the attractive foliage more than compensates for this. Growth is also very much slower, but plants will require similar conditions and treatment to that recommended above. With both plants a watch should be kept for mealy bugs which may establish themselves between the twining stems.

Increase by firm cuttings with two leaves and 1 or 2 in (2·5 to 5 cm) of stem inserted into peaty compost.

Hydrangea

Hydrangea is another example of a dual-purpose plant that may be grown in a pot or in the garden; certainly it may be purchased as a spring-flowering plant and enjoyed while in flower before being planted out of doors.

From the time it is acquired as a pot plant it is essential that the compost should at no time dry out. The hydrangea, in fact, is one of the few plants that does not object to being watered every day while it is in active growth – whereas the majority of indoor plants soon show their displeasure if given such treatment. Also essential is the need for good light and reasonably cool conditions.

Following flowering hydrangeas may well form part of the patio scene out of doors, and they will develop into fairly large shrubs in time if potted on regularly and eventually established in garden tubs or large ornamental pots. After flowering the dead heads should be removed with about 6 in (15 cm) of stem in order to improve the overall appearance of the plant. Plants can be potted into slightly larger pots after they have flowered using John Innes potting compost No. 2 or 3 depending on the size of the pot.

Over winter the plants should be kept fairly dry and in a minimum temperature in the region of 7°C (45°F), and may be encouraged to flower earlier than normal by increasing the temperature in January and the amount of water. New plants can be made from cuttings taken in April, preferably from blind shoots; the best flowers are always to be had from plants which have been raised afresh in this way each year.

When planting out in the garden a position should be chosen that will provide the plants with a little shelter from spring frosts as these damage tender growth and lessen the chances of a good display of flowers. It is also important to water the area around where the plant is to be put, and to water the plant well before it is taken from its pot.

The hydrangeas used for pot-plant culture are varieties of the double-flowered or Hortensia group of *Hydrangea macrophylla.* These are the kinds with domed heads of bloom in shades of blue, purple, pink, red or white. However, an interesting fact is that although to some extent the colour depends on variety, good blue flowers are only produced when the plant is growing in acid soil or compost. In alkaline or neutral soils the flower colours range from bluish pink to pink and crimson; white varieties remain white whatever the soil. In order to get blue flowers, therefore, the compost will need to be treated with one of the proprietary 'blueing' compounds or with alum.

When plants grown in pots are about to flower the branches tend to become heavy and bend over; to counteract this tendency a single thin cane should be pushed into the soil to support each branch and the head of the plant tied to the cane just below the flower.

51

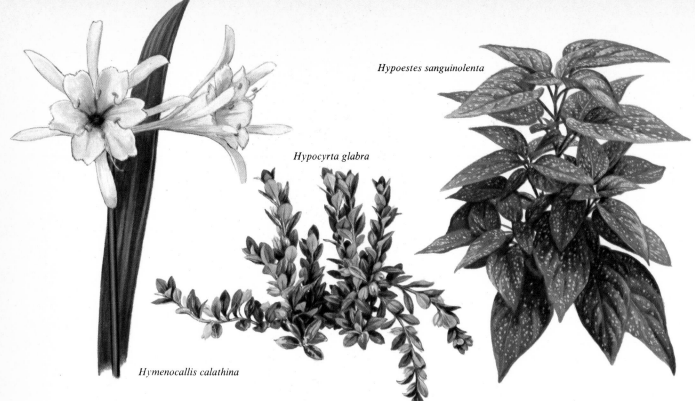

Hypoestes sanguinolenta

Hypocyrta glabra

Hymenocallis calathina

Hymenocallis

These are tropical bulbous plants that require temperatures in the region of 20°C (68°F) if they are to do well, although they will tolerate slightly lower temperatures in winter when the compost is kept drier than at other times. Mature plants in 10-in (25-cm) pots grow to a height of about 3 ft (1 m) and have a similar spread. The leaves are 4 to 5 in (10 to 13 cm) wide and are strap like in appearance; the principal attraction, however, is the flowers which are carried on stems about 3 ft (1 m) tall. In *Hymenocallis calathina* these are a beautiful clear white and are very heavily scented, quite strong enough for the fragrance of one plant to pervade the atmosphere of a large greenhouse or dwelling house. Unfortunately, the flowers last for only about ten days.

Hymenocallis do set seed but the usual method of propagation is by means of offsets which may be teased away from the side of the parent bulb when they are large enough. In the early stages plants can be potted on as they fill their pots with roots until such time as they are in 10-in (25-cm) pots when feeding will keep them going for several years without any further repotting. After plants have been in these larger pots for some time it is usually advisable to divide the bulbs and plant them up individually in smaller pots. Feed established plants regularly and keep the compost moist but avoid too wet conditions in winter.

Acquiring plants is not easy, and one is advised to keep an eye open for them in the catalogue of the specialist who deals in unusual plants.

Hypocyrta

Hypocyrta glabra is a neat plant with lots of little, fat, dark green, glossy leaves and unusual-shaped orange flowers that give the plant the common name of clog plant. They are grown from cuttings a few inches in length that have had the lower two or three leaves removed. Put several cuttings in a small pot filled with John Innes potting compost No. 1 and keep them warm and moist in a propagating case. If a propagating case is not available, a polythene bag can be used for a small number of cuttings. The best way to go about this is to insert the cuttings, water them in and then put a short cane in the centre of the pot and pop the whole lot into the polythene bag, sealing it at the top. Sealing the bag will cut down transpiration and the cuttings will root much more quickly – it will be wise, however, to have a peep inside occasionally to make sure that everything is in good order.

The polythene bag should be removed at the first signs of growth and, once well rooted in the small pots, the plants can be transferred to slightly larger pots using a mix of two parts of John Innes potting compost No. 2 and one part of sphagnum peat. If plants are plentiful it would be worth trying the experiment of placing four or five potfuls in a hanging basket or a fairly large shallow container. Hypocyrta needs a light position in rooms that are not too hot and moderate watering. The flowers are produced over a long period in spring and summer.

Hypoestes

Hypoestes sanguinolenta is one plant for which I cannot raise very much enthusiasm, but it is easily grown from seed and so finds its way into many a home or greenhouse. Seed should be sown in the spring, the seedlings being potted on as soon as they are large enough to handle. Alternatively, it can be raised from cuttings taken in the spring or summer and rooted in a propagator. In both cases once the plants have attained a height of some 6 in (15 cm) the growing points can be removed to encourage branching.

Hypoestes is mainly remarkable for its unusual foliage. The oval green leaves are heavily splashed with bright pink spots, which is the reason for the very descriptive common names polka dot plant and freckle face. For some reason even well grown plants seldom have a really healthy look and perhaps this is why I am put off them. Reasonable light, warmth and moisture are required when growing them indoors and as they are prone to attacks from scale insects a watch should be kept for these.

Ipomoea tricolor

Impatiens wallerana petersiana

Iresine herbstii

Impatiens

Recently we have seen some great improvements among the busy lizzies, *Impatiens wallerana*, in particular the F$_1$ hybrids with their larger flowers. This is a sign that more interest is being taken by the breeders in these colourful little plants. The species most often seen are *I. w. sultanii* with light green leaves and scarlet, white, orange, pink or magenta flowers, and *I. w. petersiana* with dark leaves and red flowers.

In the small cool greenhouse they will flower for months on end, and give excellent value for the modest amount of attention that is required. Indoors it is most essential that they should have ample light, and fresh air will not go amiss unless the day is very cold. Watering must not be neglected. As light is so important if plants are to retain their flowers it will do no harm to place them under a wall light in the evening.

Plants may be raised from seed or cuttings; the latter will usually root in water, but will do better in peaty compost. Seed may be sown in March for plants to flower in summer and in July for plants wanted in the winter. When potting use John Innes potting compost No. 2 or 3, and though larger plants may be grown in very large pots the plants will be more floriferous when the roots tend to be pot bound in smaller pots.

Ipomoea

Better suited to the cool greenhouse, ipomoea, morning glory, can, nevertheless, be grown indoors if it has the lightest possible window position where it can get full sun for as much of the day as possible – it will also be an advantage if the window can be opened to admit fresh air on warmer days. Hard seed should be soaked in warm water for several hours, or be nicked with a sharp knife before sowing – this will encourage germination. Five or so seeds can be sown, evenly spaced, in 5-in (13-cm) pots filled with John Innes potting compost No. 1 in the spring.

Once under way the plants grow very rapidly and will need some form of support from an early stage. The individual flowers last for only a day, but there is an endless succession of them throughout the summer that will give much pleasure over a long period. Besides the conventional blue kind, *Ipomoea tricolor*, there are red, white and even multicoloured sorts available.

A potful of morning glory at either side of a light window will present an attractive sight when plants come into flower. They may also be grown in a sheltered, sunny spot out of doors. When no longer attractive the plants should be discarded.

Iresine

Grown principally for their predominantly brilliant red foliage, iresines are often seen forming part of bedding schemes out of doors during the summer months. This indicates that there is not too much of a problem when it comes to caring for them indoors or in the greenhouse, and they respond very well when offered reasonable conditions and treatment. Plants may be increased by taking cuttings at almost any time, although it is advisable to avoid adventures into propagating during the bleaker months of the year unless ideal conditions are at hand.

Being fairly compact low-growing plants that seldom reach more than 1 ft (30 cm) in height, they do not need to be potted into pots that are larger than 5 in (13 cm) in diameter. Use John Innes potting compost No. 2 and pinch out the growing tips frequently to maintain a bushy compact habit. These are plants which do better in the rather cooler temperatures and in good light as they can quickly become etiolated and leggy. Water freely in the spring and summer, moderately during the rest of the year.

Jasminum polyanthum

Isolepis gracilis

Kalanchoe blossfeldiana

Isolepis

Isolepis gracilis (syn. *Scirpus cernuus*) is an amusing little plant with hollow, pointed stems that at first sight gives the impression of belonging to the grasses, but closer inspection will show that it is, in fact, a miniature bulrush. The small white flowers are carried on the tips of the stems and are similar to those of the bulrush. The stems are dark green in colour and somewhat slender and drooping, which makes the plant a good subject for placing in the forefront of planted arrangements, or for putting along the front edge of shelving in either greenhouse or garden room.

Moist conditions are essential, so the pot should be stood in a dish of water, and the growing position should be reasonably shaded, but the temperature is not important provided it does not drop too low. The best means of propagation is to divide clumps of mature plants and to pot them up individually in John Innes potting compost No. 2, using small pots to begin with and gradually potting into larger pots as the plant matures, but there should never be any need to put plants into very large containers. Although almost any time of the year is suitable for dividing plants of this nature, it is usually better to tackle the job during late spring or early summer when growth will be more active.

Jasminum

Plants that flower in winter are always useful to have around, and those that produce their flowers in January and February, as *Jasminum polyanthum* does, are probably even more rewarding as much of the Christmas galaxy of colour will by then have disappeared. This plant is frequently offered for sale as a pot plant in 5-in (13-cm) pots, and has attractive white flowers that are tinged with pink in the bud stage. The great attraction, however, is the very pleasing fragrance.

These are vigorous plants that may be potted on after they have finished flowering, and at the same time any untidy growth can be trimmed to shape. It is important to use a compost with some body in it, John Innes potting compost No. 2 for example, and when potting it will be wise to provide a framework of some kind that climbing growth can be trained to. It almost goes without saying that, along with all the winter-flowering plants, jasmines should have ample light if the maximum is to be got from them in the way of flowers. Regular syringing of the foliage with a fine spray will also be beneficial to them. Placing plants out of doors during the summer months in a sunny position will encourage them to flower better during the ensuing winter.

Kalanchoe

Kalanchoe blossfeldiana is a small flowering plant that is produced in large quantities, mainly at Christmas, by growers who use black polythene to control the amount of daylight available to it, so inducing it to flower at what is an unnatural time of the year. February to May is the normal flowering period.

Propagation is by seed sown in March and germinated at 20°C (68°F), or by stem cuttings taken from late spring to summer. The cuttings should be allowed to dry for a couple of days before being inserted in pots of John Innes potting compost No. 1. As the plants grow they can be transferred to 4-in (10-cm) pots in John Innes potting compost No. 2 or 3.

The care of the kalanchoe amounts to little more than ensuring that a reasonable temperature is maintained, that the plant is kept in a light position and that the compost is never allowed to become excessively wet – this is especially important in the winter.

There are a number of named forms and hybrids of this species with pink, red or orange flowers.

Kentia fosteriana

Lantana camara

Laurus nobilis

Kentia

The parlour palm, *Kentia fosteriana* (syn. *Howeia fosteriana*) was a great favourite in Victorian times and is still much in demand today, but its relatively high price has a purse-controlling influence on sales. The reason for the high cost is the fact that the plants take many years to reach maturity, during which time temperatures in the region of 20°C (68°F) are essential if plant growth is to be kept on the move. Once the plants have matured they may be grown at lower temperatures without harm, but the rate of growth will be slower.

In the greenhouse the palms prefer to be warm, moist and shaded, and one should endeavour to emulate these conditions when growing them indoors. Established plants will also benefit from regular feeding with a balanced liquid fertilizer. Potting should only be necessary every second or third year, and when performing this operation use John Innes potting compost No. 2 or 3 depending on the size of the pot. Good drainage is important, so ensure that clay pots have a layer of crocks in the bottom of the pot – 'crock' is the term used for pieces of broken flower pot used in the bottom of pots for drainage. When confronted recently with a very sick potted palm I discovered, on knocking the plant from its pot, that a worm had found its way into the soil, and accumulated worm casts in the bottom of the pot had completely blocked the drainage outlet and had, in fact, killed off the plant. There is a lesson to be learned here in that it is worth inspecting the root system for the possible presence of worms when water applied to the compos does not drain freely away.

Lantana

Many of the plants that are grown in pots for indoor decoration would be looked upon as weeds in the regions where they are grown naturally. Those of us who spend much of our working lives trying to grow bigger and better *Begonia masoniana*, sansevierias, and such like, are often a little nonplussed when the visitor from tropical regions asks with a touch of wonder in his voice if we are really serious about it. On questioning the visitor we often find that the plants mentioned are troublesome weeds in his tropical garden!

The lantana is one of those plants that has limited appeal as a pot plant, and is a tropical weed into the bargain. In its favour it can be said that it flowers all the summer through, and if whitefly can be kept under control it is not too difficult to care for. The foliage is not particularly interesting, but the flowers are neatly globular in shape and come in a wide range of colours – pink, yellow, red and orange.

Plants in pots are not very demanding in their needs, and should be potted into John Innes potting compost No. 2 as soon as they have filled their existing pots with roots. Lantana may be raised from seed sown in early spring, or from cuttings a few inches in length taken at the same time. Good light, modest temperature and regular feeding of established plants is all they require in order to do well.

Laurus

The leaves of the hardy bay tree, *Laurus nobilis*, are much sought after for flavouring and, though they may be bought dried, there is a lot to be said for plucking them from your own tree. This plant may be grown as a house plant on a sunny window-sill indoors, as part of the garden scene where it may attain a height of some 30 ft (9 m) in ideal conditions or, what is more likely, it can be grown as a clipped bay. Although costly the latter type of plant grown in a tub or ornamental pot is in keen demand for the patio, or for framing the entrance of the doorway to the street.

New plants can be propagated from cuttings taken in September and placed in a glass-covered frame out of doors – the compost should be on the sandy side and the cuttings some 3 to 4 in (8 to 10 cm) in length. Alternatively, longer pieces of growth can be pegged down in the soil close to the plant and allowed to make roots of their own before being cut from the parent plant and potted up in John Innes potting compost No. 2. The attraction then is to grow the plants, over a period of years, into pyramid shapes or as mop-headed standards. Bay trees can be kept under control and of pleasing shape by regular trimming with a pair of garden shears.

Plants will require more water in the summer than they do in the winter. Although perfectly hardy it is wise to provide some shelter for them during the winter months from strong winds which tend to scorch the leaves.

55

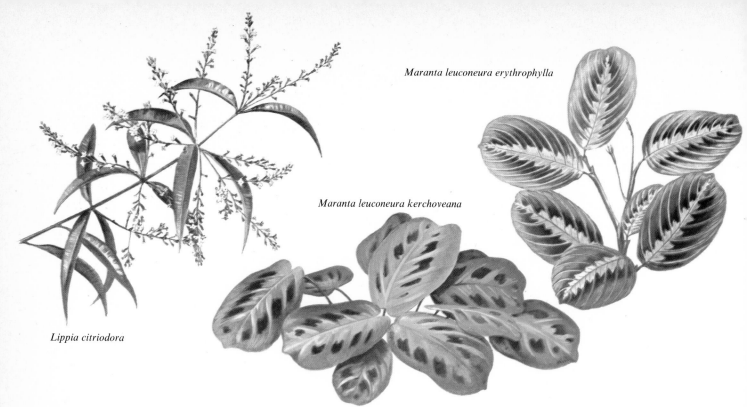

Maranta leuconeura erythrophylla

Maranta leuconeura kerchoveana

Lippia citriodora

Lippia

Lippia citriodora is a vigorous-growing deciduous shrub that is hardy in sheltered areas in warmer climates. It can be raised from cuttings that should be taken in the spring from early growth; pieces about 4 in (10 cm) in length with a heel of old wood are the best. Insert these in sandy compost or John Innes potting compost No. 1 in a propagating case heated to around 18°C (65°F), and pot on into John Innes potting compost No. 2 when the cuttings have developed sufficient root.

During the spring and summer plants will require copious watering and a light position in which to grow, and could well be regarded as another addition to the range of patio plants. Being of vigorous habit lippia will need annual winter pruning when the shoots should be cut back to within a few inches of their base.

These are not particularly attractive plants but, as the common name lemon-scented verbena suggests, they are grown mostly for their scented leaves although they do produce sprays of pale pinkish white fragrant flowers in summer. During the winter months they will need only the minimum amount of water.

Maranta

Grown essentially for their foliage, the marantas form an important part of the house-plant scene and have many uses both as individual plants and as part of a group planting.

There are a number freely available and all of them when grown indoors require shaded positions, as direct sunlight quickly gives them a miserable appearance. However, some light will be necessary, so avoid placing them in the darkest and most unpleasant part of the room. Reasonable warmth is also essential, so the aim should be to keep a fairly even temperature in the region of 18°C (65°F). It will also be helpful if the area immediately surrounding the plant can be kept fairly moist by placing the plants on moist gravel, or by plunging the plant pots in a moisture-retaining material such as peat or sphagnum moss. Although moisture is important, it is equally important when using peat for plunging pots to ensure that the medium does not become very wet and soggy.

Potting plants on into larger containers is an operation that is seldom required more than once every second year, as the marantas do not make a very great amount of root. With almost all the plants that are less free rooting it is important that the growing medium in which they are being potted should not be too heavy, so something akin to equal parts of John Innes potting compost No. 2 and peat mixed together is suggested as being suitable. At all costs avoid the temptation to use very heavy mixes which do not give the roots a chance. Established plants will benefit from feeding with a weak liquid fertilizer each week during the summer months.

Maranta leuconeura kerchoveana has pale green leaves with darker blotches that are said to resemble rabbit's footprints, hence the common name of rabbit's tracks. Another common name is prayer plant, which is derived from the manner in which the leaves fold together like hands in prayer when darkness descends. It is not at all a difficult plant to care for if reasonable conditions are provided.

Commonly named the herringbone plant, *M. l. erythrophylla* has all the appearance of being a delicate plant with its exquisitely patterned leaves. But this is far from the truth as it is one of the most accommodating of plants if one appreciates that it requires just that little bit of extra care in the home. There are a number of other marantas that one is likely to come across – all of them require the same sort of treatment.

Both plants may be increased by cuttings of the top section of the plant with about three leaves attached. These may be taken at any time but will root more easily in a heated propagator.

Mimosa pudica

Monstera deliciosa

Mimosa

Of these, far and away the most popular is the sensitive plant, *Mimosa pudica*, a perennial plant that is usually grown as an annual. Seed is sown in a fairly high temperature in the spring, or plants may be grown from cuttings taken at almost any time and placed in a warm propagating case. Indoors, it is absolutely essential that the plants should enjoy a light position and even then they will not make up into very robust subjects. As they seldom grow to more than 18 in (45 cm) in height mimosa do not need very large pots, but when potting use John Innes potting compost No. 2.

The sensitive nature of the feathery leaves of *M. pudica* is by far the greatest attraction of the plant – when touched they have the most fascinating habit of collapsing as if the plant had suddenly died; it takes a little time for them to regain their turgidity. An old gardener I was talking to recently told me that a past employer used a mature plant of *M. pudica* to mount guard at each doorpost at the entrance to his greenhouse full of hothouse grapes; the wily employer knew that if the leaves were seen in a drooping condition someone had gone beyond the door and trodden on forbidden ground!

Monstera

Quite one of the most important of all the purely foliage house plants, monstera, the Swiss cheese plant, has more than retained its popularity over the years and, if anything, strengthens its position. There is little doubt that much of its success is due to the fact that the plant has naturally glossy leaves with deep serrations along their edges. The vast majority of these plants are raised from seed that can be sown at almost any time if warm shaded conditions can be provided. In the early stages of growth the young leaves are entire, but usually when the third leaf has been produced the first signs of serrations begin to develop. Leaves of mature monstera plants are among the most fascinating of all plant foliage and, even when grown in pots, plants may have leaves measuring 3 ft (1 m) in length and all of 2 ft (60 cm) wide. By this time, besides having serrations, they will also have perforations that start at the midrib of the leaf and gradually become smaller as they extend outwards. When growing in their natural habitat they will produce leaves that are very much larger.

Older plants growing in a warm, humid atmosphere will also in time bear fruits which are preceded by exquisite creamy white inflorescences that are similar in shape to those of an arum lily. The white spathe lasts for about one week then gradually dies and as this happens the spadix in the centre of the flower increases in size and eventually becomes the very delicious fruit. In my experience the fruit should be left on the plant until it is seen to be disintegrating, by which time it is fully ripe and ready to be eaten. Said to have all the flavours of a fruit salad, it does not look especially appetising, but does in fact live up to its fruit-salad likeness.

Monstera deliciosa is the biggest kind and should be considered as a plant for a large room only. *M. pertusa* (syn. *M. deliciosa borsigiana*) has a more compact upright habit than the species just mentioned and is a better plant for a limited space.

Monsteras are fairly quick growing and active plants and must be potted into slightly larger pots each year until they are in the 10- or 12-in (25- to 30-cm) size; from then on they may be kept going for some years by regular feeding. However, it is important that fertilizer should be given in frequent weak doses rather than infrequent heavy applications. The aerial roots of older plants become quite numerous as they protrude from the main stem and should be directed into the compost when they are long enough. Where roots are forming in quantity it will do no harm to cut some of them away. Potting compost must contain a good proportion of peat, and potting should be undertaken in early summer. Monsteras should be kept out of direct sunlight and watered so that the compost is moist without being allowed to remain saturated for long periods. If the compost becomes too wet the plant will sometimes exude drops of water from the edges of the leaves and if this does happen watering should be reduced.

Nephthytis Emerald Gem

Nephrolepis exaltata

Neanthe bella

Neanthe

Also known as _Chamaedorea elegans,_
Neanthe bella is one of the most charming of
the smaller house plants and is not difficult
to care for. In every respect it is a miniature
palm tree that is useful for many aspects of
indoor-plant cultivation and, being so compact, it is especially suitable for those
householders with limited space. For terrarium gardens and bottle gardens neanthe
is indispensable, giving that important
exotic appearance to the finished arrangement.

Plants are raised from seeds that are
normally sown in very warm beds of peat at
a permanent temperature in the region of
27°C (80°F) – high temperature is most
important if the seeds are to germinate satisfactorily. From the propagating beds the
seedlings are transferred to small pots filled
with a peaty mixture in which they are
grown on either to be sold, or until such
time as they are potted on into slightly
larger pots. Strangely enough, although we
are ever expounding on the dangers of potting plants into containers that are too
large in relation to their size, the neanthe is
one of those plants that does not seem to
object to pots that would seem dispropor-
tionate. It is, however, most important to
ensure that the compost is open – good,
clean leafmould is an excellent material that
may be added with advantage to the compost for this plant. Browning of the leaf
tips can be a result of keeping the plants in
cold and wet conditions.

Nephrolepis

Nephrolepis exaltata is another plant which
brings an echo of the Victorian era when
this and many other varieties of fern were
grown in vast quantities. Many of them, no
doubt, holding pride of place atop one of
the incredible range of pedestal pots that
were manufactured in that opulent age
when ornamentation seems to have got out
of hand.

Propagation of fresh plants is probably a
task best left to the professional as high
temperatures in the region of 27°C (80°F)
are necessary. Spores may be sown on a
peat and sand mixture at any time of the
year, but as these are not viable in the cultivars of _N. exaltata_ a better method is to
peg the creeping stems into peat, removing
and potting up the young plants once they
have developed sufficient root. Plants can
also be divided in the spring.

Although nephrolepis are fairly easy ferns
to grow they require a moist atmosphere
with a minimum temperature of 10°C
(50°F) and, most important, a position well
away from draughts. Use John Innes potting compost No. 2 and pot on the plants
until they are in 8-in (20-cm) pots or
baskets.

There are many fine cultivars of _N. exaltata,_ among them _N. e. bostoniensis_, the
Boston fern, which has wide green drooping
fronds that may attain a length of some
3 ft (1 m). _N. e._ Teddy Junior is more compact in habit and very free growing with
fronds that are attractively waved. There
are many more, some coarse in appearance
and others more delicate, but all of them
extremely useful and beautiful plants.

Nephthytis

In common with almost all the indoor
plants belonging to the family _Araceae_ and
known collectively as aroids, nephthytis
requires warm, moist and shaded conditions. The compost should also be of a peaty
nature, and weak liquid fertilizer should be
given when the plants are actively growing.
Cuttings are an easy means of propagation.

Nephthytis are climbing or creeping
plants and will do better if the growth can
be pinned to a moist support of some kind.
The simplest way of providing this is to
bind sphagnum moss to a stout cane;
alternatively, three or four bamboo canes
used together will make a more robust support. Wet sphagnum moss that is fresh and
spongy should then be wound around the
support and tied in position with plastic-
covered wire. The thickness should be in
the region of 1 in (2·5 cm) all the way round.
A greater thickness of moss may be used
for larger plants. Use a hand spray to keep
the moss permanently moist and the roots
will find their way into it and greatly assist
the growth of the plant.

One of the best varieties is _Nephthytis_
Emerald Gem (syn. _Syngonium podophyllum_
Emerald Gem), although other hybrids with
variegated foliage are available. The spathes
are pale green or yellowish in colour and
not especially showy. The common name
given to all the nephthytis is goose-foot
plant, which is derived from the shape of
the leaves.

Nerine bowdenii

Nerium oleander

Nolina recurvata

Nerine

Native to South Africa, nerines are slow-growing bulbs which, because of their slow rate of growth, will never achieve great popularity and are seldom offered for sale. Therefore, acquiring plants is not easy – probably the best method is still the age-old one of seeing plants in the home or garden of a friend and showing interest in the hope that the hint will be taken! Fortunately new plants are grown easily enough from small offsets from parent bulbs which may be removed at almost any time.

Nerine bowdenii is still the species most frequently seen, but as nerines become increasingly popular as cut flowers there is much more interest being taken in them and improved plants are appearing. The flowers, which are produced in the autumn, are mostly in shades of red and pink with a lovely glistening silver sheen and are borne on stems that may be as much as 2 ft (60 cm) in length.

The plants are dormant from May to September, during which time they should remain dry and occupy the hottest possible position near the glass in an airy greenhouse or conservatory. The flowers come before the leaves, and as they appear the compost should be watered but this should at no time be excessive. When planting put several bulbs in each pot.

Use John Innes potting compost No. 2 and make sure that the pots are well drained.

Nerium

Nerium oleander, commonly known as oleander, becomes a substantial plant in time, so is not suitable for other than spacious rooms. It is also essential that it should have the maximum amount of light. Oleanders may be placed out of doors in the summer in a place where they can enjoy the maximum amount of sunlight. During the summer months plants will require copious watering and regular feeding once they are established in their pots.

Large tubs suit the oleanders best and they should be potted into John Innes potting compost No. 3 early in the year. The thin, willow-like foliage is not particularly attractive, but there is ample compensation for this in the terminal flower clusters that are available in single and double forms, mostly in shades of pink. Growth that appears immediately below the flower trusses should be removed to get the maximum effect from the flowers. Although they may be grown indoors oleanders are better subjects for the greenhouse or garden room where they will have more light and space to develop. Hard pruning almost to pot level immediately after flowering is often recommended but this may stop a possible second flush of flowers. It is better to leave the pruning until late autumn.

Propagate new plants from cuttings about 4 in (10 cm) in length taken in spring or summer and inserted in a peat and sand mixture in small pots in warm conditions.

Nolina

Indigenous to Mexico *Nolina recurvata* is also known as *Beaucarnea recurvata*, with the interesting common name of pony-tail plant, which it presumably gets from the way in which the leaves splay out like the tail from the pony's rump. Leaves of the pony-tail are thin, stiff and numerous and radiate out from the top of the large bulb that forms like a super onion as the plant ages.

Plants are raised from seeds sown in a warm propagating case in early spring, the resulting seedlings being firmly potted in John Innes potting compost No. 2 when large enough. In time the plants develop into small trees, but this is a very slow process when they are confined to pots.

This plant is seen at its best when about 4 ft (1·25 m) in height with leaves emerging from the bulbous base in the form of a fountain. At this stage it is ideally suited to a pedestal position on the top of a single plant stand. When grouped with other plants nolina loses much of its individual beauty.

Indoors it requires a position offering reasonable light and warmth, and the compost should be kept moist all the time with a little less water being given during the winter months. Established plants will need fertilizer during the spring and summer months only.

Oplismenus hirtellus variegatus

Pandanus veitchii

Passiflora caerulea

Oplismenus

This attractive grass, *Oplismenus hirtellus variegatus*, is often confused with tradescantia as the growth is very similar in colour and habit. The colour is a pleasing mix of green and silver with touches of pink, and growth is very fast indeed if conditions are agreeable.

As older plants become untidy and straggly in appearance it is a simple matter to raise fresh plants from cuttings. Several cuttings a few inches in length should be put in small pots of potting compost in reasonable warmth and normally they will root with little difficulty. These are ideal edging plants, be it along the front of the staging in the greenhouse or along the front of planted containers filled with assorted plants indoors.

By their very nature oplismenus are also eminently suited to planting in hanging baskets, or in pots on the wall that will allow the natural trails to hang down. If cuttings are struck directly into pots of about 4 in (10 cm) in diameter there should be no need to pot them into larger containers during the season as the resulting plants may well produce trails of some 3 ft (1 m) or more.

During the summer months oplismenus should be kept moist and fed, and should have as much light as they will agreeably tolerate; the foliage colour will be much more brilliant than that of plants that have been growing in poor light. It must be mentioned, however, that there is the danger of leaf scorch if plants are exposed to full sunlight.

Pandanus

Seeing pandanus growing in a pot to a height of some 10 ft (3 m) with long saw-edged leaves radiating in all directions, you could well be excused for thinking that it is probably one of the most spectacular of all the purely foliage plants that you are ever likely to encounter. Pandanus is commonly named the screw pine because of the way in which the leaves at their base spiral around the short trunk of the plant.

Pandanus veitchii is the species most commonly seen and this is grown entirely for its foliage, which is green, variegated white and green or amber and green. Pandanus demands considerable space when well matured but fortunately it is reasonably slow growing so will not push one out of the house and home too quickly. It is not a particularly pleasant plant to handle on account of the close-set spines on the edges of the leaves and similar spines from the base to tip of the leaves on their underside. Essentially it is an individual plant that has a most exciting appeal when placed on its own to be admired from all angles.

Growing conditions need not be too exacting, as pandanus are not too demanding, needing good light and reasonable temperature allied to a watering programme that errs very much on the side of dry rather than wet conditions. New plants are raised from offshoots that develop at the base of the parent plant – these should be peeled off when large enough and potted up in John Innes potting compost No. 1 to begin with.

Passiflora

Given their head passion flowers can become rampant and untidy plants that are only suited to areas where ample overhead space can be provided to accommodate the invasive climbing growth. They are frequently sold in medium-size pots for home decoration with the growth wound around canes or hoop-shaped supports. Being vigorous plants the best treatment on purchasing them is to repot them into slightly larger containers – if purchased in 5-in (13-cm) pots then they should be transferred to pots of some 7 in (18 cm) in diameter. At the same time a taller and possibly wider framework should be provided for the anticipated growth. Treated in this way the plant can be seen to prosper as it roots into the new compost, whereas, if left in the smaller pot, it might equally well decline in vigour. Potting can be done at any time between spring and the end of the summer and the compost should be reasonably heavy, John Innes potting compost No. 3 for example.

The foliage is not very exciting but the flowers more than compensate for this when they appear. *Passiflora caerulea* is the one most often seen with flowers that are pale pink, purple and white and of the most intricate design. The lightest possible position should be provided indoors and during the warmer summer months it is most important that the compost should at no time dry out, though it can be allowed to become a little dryer in winter.

Pelargonium (Ivy leaved)

Pellaea rotundifolia

Pelargonium (Regal)

Pelargonium

These provide a wealth of summer colour, with the exception of the scented-leaved varieties that are grown for this purpose and are not especially attractive. The others are the Regal, Zonal and Ivy-leaved types, all of which are most rewarding plants.

The last are particularly valuable as basket plants, and are at their most effective when the basket is completely filled with them. In this way they can be grown without being fed, which would be a requirement if other plants were included; if variegated ivy-leaved pelargoniums are fed and grown too lush they lose much of their sparkle as variegated plants. At the end of the summer they should be hard pruned. As an alternative to trailing, the plants may be encouraged to climb, and can be superb against the wall of the garden room – when grown in this way the pruning should not be so harsh as the main stems of the plant ought to be left trained to the wall to give plants a good start the following year.

Zonal pelargoniums are the ones with dark markings to their leaves which are much used as part of the summer bedding display in the garden. As well as their garden use they make excellent pot plants for a light window position indoors, or on the patio outside during the summer months. When grown in large pots zonal pelargoniums may also be encouraged to climb and will provide a bright display throughout the summer months. When purchasing plants look for firm, stocky ones that can be moved on to slightly larger pots almost as soon as they are taken home. However, it is not necessary to use pots of

excessive size as plants can be repotted in the same container in the spring by removing the plant from its pot and shaking off much of the old soil before potting again with John Innes potting compost No. 2. Whatever the location plants will need ample light and air about them if they are to do well, and in winter they must be kept in a cool, airy place.

The regals with their green leaves and mass of flowers, many of them bi-coloured, make fine pot plants that are not difficult to manage in conditions that offer modest warmth, good light and fresh air around them whenever the weather permits. After flowering it is advisable to hard prune plants so that they grow more sturdily and compactly the following year. The winter temperature need only be in the region of 10°C (50°F) provided conditions are not damp.

Cuttings of all these will root in late summer, and should be about 4 in (10 cm) long, shorter in the case of the ivy-leaved ones, and have the lower leaves removed. The cuttings should be cut cleanly just below a leaf joint and the severed ends treated with rooting powder before being inserted in appropriate compost around the outer edge of 3½-in (9-cm) pots. When rooted, plants can be individually potted in containers of similar size.

Much work has been done on pelargoniums in recent years and it is well worth keeping an eye open for better types.

Pellaea

Although the numbers of available fern varieties have diminished in recent years there are still sufficient of them about for the keen plantsman to make up an interesting collection. Admittedly scope for growing a wide selection of ferns indoors is limited, but for anyone with a small, heated greenhouse there is much to commend it.

Pellaea rotundifolia is a compact and attractive fern with small rounded leaves which is seen at its best when growing in a hanging basket. Conditions should be moist and must be shaded, and the minimum temperature should not fall below 10°C (50°F). It seems quite happy to tolerate higher temperatures provided the atmosphere does not become excessively dry.

When new plants are being raised the temperature should be in the region of 20°C (68°F) – spores are sown on the surface of seed boxes filled with a peat and sand mixture. Alternatively, and more easily, plants may be increased by dividing existing clumps, in which case the temperature is not so critical.

Peperomia magnoliaefolia

Pellionia daveauana

Peperomia caperata

Pellionia

In the cool greenhouse the tradescantia is in all probability the most useful of all the purely foliage plants – mainly because it is very easy to grow and equally easy to propagate. For the warmer greenhouse *Pellionia daveauana* could well be the equivalent, in that it is very easy to propagate and grows reasonably quickly. It is also extremely useful for all sorts of purposes in association with small displays of plants indoors, especially as a trailing plant in troughs and baskets.

To describe the colouring is almost an impossibility, as it varies so much according to the amount of light that the plant is subjected to, but pink, grey, green, brown and a number of mottled shades of these four are all possible. Although shaded conditions are normally recommended for this plant it is interesting to experiment in order to determine just how much strong light it will tolerate before there are signs of leaf damage. Loss of a few plants as a result of experimenting will be no great tragedy as the plants are so easily raised from cuttings.

The minimum temperature suggested is 13°C (55°F), but plants will do that much better if the minimum can be raised above this level. Higher temperatures are not particularly harmful if there is at the same time a reasonably high humidity level.

Indoors, the pellionia requires warmth, moisture and light shade and, in a peaty compost, cuttings will root very readily. To obtain a well shaped plant several cuttings should be put in each pot.

Peperomia

Another of the small and important house plants that are produced in vast numbers annually. Although no more than four or five varieties are offered commercially in any quantity, there are many other fascinating sorts that are occasionally seen. For the person with sufficient interest peperomias might well form a small and interesting collection to be grown alongside other indoor plants, in the knowledge that unusual plants will always attract attention. A point much in their favour is that they are all compact plants that will take up very little space, and the few more robust ones can easily be reduced in height by cutting them back, or new plants can be propagated from cuttings of leaf or stem at almost any time of the year and older plants can then be discarded. All the peperomias require reasonable warmth, a fairly light window position with protection from strong sun, and moderate watering. Most of them abhor heavy composts and grow very much better in soilless mixtures.

Many of them do produce a rat's tail stalk of flowers, but all of them are grown specifically for their foliage. Some have thick fleshy stems and equally fleshy leaves, while others develop into compact rosettes with leaves radiating from a small, chunky stem. *Peperomia caperata* is one of the latter type and has most attractive dark green crinkled leaves. There is also a variegated form of *caperata* that is much more troublesome to propagate and care for. The first mentioned is propagated by means of leaf cuttings, which are ever plentiful. The variegated form is raised from cuttings that must have a piece of the main stem of the plant attached; cuttings taken with a piece of stem will continue to produce variegated leaves while leaf cuttings will revert to the all green kind. Another rosette-forming peperomia is *P. hederaefolia*, which is an attractive grey colour and is also propagated from leaf cuttings.

Of the stemmed sorts *P. magnoliaefolia* with its cream and green colouring is by far the best known – when purchasing these seek out the plants with better colouring as there is a lot of variation. One of the larger types is *P. obtusifolia* which has fleshy leaves that are a rich burgundy red in colour.

Seen less frequently these days is *P. sandersii*, which has attractive rounded leaves with dark green stripes and silver-grey base colouring. It is a little more difficult to raise and care for, but this does not seem a good reason why it should be less popular than many of the much less attractive house plants that are sold in vast quantities annually. An interesting feature of this plant is that the leaf cuttings can be prepared by dividing the leaf into equal quarters by cutting down and across with a sharp knife and inserting the pieces perpendicularly in warm beds of moist peat.

Philodendron tuxla

Philodendron scandens

Philodendron wendlandii

Philodendron

Conditions that are very hot and dry are alien to the majority of indoor plants, and this is particularly so´ in respect of the moisture-loving philodendrons. In their natural jungle habitat they enjoy conditions that are moist and shaded, with their roots travelling over a wide area in search of nourishment. Although it would not be easy to simulate jungle conditions in the living room it is as well to remember that shade and moisture are essential needs of these members of the *Araceae* family, and that any drying out of the compost or a dry surrounding atmosphere can be fatal.

The majority of the philodendrons can either be encouraged to climb or trail, but climbing is their more natural function. *Philodendron hastatum* has large arrow-shaped leaves that are among the largest to be found in the easier philodendrons and it is essentially a climbing plant. Indeed the stout stems and large leaves will require adequate staking with a support of the sort that one would normally associate with young outdoor trees. *P. tuxla* has leaves of a similar arrow shape and grows in much the same way as *hastatum*.

All the taller growing plants of the *Araceae* family will grow better if the supporting stake is wrapped in a thick layer of wet sphagnum moss into which the aerial roots can penetrate to draw moisture. When the aerial roots are long enough they should be directed into the compost in the pot. Removal of these roots should only be contemplated if there is a very large number of them, as loss of such roots will impair the well-being of the plant.

Not all philodendrons are of a climbing habit, and in *P. wendlandii* we have a plant that is supremely elegant as a low-growing subject. The leaves are a rich dark green with short petioles that are compactly arranged around a short stump that gives the plant the appearance of a large green shuttlecock. The plants occasionally produce attractive spathe flowers, but the principal attraction is in the foliage and the way it is arranged around the stem of the plant. Another non-climbing type is *P. bipinnatifidum*. This has fingered leaves that radiate from a central stumpy growth and is a fine architectural type of plant that will also need reasonable space in which to expand its majestic leaves.

Far and away the most popular among the easier philodendrons, however, is the sweetheart plant, *P. scandens*. The leaves are heart shaped and a pleasing shade of green, but the most appealing characteristic is its ability to tolerate a very wide range of indoor conditions without seeming to suffer unduly.

Most of the philodendrons can be raised from cuttings or from seed, in either case in the warm and moist conditions of the propagating case. At all stages of potting a peaty compost is necessary – a suggested mixture is two parts of John Innes potting compost No. 2 and one part of sphagnum peat. Although plants approve of ample moisture surrounding them, it is important that the potting compost should be free draining. Feed regularly with a weak liquid fertilizer to keep the plants in good order once they have become established in their pots. Much depends on the development of the individual plant but potting on is not usually needed more than once every second year.

All the philodendrons with glossy foliage will benefit from having their leaves cleaned occasionally with a damp sponge. Frequent syringing of the foliage will help in maintaining a moist atmosphere around the plants.

Other philodendrons are described on page 81.

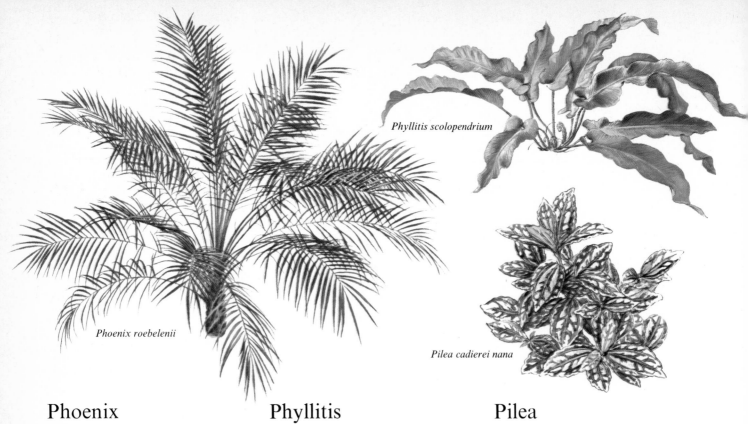

Phyllitis scolopendrium

Phoenix roebelenii

Pilea cadierei nana

Phoenix

These are splendid palms with a grace that is all their own. The leaves have a silver sheen that is seen at its best when the plants are more mature at an age of about five years. Even at this age the palms are less than 5 ft (1·5 m) tall, so in spite of the fact that high temperatures are required to keep them on the move there is not much to show for the effort involved. However, small plants are occasionally available and if time is on your side then go ahead and watch the development of your very own phoenix palm.

The two most likely to be seen on sale are *Phoenix canariensis* and *P. roebelenii* – the latter is less coarse than the former and is the one to have if a choice is being offered. Both are commonly known as date palms. Indoors they require good light, warmth and ample watering during the spring and summer months with less water in winter. Water should be seen to drain freely through the compost almost as it is poured over the soil. Masses of roots are produced, so annual potting on is required in the first few years and John Innes potting compost No. 3 should be used at all stages. New plants are raised from seed which must be sown in peat in very warm conditions, temperatures somewhere in the region of 25°C (77°F).

Phyllitis

The hart's-tongue fern, *Phyllitis scolopendrium,* is quite hardy and very adaptable in that it may be planted in numerous locations in the garden where it will enjoy shade from strong sunlight; it may be used to decorate the patio, or it will be equally at home indoors. Eventually the plant will develop strong rhizomes which may be divided early in the year, March to April, if required. The bright green leaves are strap like with undulating margins but there are several forms of *P. scolopendrium* which vary slightly in appearance.

Indoors they are ideally suited to the cool room that is reasonably light, but not too sunny, and they are not too demanding in respect of care and attention. The compost should be kept moist during the spring and summer months, with a little less water being given at other times. Potting on into larger containers is best undertaken in early summer and the compost should consist of equal parts of peat and loam with some sharp sand added to assist drainage, the addition of a small quantity of old mortar rubble will also be helpful in improving the plants' performance. Propagation is by spores or by division.

Adaptable plants of this sort that can be put out in the garden in a sheltered spot are most useful in homes where space for potted plants is limited. However, even though phyllitis is completely hardy, it is unwise to remove a plant from a room that is inclined to be overheated and to put it out of doors when there is a sharp difference in the temperature. It is much better to acclimatize it gradually to outdoor conditions by leaving it first in a cooler place for a week or two.

Pilea

Among the easiest of the smaller foliage plants, the pileas should be well within the scope of the beginner with house plants. Starting with relatively inexpensive plants that are not difficult to care for is the best policy for the newcomer to indoor-plant growing. It will be less costly in the event of failure, and the chance of success will be improved. These are also fine little plants to experiment with when taking the first steps into the mysteries of propagation. Almost all of them are easy to raise from cuttings, and these are usually in fair supply. Trimmed cuttings about 3 in (8 cm) in length will benefit from being dipped in rooting powder before being inserted in moist peat and sand. A propagating case heated to about 18°C (65°F) will greatly assist the rooting process. To get plants with a full appearance at least five cuttings should be inserted in a 3½-in (9-cm) pot.

One of the best to grow is the silver-leaved *Pilea cadierei nana* which is more compact and tidy that the coarser growing *P. cadierei*. With pileas in general it is advisable to remove the growing tips at regular intervals to keep the plants more compact and attractive. *P. repens* has larger, more crinkled brownish-green leaves which blend well with other plants in arrangements. A vigorous plant that, like the other pileas, needs warmth and light shade with moderate watering to succeed.

Pittosporum undulatum variegatum

Plectranthus australis

Platycerium bifurcatum

Pittosporum

Plants for indoor decoration can be acquired in all sorts of different ways and they need not all be terribly expensive nursery-raised ones. Much of the florists' foliage material commonly used to enhance the appearance of cut flowers can be used as cuttings. An example I have in mind here is the wavy edged, glossy leaved *Pittosporum tenuifolium* that is much used by florists and is hardy in more sheltered parts of Britain.

Cuttings about 3 in (8 cm) in length should be taken from firm shoots and placed in pots filled with a peat and sand mixture and kept warm and moist until they have rooted. To get a plant of full appearance several pieces may be put in one pot, and when rooted they can go into John Innes compost No. 2 and be grown on to provide glossy green plants for the living room that are much more attractive than many of the more conventional house plants offered for sale today. Even if it should fail it will not have been a costly experiment.

Slightly more tender out of doors, but equally easy in cool, light conditions indoors, *P. undulatum variegatum* is a handsome plant that will attain a height of some 6 ft (2 m) when its roots are confined to a pot. Keep the compost moist, but avoid extremes of wet and dry conditions.

Platycerium

These are ferns with a difference in that they do not have the delicate foliage which is normally associated with this group of plants. Instead they produce two types of fronds, the more interesting of the two being the firm, down-covered fertile ones that are not unlike antlers in shape and are responsible for the plant having the common name of stag's-horn fern. The other fronds are sterile and are known as the anchor fronds as they attach the plant securely to whatever tree or other support it is growing on. In time these leaves change to an unpleasing dry brown, but when young they are beautifully smooth and pale green. Neither type of frond should be handled or cleaned in any way as this will mar its natural downy appearance.

To do well these ferns require warmth, shade and moisture, but at no time must they become waterlogged. Being natural epiphytes they are seen at their best when attached to a piece of bark or old tree stem – sections of bark can be purchased and plants do look better when set off against this clean and natural backing. To attach a plant knock it from its pot and bind the root ball with wet sphagnum moss, then fasten it to the bark with plastic-covered wire, and thereafter keep it moist by periodically plunging both plant and anchorage in a bucket of water. In time the anchor leaves will completely envelop the bark and a most pleasing plant will be the result. *Platycerium bifurcatum* is the most commonly available kind.

Plectranthus

Belonging to the same family of plants as the humble coleus, *Labiatae*, the plectranthus are equally easy to care for. There are four in cultivation, but only two that one is likely to come across in the normal course of events; these are *Plectranthus australis* and *P. oertendahlii*. The first has rounded glossy green leaves that are deeply crenated along their margins and is of natural creeping habit. *P. oertendahlii* has leaf margins that are only slightly crenated and the leaves are less waxy in appearance, but this is more than compensated for by their attractive silvery veins.

Both plants are extremely easy to care for indoors, needing only a light windowsill position in reasonable warmth and watering that is moderate but never neglected. To retain their attractive crisp appearance it will be necessary to feed them with a balanced liquid fertilizer at regular intervals once they have become established in their pots. If a proper feeding programme is maintained plectranthus should only need potting on into larger containers every second or third year. In any event, plant pots should never be too large, and it is usually better to start new plants from cuttings rather than pot the old favourite into larger and larger containers. Cuttings require very little preparation as almost any piece will root in peaty compost in warm conditions.

If you are green fingered, or lucky, there may be the bonus of white or whitish-lavender flowers in the autumn.

Polyscias balfouriana marginata

Podocarpus macrophyllus

Primula malacoides

Podocarpus

Podocarpus are very slow growing and would seem to have little appeal for the present-day pot-plant owner who wants plants that grow at a reasonable pace. The attraction, therefore, lies in the fact that podocarpus has something different to offer, the leaves being slim and green and very congested. It is also a fairly tolerant plant that will accept lower temperatures without too much discomfort provided the compost is not allowed to become too wet. It requires annual potting in John Innes potting compost No. 3 until it is in 10-in (25-cm) pots and must then be fed regularly.

Acquiring plants has become a difficult matter, although podocarpus may be raised from seed if this can be obtained in the first place. There are a number of these trees, but *Podocarpus macrophyllus* is probably best as it is very compact and would make an ideal plant for the patio or balcony during the summer months. Plants are in no way demanding.

Polyscias

Belonging to the *Araliaceae family* these are plants that develop into tall evergreen woody shrubs with attractive green or variegated foliage. To grow them well they need lightly shaded conditions in a warm room that is maintained at an even temperature in the region of 18°C (65°F). Plants will be less inclined to be top heavy if, as they increase in size, they are transferred to clay pots rather than the lighter plastic ones. It will also be necessary to use a fairly heavy compost such as John Innes potting compost No. 3 and to ensure that it is freely drained by placing a layer of crocks in the bottom of the pot.

With green and cream coloured leaves, *Polyscias balfouriana* is probably the best known, but *P. b. marginata* has much softer and more attractive colouring in a mixture of green and yellowish green with touches of cream. When grown in large pots in ideal conditions both plants will attain a height of some 15 ft (4·5 m), but the upward progress of polyscias can be curtailed by removing the growing tips.

There are several more compact species, such as *P. dissecta*, *P. filicifolia* and *P. fruiticosa elegans*, all of which have more delicate foliage and are of more manageable size for smaller size rooms.

All can be rooted and grown from cuttings about 4 in (10 cm) in length taken in the spring, or they may be increased by means of cuttings of fleshier root sections taken at the same time of the year.

Primula

During the winter and spring months there can be few potted plants that match the graceful appearance of the primulas, which are available in a very wide range of delicate colours. With greenhouse facilities that offer a minimum temperature of around 10°C (50°F) it is not difficult to raise plants from seed sown between February and May according to variety. Sow the seed very finely on the surface of John Innes potting compost No. 1 and place the seedboxes or pots in a warm propagator, temperature 16°C (60°F) if possible. Once the seedlings can be handled they should be transferred to small pots, or spaced out in seedboxes and put in pots at a later date. Keep the compost and surroundings moist, but avoid splashing water over the foliage, particularly during the colder weather.

In common with many flowering plants it will be better to remove the early flowers that develop as this will help to build up the plant so that a much better show is provided later. Once the plants have become established in their final pots they should be fed regularly with liquid fertilizer at least once each week.

Although essentially winter- and spring-flowering plants, it is not uncommon to find that *Primula obconica* will often flower for ten months of the year. There are few flowering pot plants, other than the saintpaulia, that can match this sort of performance. A disappointing aspect of this plant, however, is that after handling it many people suffer skin rashes and irritation, and one would certainly suspect *P. obconica* if anyone in the homestead complains of skin

Primula obconica

Punica granatum nana

Pteris cretica

Pteris

Punica

irritation following the introduction of the plant. In fact, it is not even necessary to handle the plant, susceptible people will be affected simply by being in the same room as one. This is, no doubt, one very good reason why this superb plant, with its flowers in a range of pink, lilac, blue, and white, has been less popular in recent years.

Primula malacoides is another favourite that has been improved in recent years with the introduction of many new colours – lavenders, pinks, reds and white. It is also easy to care for indoors and only requires a light position in a cool room to give of its best.

There are a number of other primulas that can be raised from seed or purchased as mature plants – among them *P. sinensis* and its several forms, and the yellow-flowered *P. kewensis* which, alas, seldom seems very popular. There is also *P. acaulis* which is not unlike a miniature form of polyanthus and may be planted in the garden after flowering.

Of these the most commonly available are *Pteris cretica*, with fronds about 1 ft (30 cm) in length, and *P. ensiformis* which has slender fertile fronds to about 20 in (50 cm), and shorter sterile fronds. There are several forms of both of these, all of them attractive and not difficult to manage.

Protection from strong light is necessary and temperatures in the order of 16°C (60°F) will suit them, though lower temperatures will not be damaging if the plants are not left cold and wet for long periods. Almost the best way to be rid of any plant that prefers reasonable warmth is to keep the compost very wet and to lower the temperature at the same time – wet and cold conditions are never a very satisfactory combination as far as indoor plants are concerned. All ferns when growing in reasonable warmth should be kept moist all the time, care being taken to avoid extremes of wet and cold.

Plants may be propagated by sowing spores on a mixture of sand and peat in a temperature in the region of 27°C (80°F), but this is a business requiring a degree of skill and is best left to the experienced nurseryman. It is also possible to increase plants by means of division. Do this carefully and pot up the divided pieces in John Innes potting compost No. 1; do not overwater plants while they are settling into the new compost and keep them warm.

This is the pomegranate and it is another of the plants that may form part of the patio scene during the summer months, or all the year round if the patio is sheltered and very severe weather conditions are not experienced. In milder areas the pomegranate is relatively hardy, but should have the protection of a wall when planted outside.

There are several varieties, but for pot culture *Punica granatum nana* is by far the best as it seldom attains a height of more than 3 ft (1 m), while *P. granatum* is much larger, coarser and less attractive. Growth is very woody, the leaves are small and green and the attractive flowers, which are produced in summer and early autumn, are double and a pleasing shade of orange. Plants may be raised from seed sown in the spring, or increased by means of firm cuttings taken in the summer and inserted in John Innes potting compost No. 1.

Getting stock and seed may, however, be a problem as they are in short supply but if you have the space to accommodate a plant they are worth keeping an eye open for, and with luck you may be able to grow your own pomegranate fruit. However, even when pot-grown plants fruit they are not very exciting as the fruits seldom swell to more than large marble size. When caring for them well-drained compost and good light are essentials, keep them moist in the summer and a little on the dry side in winter.

Rhoeo discolor

Rhoicissus rhomboidea

Ricinus communis

Rhoeo

Rhoeo discolor belongs to the diverse tradescantia tribe (*Commelinaceae*), and anything less like the conventional image of a tradescantia would be difficult to conceive. It is also a rather more temperamental plant, needing a minimum temperature of about 18°C (65°F) and careful watering that ensures moistness without extremes of wet and dry conditions. It prefers shade and should be fed once it is established in 5-in (13-cm) pots – larger pots are not usually necessary.

The leaves, which are about 10 in (25 cm) in length and arranged in a rosette, are unusual in colouring. The undersides are purple and the uppermost sides are brownish-green with attractive cream stripes. In spite of this rhoeo has never been a very popular house plant, although for the person looking for something different it is well worth seeking out.

The reason for the two common names, Moses-on-a-raft and three-men-in-a-boat, is an added interest. These relate to the way in which the typical tradescantia-type flowers nestle in the boat-shaped bract that is borne low down on the plant.

To increase the plant take cuttings from firm young growth and insert them in John Innes potting compost No. 2 in warm conditions; the cuttings can be taken at any time other than in winter.

Rhoicissus

Rhoicissus rhomboidea, grape ivy, is one plant which will frequently survive in what would seem like impossible conditions. It is an attractive climber with three-lobed, glossy dark green leaves which can be used in conjunction with a trellis or similar support to divide one room from another, a dining room from a living room for example. For such a position it is much more satisfactory to select a tolerant plant that will thrive in rather inadequate light rather than pick those that in a short time will be hanging to the supports for dear life. And rhoicissus is just such a plant in that it will be little bother if given reasonable care. A minimum temperature of 7°C (45°F) is all that is required, although it is able to withstand central heating, and the plant is better out of strong sunlight but in a well ventilated room. Water freely in the summer and keep just moist in winter; feed when new growth is being produced. The ideal compost for all stages of potting is a mixture of two parts of John Innes potting compost No. 3 and one part of fresh peat. As the plants grow some pruning may be required to keep them in check.

Propagation is easy from cuttings of two leaves taken about half an inch (1 cm) below the lower leaf joint.

Ricinus

Ricinus communis, the true castor oil plant (once described to me as the castrol plant – an understandable error perhaps), is a most accommodating subject as it may be grown to maturity in the same year as seed is sown. Prior to sowing, the seed should be soaked in tepid water to assist germination. Sowing should be done in April and the resultant seedlings potted as soon as possible, and thereafter potting on should not be neglected until the plants are in 7-in (18-cm) pots of John Innes potting compost No. 3. Ricinus may be grown indoors, or they may become part of the patio display during the summer months.

The shape of the leaf is very similar to that of *Aralia sieboldii*, a plant with which it is often confused. The leaves tend to take on a reddish-bronze colour as they age and this makes the plant a most attractive member of a group arrangement.

Ricinus are useful plants for those who seek something with size and maturity for a summer display, yet do not have the facilities to house them during the winter. When grown as an annual ricinus will attain a height of 4 ft (1·25 m) but if, instead of being discarded in the autumn, it is rehoused and grown on indoors as a perennial it will eventually reach 15 ft (4·5 m). Indoors ricinus will need good light if they are to retain their colouring, ample watering and feeding.

Ruellia macrantha

Sansevieria trifasciata Golden Hahnii

Ruellia

One seldom hears of plants being referred to as 'stove plants' these days – stove being an old gardening term that implied that the plants so defined were in need of very high greenhouse temperatures in excess of 20°C (68°F) and that they were among the most difficult of potted plants to care for. Personal experience suggests that the term has fallen out of favour and that many of the plants that were in the past treated as stove subjects could have been grown equally well, and with considerably less expense, at very much lower temperatures.

There are a number of ruellias, family *Acanthaceae*, which can be comfortably grown at temperatures in the region of 16°C (60°F) if the compost is kept a little on the dry side during the winter months when lower temperatures are likely to prevail. There are both annual and perennial species; the latter can be increased by means of cuttings taken in the spring, and seed is sown in February to provide annual plants. In both respects it is an advantage to use a heated propagating case or frame.

Either when growing indoors or in the greenhouse, it is essential that plants should enjoy a shaded position and that the compost be kept moist at all times, with just a little less water being given during the colder months of the year. The potting medium should be very light and peaty, so the heavier John Innes type compost should not be used unless a considerable amount of extra peat is added.

The flowers are mostly trumpet shaped, rosy purple, blooming from winter to spring in *Ruellia macrantha* and in summer or winter for *R. amoena*.

Sansevieria

Old indestructible – the reader who has difficulty in maintaining this plant really has got a problem, and the probable reason for failure is misguided kindness. Consideration may be all very well with the more tender plants, but *Sansevieria trifasciata laurentii*, to give it its full name, will do very much better if it is forgotten rather than fussed over. Its main need is for reasonable warmth and good light in which to grow – there is no necessity for frequent watering, feeding and the usual fussing that other house plants appreciate.

Knowing when to pot on is no problem as the plant should be left until it actually breaks the pot in which it is growing before finding a slightly larger clay pot and John Innes potting compost No. 2 in which to repot it. Clay pots are needed to provide reasonable anchorage for the top-heavy foliage that is of a succulent nature and stores considerable moisture, hence the need for giving the plant a good watering at infrequent intervals.

In different parts of the world the plant has different common names, two of them being descriptive while the common name in Britain of mother-in-law's tongue is less easy to understand. In America it is the snake plant, this for the obvious reason that the leaves have a snake-like pattern in them. A West Indian once informed me that in his part of the world it is commonly referred to as donkey's ears, again obvious when one isolates two leaves and sees the resemblance between them and the ears of the donkey.

New plants may be made by dividing the leaves into sections of about 3 in (8 cm) in length and rooting them in warm conditions – unfortunately plants resulting from this form of propagation do not have the yellow margin of the parent plant and are much less attractive. To retain the margin plants should be propagated by taking the young shoots that grow up beside the larger ones and potting them individually. To do this the plant should be removed from its pot and the young shoot taken off with a piece of the rhizome and as much root as possible. It will also be beneficial to dust the cut mark with rooting powder to reduce the possibility of rotting.

Older plants of sansevieria will frequently produce lime-green flowers in the summer, these are pleasantly scented and quite attractive.

Sansevieria t. Hahnii and *S. t.* Golden Hahnii are extremely slow-growing rosette-forming plants, and are equally easy to care for. This also applies to *S. gigantea* which has broad mottled green leaves that grow to a height of some 18 in (45 cm).

Saxifraga sarmentosa

Schizanthus hybrid

Schefflera actinophylla

Saxifraga

Saxifraga sarmentosa is another of the friendship plants, also the sort of plant that will excite the curiosity of the child who may be showing an interest in plants. Easy propagation and reasonably quick growth are its attractions – ease of rooting making it simple to give plants to friends (hence the friendship angle), besides encouraging the younger gardener to take an interest.

The plants grow as small rosettes of almost indeterminate mottled colouring, and from the young plants similar small rosettes appear on slender stalks. These can be most attractive when hanging down from a well grown specimen. The best way of propagating numbers of plants is to place the plant pot in the centre of a box filled with John Innes potting compost No. 1 and then to peg the young plants into the compost as their stalks become long enough. When these have obviously rooted and begun to make new growth they may be snipped from the parent plant before being lifted and potted into individual containers of John Innes potting compost No. 2.

The trailing saxifraga will grow in most conditions but is seen at its best when suspended about eye level, either in pots or hanging baskets. When baskets are used for smaller-leaved plants of this kind it is important to use ones of small dimension that will be in keeping with the size of the plants being put in them. In this respect it may be wise to choose the more modern plastic baskets that have drip trays fitted on to their bases, so making it possible to use them indoors without getting a shower bath every time the plant is watered.

Schefflera

The resilience of plants is something that many of us find difficult to understand, and we frequently hear of plants that suffer incredible hardship only to spring back to life when the conditions improve. One would not normally associate the tall and elegant schefflera with being the most durable of plants, although it is not by any means a problem. Yet a friend who manages a house-plant nursery has told me the following story of a very large schefflera that had been cut down and seemingly disposed of. From the wreckage he cut a piece of leafless stem some 3 ft (1 m) in length with the thought that it would make a good walking stick. This he used daily around the nursery for nearly two months; until, in fact, he pushed it into a large pot of compost with instructions to an astonished member of staff that it should remain there to see if it would root! Some weeks later, to everyone's amazement, leaf buds were seen swelling at the top of the stick – the plant is now a treasured possession of beautiful standard shape and is clearly very pleased to have a new lease of life.

The schefflera is very much an individual sort of plant that should stand on its own and have ample space in which to develop. Mature plants should be in pots at least 10 in (25 cm) in diameter, and the standard growing conditions of warmth, light, and moisture will suit them fine. The two species most often seen are *Schefflera actinophylla* and *S. digitata*. Propagation is from seed.

Schizanthus

This is a potted plant that is very much of a temporary nature; a plant that will provide added colour for a limited period as opposed to the conventional house plant that can be kept indoors throughout the year.

The ornate Victorian conservatory was a costly structure to heat and maintain and is now very much a thing of the past, but in recent years we have seen a tremendous increase in the number of garden rooms or sun lounges of both permanent and temporary nature. With the addition of comparatively few plants these garden rooms can take on a new dimension, and if the room is heated then so much the better. With just a little thought given to the selection of plants and furniture such rooms can enhance the appearance of both the garden and the home. And it goes without saying that as the light factor in the garden room is so much better than indoors many plants can be grown that would otherwise present problems.

In this respect we could well consider the poor man's orchid or butterfly flower as the schizanthus is commonly known. They are available in a brilliant array of colours, are no great problem to manage and, a considerable asset, they will do perfectly well in cool conditions. For the few plants required for the garden room it is probably better to purchase young plants than to grow them from seed only to find that there are many more than can be adequately handled – having too many invariably leads to few of the plants doing as well as they would if there was less of them. When purchasing, to give some variation, try to select some from

Senecio macroglossus variegatus

Schizanthus hybrid

Setcreasea purpurea

Senecio

Setcreasea

the taller strains and some of the dwarf varieties. Plants can be raised from seed simply by following the directions on the packet in which the seed is bought.

To spread the flowering period it is possible to have plants which will flower in the spring from seed that was sown in September, and a further batch from spring-sown seed that will flower in late summer. Plants should be potted on as they fill their existing pots with roots, using John Innes potting compost No. 2; the final potting should be into 7- or 8-in (18- to 20-cm) pots. Thereafter feeding should not be neglected if yellowing of the foliage is to be prevented. Young plants must have their growing points removed to produce full and compact specimens. The growing atmosphere should be buoyant, so stuffy and hot conditions should be avoided by regular ventilation; even on colder days this will do no harm if the temperature does not drop below 7°C (45°F).

It is important to ensure that as plants develop they are provided with cane supports and larger plants will need several canes around the edge of the pot. Following flowering plants are of no further value and should be discarded.

There are two of these that the house-plant grower is likely to come across, one dark green and somewhat coarse and the other with variegated glossy leaves that are pleasantly colourful. Both occasionally produce attractive daisy-like flowers.

The green one is *Senecio mikanioides*, commonly named German ivy, which is deceptive as it is not an ivy. However, it is a most useful plant indoors and in its way is probably far more practical as a trailing plant on the wall of the living room than any of the ivies are ever likely to be. Where ivies abhor hot, dry conditions the senecios will be much more at home and will provide an equally good effect and grow at twice the pace of the ivies. I frequently wonder why there are not more compact trailing plants on the market, especially as there is a keen demand for them and lots of wall brackets and pot holders about for putting them in. However, it must be added that when choosing plants for wall positions only the more durable ones should be selected.

The variegated form is *S. macroglossus variegatus*, Cape ivy. This is a pretty little plant that roots like a weed when put in almost any compost as a cutting, and naturally climbs any support that may be available. If all the growing points are removed when young it can be used as a trailing plant, but the tendency is for it to climb. Pot in John Innes potting compost No. 2 with a little extra peat, and keep a careful watch for greenfly on the young growth.

Setcreasea striata and *S. purpurea* belong to the tradescantia tribe, and are as little trouble to raise from cuttings as are most of the smaller-leaved tradescantias. The first, as the name suggests, has green leaves with prominent white stripes, whilst the second has unusual purple colouring which gives it the common name of purple heart. Both can be raised from cuttings a few inches in length, but better looking plants will be produced if several cuttings are put in each pot and the growing points of each cutting removed when it has rooted and begun to grow away.

Both are easy plants for a position in good light but away from strong sunlight. They need watering fairly freely in summer and should also be given regular applications of fertilizer then. Keep the compost only just moist in the winter.

The flowers of *S. striata* are white, those of *S. purpurea* lilac, and all are produced in the summer. The flowers are, however, very insignificant and these plants must be regarded primarily as foliage plants.

Solanum capsicastrum

Sparmannia africana

Strelitzia reginae

Solanum

The winter cherry, *Solanum capsicastrum*, is one of those plants that is normally purchased in late autumn and winter, its bright orange-red berries doing much to cheer the winter scene both in the greenhouse and indoors. Although the plants may be kept from one year to the next it is much better to start with fresh ones annually by sowing seed in February or March, or by taking cuttings in spring from plants saved from the previous year. The seed may be saved from berries which have been allowed to ripen fully.

Seed should be sown in the conventional manner in a temperature around 18°C (65°F) and the seedlings pricked out and potted on as they become large enough. The tip growth and subsequent sideshoots of young plants should be pinched out to encourage a more bushy habit. During the summer months the plants in their pots may be placed out of doors in a sheltered spot, to be brought in again about mid-September. To assist pollination it is important that the plants should be sprayed over daily with water while they are in flower – failure to do this may result in a much less satisfying crop of berries.

While solanums are indoors it is most essential that they should enjoy the lightest possible location. This is particularly important once the berries have developed as poor light may result in them being shed.

Sparmannia

The African wind flower, *Sparmannia africana*, has lime-green colouring, is a vigorous-growing plant and, in my humble opinion, very beautiful when well grown. Being a vigorous grower it can well do with potting on annually into John Innes potting compost No. 3 until such time as it is in a 10-in (25-cm) pot, thereafter it should be sustained by regular feeding. After two or three years it will show signs of deterioration and may have to be replaced by a new plant grown from easily rooted cuttings. Alternatively, take the plant from its pot and with a sharp knife remove a good proportion of the root system before replacing in the same pot with fresh compost – once potted give a thorough watering.

This is a plant for average indoor conditions, although it does best in the slightly cooler temperature range and will tolerate a minimum temperature of 7°C (45°F). Keep the compost moist at all times.

The white flowers are produced in May and June, the pistils in the centre of the flowers open outwards in the slightest movement of air and give the plant its common name.

Strelitzia

Strelitzia reginae, bird of paradise flower, has a fantastic exotic-looking flower which it takes in the region of five years to produce from the time the seed is sown, and there seems to be no short cut to success. Seeds are not difficult to germinate in a high temperature in the region of 21°C (70°F). Once the plants have got under way they can be transferred to small pots to grow on, but avoid the temptation of putting them into pots that are of excessive size. Let them become well established in their existing pots before moving them on to the next size up. Do not be tempted into thinking that the larger the pot the plant is growing in then the better the growth must be; the reverse is often the case as a small amount of root in a great bulk of soil leads to waterlogged compost and indifferent results.

Strelitzias will require the lightest possible position indoors, and will not come to any harm out of doors during the warmer summer months. Moderate temperature is needed once plants are in pots of the 7-in (18-cm) size and there they should remain as they flower very much better when pot bound. Water freely in summer, less often in winter. Increase older plants by division early in the year.

Besides being agreeably attractive as potted plants there is also a keen demand for strelitzias as cut flowers both in the amateur and professional sector. Indeed, if flower production is the most important requirement it is often better if the plant is removed from its pot and planted in the ground. In this event a heated greenhouse offering the conditions described earlier

Streptocarpus hybrid

Streptocarpus Constant Nymph

Streptocarpus

will be an essential requirement. Rather than putting a single plant in an odd corner where it will almost inevitably suffer indifferent treatment, it is very much better to plant a small group of about six plants in soil which has been well dug and fertilized. Mature plants will give much better results than tiny ones that will take much longer to develop.

Having taken some care with the planting, strelitzias can be left for many years with only the occasional attention of cleaning them over and giving them a dressing of bonemeal in the winter. They will not be harmed if the greenhouse glass is lightly shaded in the summer, but in winter it is important that the glass should be absolutely clean in order to obtain the best results.

Strelitzia reginae is the more compact species and better suited to the limited height of the average small greenhouse. There are taller, much bolder types such as *S. augustifolia*, which attains a height of some 15 ft (4·5 m) and takes as many years to produce its first flower.

Although much work has been done in recent years on developing new varieties of this plant, varieties which are very free blooming and with a much wider colour range, my preference is still for the old established *Streptocarpus* Constant Nymph. This has spear-shaped leaves and beautiful violet-blue flowers.

All the streptocarpus flower throughout the spring and summer months; in fact, with reasonable warmth in a small greenhouse some flowers are produced at almost any time of the year.

Indoors they require ample light, needing shade from strong sunlight only. An airy position that offers a reasonable temperature will also be an advantage. The compost should be moist all the time, with slightly less water being given during the winter months. Regular feeding will be the order of the day during the spring and summer months once the plants have become established in their pots.

Plants may be propagated from seed sown in February or midsummer to provide plants at different times of the year – for seed sowing a temperature of about 18°C (65°F) will be required. Plants may also be increased by dividing larger clumps in the spring of the year and potting them up individually.

Should a greater number of plants be needed then individual leaves may be removed and inserted in a peat and sand mixture at a temperature similar to that suggested for seed raising. Small clumps of new leaves will form at the point of insertion and when these are large enough to handle

they should be potted up individually.

Apart from the well established Constant Nymph, there is a range of new varieties that I mentioned earlier. These have been bred from *S* x *hybridus* and *S. johannis* and they are all known by girls' names – Tina, Helen, Louise, etc. They are notable for massed displays of bloom in shades of pink, rose, mauve, blue, purple, and white.

Although streptocarpus, commonly known as Cape primroses, make fine plants for indoor decoration they are also superb plants for the small greenhouse that is moderately heated. The cost of heating a small greenhouse or garden room is often frowned upon as being extravagant, but when compared to the cost of other hobbies and pastimes it is not such an expensive item considering the amount of pleasure that the enthusiast can derive from growing the things he likes.

Tolmiea menziesii

Tetrastigma voinierianum

Thunbergia alata

Tetrastigma

The young growth of this plant has a slightly menacing look as it projects from the parent plant almost at right angles and the leading tendrils stand out like antennae in search of prey. Behind these the older tendrils hang down and resemble thin spidery legs that give this section of the plant a somewhat awesome appearance.

Belonging to the vine family *Tetrastigma voinierianum*, when it decides that it likes you and is prepared to grow, is one of the most rampant of the larger house plants and will very quickly fill its allotted space. Seen at its best when interwoven through a trellis or similar framework it is one of the most rapid-growing plants, but will at times, often for unaccountable reasons, remain static for months on end. During these periods it is wise not to be too heavy with the watering can, but at other times the compost should not be allowed to dry out. Active plants will quite quickly, as a rule, grow to the point where they should be in pots of a 10-in (25-cm) size and will need regular feeding. Potting into larger pots than this is seldom necessary for plants in the home. When potting on use John Innes compost No. 3.

The foliage is covered with a natural downy substance. Plants with leaves of this sort should at no time be cleaned as the rubbing action on the leaf mars their appearance. The temperature should be maintained in the region of 18 to 21°C (65 to 70°F), and a shaded position is best.

Thunbergia

With facilities such as a heated greenhouse or garden room it will be found that seed of many plants can be sown at differing times of the year in order to spread the flowering period over many more months. For example, schizanthus seed can be sown in late autumn to flower in the spring, and seed sown in February or March will flower in late summer.

Black-eyed Susan, *Thunbergia alata,* is a more unusual plant that may be treated in similar fashion, the period from seed sowing to flowering is about six months. The common name is derived from the appearance of the flowers which have orange petals with black centres and are very attractive when seen *en masse* on well grown plants. Only a few seeds need be sown at a time, and an excellent method of doing this is to fill a 5-in (13-cm) pot with a good house-plant compost and then to sow six seeds in the pot; when these are established the three weaker seedlings should be removed, leaving the stronger ones to grow on.

Thunbergia is a natural climbing plant, therefore some form of support must be provided – it need not be too tall as plants seldom attain a height of more than 6 ft (2 m) before they lose their appearance and need replacing. Provide good light and reasonable warmth, and keep a watchful eye for red spider mite – plants that are badly affected by this should be destroyed.

Tolmiea

Tolmiea menziesii has acquired its amusing common name, the pick-a-back plant, from the tiny plantlets which are formed and carried on the backs of the older leaves. These plantlets provide an easy means of propagation and if removed and placed on pots of ordinary compost they will root with no difficulty.

Tolmiea is also one of the few indoor plants which is completely hardy in Britain. It is, in fact, a hardy herbaceous perennial and will survive out of doors, although in common with other perennials the foliage dies down in the winter. Its hardiness is a useful feature when contemplating holidays as it will be quite all right if it is planted in the garden and well watered before departure, but preferably not in midwinter.

Indoors it is evergreen and requires only cool and light conditions to do well and produce its hummocks of bright green leaves. Temperature is not important but something in the region of 10°C (50°F) will be the most suitable. In hotter and dryer conditions this plant may well be attacked by red spider. Larger plants tend to become too large and untidy and it is better to discard them when this happens and start afresh.

Tradescantia blossfeldiana variegata

Tradescantia fluminensis Quicksilver

Zebrina pendula

Tradescantia

Another of the friendship plants that can be acquired as cuttings or small plants from friends, rather than from the flower shop where there seems to have been a dwindling supply in recent years. However, there is little reason to go short of these plants as there must be millions of them around and it is simply a question of keeping one's eye open for them in a shop, or on a windowsill when visiting.

Cuttings acquired on request, or by accident when they fall off in the hand (these always root better!) should be placed in a polythene bag, care being taken not to crush them. On getting them home the best way to root them is to insert five or six cuttings in 3½-in (9-cm) pots of John Innes potting compost No. 2, and to remove the growing tips when they have begun to grow well. Alternatively, single cuttings can be suspended in the narrow neck of a bottle filled with water. Once rooted they can be potted up in compost. However, except for the interest of seeing roots develop, this seems to be a waste of time as the cuttings may just as well go directly into the pot where they must grow eventually.

When kept moist, well fed once they are established, and in good light, they make fine plants in very little time. In good light they are more likely to retain their variegation, and to help this any green shoots should be removed as soon as they are seen. The plain green shoots are much more vigorous and will quickly take over if left on the plant.

The temperature is not especially important provided it does not become very hot or very cold – tradescantias will do best in the middle range. Being durable and adaptable they will grow almost anywhere that is warm and moist. Grown conventionally in pots they will do well, or they are equally at home when pieces break from the plant and grow in the gravel on the greenhouse staging. They will also grow on the floor of the greenhouse under the staging where they will keep down the weeds and provide a continual supply of cuttings from which to propagate fresh plants.

There are many varieties; besides the usual silver, there are golden as well as pink, cream and russet-brown forms. Most are varieties of *Tradescantia fluminensis*, which is a trailing plant with bright green leaves. Much more spectacular is *T. f.* Quicksilver with silver variegation. *T. blossfeldiana* is a more erect plant, rather hairy, with dark green leaves with purple undersides. Once again there is a more attractive variety – *T. b. variegata* – with cream-striped leaves.

Zebrina

Zebrina pendula, a humble member of the tradescantia tribe, is often passed over without so much as a second look when seen growing among a collection of other plants. Next time have a closer look and you will see that there are some fascinating colours in the leaves – green, purple and brown with an overall sheen of silver in really healthy plants. The undersides of the leaves are a greenish purple.

Treatment is the same as for the tradescantia, but to see plants of zebrina at their best they should be grown in hanging baskets where they will have ample space for both root development and leaf growth. Many is the time I have stood on duty at a flower show and seen the almost incredulous faces of visitors looking at superb baskets of *Z. pendula* – you can read these faces as they think to themselves that it cannot possibly be the same plant as the poor wee thing they are attempting to grow on the mantlepiece at home. A great deal of satisfaction can be derived from growing one of the humbler plants into something of a show stopper.

There is a good form of *Z. pendula* called Quadricolor which has rose-purple leaves with white stripes and purple undersides. *Z. purpusii* is also an interesting species with purple-flushed green leaves which once again are purple on the underneath. *Z. pendula* produces rather insignificant pale purple flowers in summer while *Z. purpusii* carries lavender flowers in autumn.

Increase by cuttings a few inches in length taken at any time of the year and rooted in John Innes potting compost No. 1.

75

Aglaonema Silver Queen

Anthurium scherzerianum

Moderately Easy Indoor Plants

Plants in this section may well be considered as a natural step up for the plantsman who has achieved reasonable success with the easier subjects. And it may well be found that some of the plants listed here are not as difficult to manage as some of those in the easier section. However, personal experience of growing these plants and of seeing them growing in other people's homes suggests that they do, in fact, present that extra bit of difficulty in average home surroundings.

Indoor conditions have changed considerably over the years and the average home is now well heated and offers abundant light for the general benefit of plants. However, excessive temperature can be a disadvantage to many plants and the cyclamen, which prefers cool and light conditions, is a typical example of a comparatively easy plant that can become a difficult subject when grown in rooms that are very hot and dry. The same applies to bougainvillea, which can be particularly difficult in conditions that are hot, dry and airless – given cool, light and airy conditions it could well be described as an easy plant. But such conditions are now becoming the exception rather than the rule.

Aglaonema

Given the warm and moist conditions that they require many of the aglaonemas will develop into fine specimen plants that will be much admired. They will also appreciate shade and a peaty compost that is free draining, so it is necessary to provide ample 'crocks' in the bottom of the pot. One common problem with aglaonemas is that the bases of their leaves curl tightly around the stem of the plant and provide a perfectly protected home for the mealy bug pests that seem to find these plants particularly appetizing. Dealing effectively with these pests will mean thoroughly drenching the areas around the stem of the plant with appropriate insecticide – to kill mealy bug direct contact with the pest is essential.

Where space is adequate and a bold plant is not an embarrassment, then consideration should be given to *Aglaonema pseudobracteatum*, a fine plant with attractive cream and green variegation. Plants are not easily come by and it may necessitate searching through the specialists' catalogues before a source of supply is located.

Much more compact and much less trouble to acquire is *A*. Silver Queen which has attractive variegated leaves in shades of grey. When purchasing this plant take the precaution of inspecting the area around the base of the leaves just to ensure that there are no pests in residence. There are a number of other varieties that may be offered for sale but not all of them are as attractive as those mentioned.

The simplest method of propagation is by division of the root clumps in spring, or at any time if a heated propagator is available.

Anthurium

Belonging to the *Araceae* family, all the anthuriums will require warm and humid conditions if they are to be seen at their best. Provided it can be obtained the keen plantsman will find that the majority of the anthuriums can be raised from seed with little difficulty if a propagating case heated to a temperature of some 20°C (68°F) can be maintained. At all stages of growth a peaty and open mixture is required. Older plants will benefit from having a little fresh sphagnum moss added to the potting mixture, and for larger plants of *Anthurium andreanum* it will be an added advantage if the moss can be soaked in liquid fertilizer prior to being added to the compost.

The easiest to manage indoors, and by far the most freely available, is *A. scherzerianum* which seldom attains a height of more than 2 ft (60 cm) and will, when carefully grown, oblige with a fine display of scarlet-coloured 'flowers'. The flower-like spathe is highly colourful and the spadix is spiralled and said to resemble the flamingo, hence the common name of flamingo plant.

Much more demanding in respect of space and attention is the very exotic *A. andreanum* with colourful flowers in many shades of pink and red; the rarer white forms are a coveted acquisition. This grows much taller than the flamingo plant and to get the best out of it is necessary to bind a thick layer of sphagnum moss around the stem of the plant as it increases in height – aerial roots will then grow into the moss and the plant in turn will do very much better. *A. crystallinum* is grown purely for its large and exotic leaves, and needs warmth, shade and moist conditions.

Asplenium nidus

Bougainvillea glabra

Camellia japonica tricolor

Asplenium

With its appealing common name of bird's nest fern, *Asplenium nidus* is almost assured of being popular. But, into the bargain, it is also a very fine foliage plant in its own right and when well grown can hold its own in almost any company. The leaves are smooth and pale green in colour and are arranged in the form of a shuttlecock. They must, however, be handled with the greatest care as they are very easily damaged. Scale insects can be troublesome and should be carefully washed off with a soft sponge that has been soaked in insecticide.

Aspleniums need steady warmth, shaded locations and fairly high humidity if they are to do well. Given these conditions and a reasonable amount of luck, plants of the bird's nest fern will attain quite majestic proportions in time with individual leaves 3 ft (1 m) or more in length. It is, however, a long, slow business to grow plants to specimen size and such grand results should not be expected in the living room. Small delicate plants can, with advantage, be confined to a growing case until they are of reasonable size. Many of the larger propagating cases, made of plastic and not too expensive, are ideal for this purpose

Potting on into larger containers should only be necessary every second or third year once plants have advanced beyond their small initial pots. A well drained peaty compost will suit them best, and when watering they will benefit if rain water can be used. New plants can be raised from spores sown on the surface of sandy peat, but this is a difficult task best left to the nurseryman.

Bougainvillea

One of the most brilliant of tropical shrubs, the paper-like bracts of bougainvillea will offer an exotic and colourful touch to any greenhouse or garden room display. Indoors, where available light is often inadequate, these can be difficult plants unless placed in the lightest window position. In ideal conditions they will grow rapidly and soon find their way into the upper reaches of the room, so some form of support will have to be provided for growth to be tied to as it develops. The flower-like bracts begin to turn colour from March onwards, magenta shades being the more usual, although there are other colours that range from deep pink to white, with a fine yellow form being a particularly worthwhile acquisition.

While the plants are dormant during the winter months they will require no water and should be housed in a warm place. When growth develops in February the compost should be watered and any untidy growth can be pruned back to shape. Pruned pieces a few inches in length can be encouraged to root by placing them in a peat and sand compost and keeping them in a warm propagating frame; by using rooting powder even the oldest and toughest pieces can be successful. When potting use John Innes potting compost No. 2 or 3, depending on the size of the plant, and make sure that ample drainage is provided.

Temperatures in the region of 10 to 16°C (50 to 60°F) will be quite adequate, with lower temperatures in winter when the plants are dormant. A good sunny position is an essential requirement, and a watchful eye should be kept for mealy bugs.

Camellia

Belonging to the same family of plants, *Theaceae*, as the tea plants of commerce, the camellias are very much more durable than was at one time supposed. In milder areas if planted in open woodland they will develop into fine specimen plants, giving a magnificent show of their waxy, single or double flowers in the spring. The varieties offered for pot cultivation are mostly hybrids of *Camellia japonica* and the colours range from white through pink to red.

When reared in pots they are probably at their best when overwintered in a cold greenhouse that gives them a little protection from the worst of the weather, and during the summer months their naturally glossy leaves will do much to enhance the appearance of the patio, or terrace.

A peaty lime-free compost is essential and it will benefit plants if all watering can be done with rain water. Being slow-growing subjects, pruning is seldom necessary and when done should be confined to trimming untidy growth to a more pleasant shape. When grown as a pot plant indoors it is essential that the camellia should have a light window position in order to encourage growth and flower production. Keeping the compost moist in summer is important, with a little less water being given during the winter months – it is, however, essential that the compost should be free draining and pots must be well crocked. Due to a slow rate of growth potting on is not required very frequently, and it is important that all plants should be confined to pots that are relevant to their size. Loss of flowers and buds may result from erratic watering, and from wildly fluctuating temperatures.

Clerodendrum thomsonae

Crossandra infundibuliformis

Columnea gloriosa purpurea

Clerodendrum

Clerodendrum thomsonae is a woody, climbing shrub that will attain a height of some 8 ft (2·5 m), and not be too difficult if reasonable growing conditions and a lightly shaded position are available. Some form of support will be needed for tying growth to as it develops. The leaves are green and somewhat coarse in appearance, but any deficiency here is amply compensated for by the excitement of the colourful crimson and white bracts that hang in large clusters throughout the summer months.

Although plants will retain their leaves during the winter months if the compost is watered, it is often better to allow the compost to dry out gradually towards the autumn and to keep it dry until new growth is evident in the spring, when watering can be gradually restarted. At this time it is wise to pot the plant on into a larger container, or to remove some of the old compost and pot the plant with fresh compost in the same container. Plants can be pruned to more reasonable size after flowering in late summer or early autumn, but if space is available they may be left and will form a fine display against a wall.

Being somewhat vigorous they will soon fill their pots with roots, so it is important that feeding should begin as soon as they are established in their pots. When potting on, John Innes potting compost No. 2 or 3, depending on plant size, will suit them; younger plants will benefit if a little additional peat is added to the compost. In a warm propagating frame cuttings of a few inches in length will not be difficult to root if taken in the spring.

Columnea

These are among the most colourful and interesting of all the subjects that may be used as trailing plants in pots or hanging baskets but they are not seen offered for sale nearly as often as might be expected. However, they are well worth acquiring and will provide a brilliant show of colour in the early part of the year when there are not a great many flowering plants to choose from.

Cuttings, a few inches in length, will root readily in a heated propagator, and when rooted several pieces should be put in 3½-in (9-cm) pots and allowed to establish before being potted on again about six to eight weeks later. An alternative to potting is to place three or four of these small plants in a hanging basket, using a peaty and open compost.

There are many varieties to choose from but it is frequently a question of getting what is on offer. *Columnea banksii* is the most usual and it is a good plant for the home with waxy dark green leaves and red flowers from November to April. *C. gloriosa* is rather more delicate with paler green leaves although producing red flowers over much the same period, *C. g. purpurea* is a good form of this. *C. microphylla* looks rather like a smaller-leaved form of *gloriosa*.

All the columneas require warmth, light shade and a moist situation if they are to do well. For a few weeks prior to flower production it will be an advantage if the temperature can be lowered to about 10°C (50°F). At this time it is also advisable to keep the compost a little on the dry side.

Crossandra

Crossandra infundibuliformis is one of those enigmas of the plant world which will oblige one person by flowering and growing quite happily, while for another it simply refuses to grow or flower. There are many plants like this and it is often said that the successful owner possesses a form of green-fingered magic that induces plants to perform extraordinarily well for them. There are also those among the house-plant-growing public who swear by the need for talking to their plants in order to get the best from them – and they may be right, who knows?

Crossandras belong to the *Acanthaceae* family, from which we get a number of worthwhile house plants, among them the aphelandra and the beloperone. New plants of crossandra are propagated from cuttings taken in the spring; these should be from firm growth and some 3 in (8 cm) in length. It will also be helpful if cuttings are treated with a rooting powder prior to insertion, and it is essential that they should then be housed in a warm propagating case as they are not the easiest of subjects to root.

The leaves are an attractive glossy green and the flowers, which vary in colour from the red to the yellow side of orange, are borne over a long period during the spring and summer months. When caring for crossandras indoors they will need moist, warm and lightly shaded conditions.

Cyclamen hybrids

Cuphea platycentra

Cuphea

Cuphea platycentra (syn. *C. ignea*) has scarlet tubular flowers with white mouths that resemble the ash on the end of a cigar, hence the common name cigar plant. New plants may be raised from cuttings, a few inches in length, taken in the spring or summer, or plants may be very much more easily raised by sowing seed in the spring in a warm propagator. Fuller and more attractive plants can be obtained if several young seedlings are put in each pot rather than grown as solitary plants.

In summer cuphea can be put out of doors. In the home they should occupy a light position and the compost should be kept moist and fed once the plants have become established in their pots. Almost any reasonable potting medium will suit them, but a mixture of two parts of John Innes potting compost No. 3 and one part of peat is suggested as being ideal.

Plants quickly become straggly and untidy and, rather than trying to keep them from year to year, it will be much more satisfactory to raise fresh plants from seed annually. The usual run of garden pests find cupheas reasonably appetising it would seem, so a careful eye must be kept on them and pests treated as soon as they appear.

Cyclamen

In spite of much opposition from the many other flowering pot plants that are available at the same time, before and after Christmas, the cyclamen is still one of the most popular. This seems even more surprising as so many people find this attractive plant difficult to care for indoors.

The commercial producer may well give a clue to their treatment once bought for indoor decoration. An essential part of the nursery growing is to ensure that plants are not subjected to hot conditions, the aim being to maintain temperatures in the region of 13°C (55°F). It is also essential that plants should be grown in greenhouses that will provide dappled shade – this means shading that is sufficient to protect them from the direct rays of the sun but will at the same time admit adequate light. So, when caring for cyclamen indoors it is best to endeavour to emulate the efforts of the nurseryman by providing a light and cool windowsill and not a very hot dry environment.

Except for plants that are being grown on to specimen size for display purposes, almost all of those offered for sale by the commercial grower will have been raised from seed sown in the autumn of the previous year, although there are new strains of cyclamen that will produce good size plants from seed sown earlier in the same year. From their seedboxes the young plants are gradually potted on into larger containers using a reasonably peaty compost that is free draining, as heavy stodgy compost will inevitably produce poor results.

The ideal place for plants indoors is the light and reasonably sunny windowsill where they will enjoy cool rather than hot temperatures. Although cyclamen must be kept moist at all times it is better to err on the side of dry conditions rather than too wet when attending to their needs. Also, when feeding plants it is better to give them weak doses of fertilizer at infrequent intervals.

Following flowering it will be natural for plants to die back gradually and rest during the summer months. As the flowers die and the foliage begins to lose its colour the amount of water should be reduced until the compost is dry. The plant pot should then be placed on its side in a cool dry place, under the greenhouse staging is ideal or in a shed or garage. During June and July the corm of the plant should be frequently inspected for signs of new growth, and when this is seen the old compost should be removed and the corm potted in a completely fresh mixture, using the same pot in which the plant has been growing. The corm should be placed in the compost to about half its depth, as burying too deeply may result in rotting.

The florists' cyclamen are forms of *Cyclamen persicum* and there is a wide range of these available, often with beautifully variegated foliage to enhance the crimson, pink or white flowers.

79

Dieffenbachia exotica

Dipladenia splendens

Gardenia jasminoides

Dieffenbachia

It would be foolish and incorrect to class all the dieffenbachias as middle-of-the-road in respect of care and attention, but *Dieffenbachia exotica* slips easily into this range. It is compact, colourfully variegated and not too difficult to care for provided the required cultural conditions are not neglected. In a nutshell these mean a temperature that does not drop below 16°C (60°F), a moist atmosphere and fairly heavy shading. However, this plant will withstand some fluctuating temperatures; the same cannot be said for the more difficult species and varieties mentioned on page 87. Watering needs to be heavier in the summer and the plants should be fed regularly then.

For the modern home the compactness of the plant is one of its most appealing features. An improvement on *D. exotica* is *D. exotica* Perfection, which has the pleasing habit of producing quantities of young plants at the base of the parent stem. Besides giving the plant a fuller and more decorative appearance these also provide an excellent source of material from which to propagate new plants.

When the plants attain a height of some 30 in (75 cm) it is usual for them to produce typical arum-like flowers with spathe and spadix. As these are not especially attractive it is often best to remove them as they open. The entire stalk of the flower should be removed since there is a tendency for any pieces that are left to rot and in time affect the main stem of the plant.

Dipladenia

The majority of these are only suitable for growing in the greenhouse or garden room where the temperature can be maintained at a minimum level of around 18°C (65°F). Allied to high temperature it is necessary to dampen regularly the interior area of the greenhouse in order to provide the maximum amount of humidity. High temperature on its own will only create a very dry atmosphere and one of the great secrets of success with plants in the greenhouse or garden room is to create the proper 'feeling'. This is done by keeping the atmosphere moist while at the same time avoiding dank, airless conditions.

Dipladenias are green foliage plants which will readily climb any form of support and will also offer a colourful display of funnel-shaped flowers over a long period. The most popular species is the pink-flowered *Dipladenia splendens*. This is also one of the easiest to grow as a pot plant indoors, but to retain a compact and attractive appearance the growth should be twined around a simple framework placed in the pot rather than allowed to grow in thin strands on a single cane. Plants can be kept in check by being pruned back nearly to the base in February.

Dipladenias require copious watering while they are growing but as this should be combined with good drainage an open peaty compost should be used. The plants need protection from strong sunlight and to be sprayed over to increase the humidity. Increase by cuttings of young growth taken in summer and rooted in a heated propagator.

Gardenia

When grown as a room plant *Gardenia jasminoides*, Cape jasmine, will require cool, light conditions. It will also be essential to keep the compost permanently moist while the plant is producing new leaves, and a little dryer at other times. Like the azalea, it is one of those plants which will benefit from being watered with rain water. Regular use of hard water will in time result in plants growing with yellow, discoloured foliage. A similar appearance will also result if the plant is potted in compost with a high lime content.

It is an advantage for any plant to have natural glossy foliage, and in this respect the gardenia is well endowed. However, the principal attraction is the double white flowers that are produced during the spring and summer months of the year – these have a heady scent.

Growth is comparatively slow, but plants that have been well cared for will develop to a considerable size in time. Pruning is seldom necessary and should be confined to the trimming back of any shoots that have an untidy appearance. Older plants are often better for being grown in clay pots that have had a liberal supply of 'crocks' placed in the bottoms to ensure adequate drainage. Leaves that take on a hard yellow appearance can also be a problem, and this is best counteracted by watering a solution of sequestrated iron into the compost. Proprietary compounds are available for this and manufacturers' directions should be followed. Premature loss of buds is due to wide variation in the growing conditions, either fluctuating temperatures or varying amounts of water.

Philodendron melanochrysum

Pleomele reflexa variegata

Plumbago capensis

Philodendron

When it comes to rather grand common names few plants can match *Philodendron eichlerii*, which goes by the appendage of king of tree philodendrons. And it is a truly magnificent plant when fully developed with arrow-shaped leaves several feet in length radiating from a stout central stem. However, it is only suited to very large rooms, and even then must have its roots confined to pots of 10 in (25 cm) in diameter. Fully mature plants are best when seen in the botanic garden where proper conditions and space can be provided for them.

Vastly different is *P. melanochrysum*, which has leaves very similar to the sweetheart plant, *P. scandens* (see page 63) in shape. However, they are much more attractive in colour, being a rich dark olive that gives the plant an almost velvet appearance. It is also a much more difficult plant to care for, and will almost certainly require a mossed support for the aerial roots to cling to, or a damp wall against which to grow.

Among the philodendrons there are many other plants that are occasionally available, all of which will need the moist, warm and shaded conditions mentioned here. Most of these plants can be propagated from either seed or cuttings, and all of them will require an open peaty compost when potting on is necessary.

Pleomele

Closely related to the dracaenas, *Pleomele reflexa variegata* has wiry stems that produce short, pointed leaves which are closely grouped on the main stem of the plant. The young leaves at the top of the branch have an exquisite lime-green colouring which changes to golden-yellow and then to cream as the leaves mature. Specimen plants with many branching stems are among the choicest of all foliage plants, and will improve the appearance of any display or collection. In common with most of the dracaenas of this type it is quite usual for these plants to shed their lower leaves as they increase in height and this, rather than marring their appearance, seems to make them more graceful with their clumps of growth atop of slender stems.

The plant originates from the regions of India and Ceylon, and the common name is song of India, which would seem to assure it of popularity if only it was quicker growing. Pleomele requires warmth, good light and conditions that are never too wet. It will also exist for a long time in the same pot, and seems to prefer this sort of treatment to the more conventional handling that would require it to be potted on more frequently. When potting is undertaken a reasonably heavy compost, John Innes potting compost No. 3 for example, should be used and there should be ample drainage provided as pleomele abhor wet conditions – particularly wet and cold situations.

Plumbago

Here we have a confession – this is one of the plants that seldom does well for me, in spite of the fact that I have tried it in all sorts of situations that would seem to be right for it. Yet a colleague with a minute greenhouse measuring some 6 by 4 ft (2 m by 1·25 m) grows it, much to my consternation, with almost nonchalant ease. Perhaps his secret is that, for reasons of economy, his plants do not enjoy minimum temperatures of more than about 7°C (45°F). Come to think of it, the finest plants of plumbago that I have ever seen were grown in the cool corridor that ran along the end of a collection of greenhouses. In this situation *Plumbago capensis* presented a sheet of incredible azure-blue flowers throughout the summer.

Indoors, maximum light is essential and cooler conditions will, it would seem, also be beneficial. When actively growing plants will need ample watering, less when they are resting during the winter months. Well-drained compost is essential; John Innes potting compost No. 2 or 3 depending on the size of plants seems to suit them if the advice of my successful colleague is anything to go by!

New plants may be raised from seed sown in the spring, or cuttings of firm shoots may be rooted at almost any time in a warm propagator. After flowering, plants can be hard pruned and will come to no harm – they will also occupy less space and be much easier to care for when treated in this way.

Varieties of *Saintpaulia ionantha*

Saintpaulia

Available in a wide range of colours, the saintpaulias (also known as African violets) have attained universal popularity as indoor plants, and plants for the garden room and greenhouse. Much of their popularity is obviously due to the fact that they are comparatively inexpensive and that they are available throughout the year, whereas most other flowering pot plants are seasonal. They are also reasonably easy to propagate from seed or from cuttings.

If a heated propagator and moist conditions can be provided, then the raising of new plants from seed is not much of a problem. However, it is usually very much better for the average person to take leaf cuttings from his own plants for propagation purposes, or to procure a few leaves from some other source. It must be emphasized here that only the best leaves should be used, as small or sickly leaves will almost certainly produce poor results. Rather than cut leaves from the plant it is better that they should be broken off ensuring that no piece of the leaf stem is left attached to the plant to rot.

Although cuttings can be rooted by suspending them in water, it is more sensible and satisfactory to use a peat and sand mixture in shallow boxes or small pots and to insert the leaves just far enough for them to stand erect. The rooting medium should be moist but not soggy, and to speed the rooting process a small propagating case heated to a constant temperature of about 20°C (68°F) will be necessary. When growth develops it will be as a cluster of small leaves at the base of the leaf stalk. Once this reaches a reasonable size the complete cluster of leaves can be potted into a small pot of peaty compost and a plant will develop fairly quickly. However, when treated in this way the finished plant has a very full heavy appearance as a result of the leaves being closely clustered together, and when the flowers are produced they have to push their way unattractively through the mass of foliage and are not seen at their best. Although it is a slower process it is very much better to tease the young plantlets gently apart when they have developed two leaves that are large enough to handle, and to space them out individually in pans or boxes of potting compost. Thereafter they may be potted into small containers when they are large enough. The principal benefit of this method is that the plant develops with a single crown, and when flowers appear they stand proudly away from the foliage.

Saintpaulias do very much better in positions that afford them the maximum amount of light, needing protection indoors from strong, direct sunlight only. The greenhouse and garden room become more intensely bright, so plants in either of these places would need a little more protection from the sun. In addition to a good draught-free window position during the day it will be found that saintpaulias respond very favourably to being placed under a wall or table lamp in the evening. They are also excellent subjects for growing in Wardian cases, or in converted tropical fish tanks, provided some form of lighting over the plants can be arranged. To prevent scorching of the foliage any lights placed over plants should be at a reasonable distance.

When watering it is important to ensure that the compost dries out a little between each application, and on no account should it remain soggy for any length of time. Watering should be done with tepid water and care taken that the leaves and flowers are not splashed, particularly if the plants are standing on a sunny windowsill. In the hot and dry atmosphere of centrally heated rooms it is beneficial to group plants together by placing them on a tray containing an inch or two of gravel that is kept permanently moist. Alternatively, plant pots can be plunged to their rims in containers filled with moist peat or sphagnum moss.

The ideal temperature is around 18°C (65°F), but it is really more important to maintain a steady temperature, even if it is slightly below this level, as wildly fluctuating temperatures are more likely to be a cause of trouble. Established plants will benefit from regular feeding with weak liquid fertilizer during the spring and summer. When potting on an open, peaty compost should be used – a mixture of equal parts of John Innes potting compost No. 2 and fresh sphagnum peat is ideal – but avoid putting plants into pots that are too large as they do less well.

There are many named varieties of African violets to be found. All are cultivars of *Saintpaulia ionantha*; the more recent introductions being much more resistant and able to withstand less than ideal growing conditions. Double- and single-flowered kinds in a range of pink, blue, deep purple and white and some bicolours are available.

Spathiphyllum wallisii

Stephanotis floribunda

Stromanthe amabilis

Spathiphyllum

For the house-plant grower any plant that produces a flower is an added bonus, so it is surprising that spathiphyllums are not much more popular than they seem to be at present. Of the two varieties that are occasionally available, _Spathiphyllum_ Mauna Loa has stately white flower-like spathes on stout stems produced over a long period but these, unfortunately, are seldom plentiful. However, plants with only one or two flowers can add considerably to any collection or display of plants. When accommodating this plant reasonable space is required for the large leaves that radiate from the centre of the pot.

More suitable for the average home is _S. wallisii_, which has smaller leaves and is very much more compact in its habit of growth. The spathes are of a similar shape and colour to the first mentioned, although smaller and more numerous; these incidentally give the plant its common name of white sails. Both plants grow as clumps of leaves that sprout directly from the soil in the pot, and both may be propagated by dividing the root clumps at almost any time of the year and potting the divisions up in a peaty compost.

At all stages of growth a peaty compost is necessary, and plants will generally do better in the conditions enjoyed by most members of the _Araceae_ family – namely, moist, warm and shaded.

Stephanotis

Specialist pot-plant growers have done much to improve the appearance and performance of _Stephanotis floribunda_, Madagascar jasmine, by using artificial light to get them to flower more freely, and to flower much earlier in the year than they would if grown under completely natural conditions. However, a word of warning is offered to the would-be purchaser who may be tempted to buy plants that are in flower too early in the year – the exotically scented flowers of these plants have a tendency to turn yellow and drop off much earlier than plants that are bought during the summer.

Stephanotis makes an ideal plant for the light, airy and reasonably warm garden room or greenhouse where the twining growth should be provided with some form of support to which it can cling. Vigorous plants will have to be fairly severely pruned each year, otherwise they will tend to take over completely and become much too congested and unattractive. Firm pieces with two leaves attached can be used for propagation purposes if a heated propagator is available. New plants may also be raised from seed but this is usually a very slow business – pollinated flowers will develop large green fruits that should be allowed to ripen completely on the plant to the point when they split open to expose the seeds attached to silky white 'parachutes'.

Keep the plants in reasonable light and avoid overwatering in winter to get the best from them. Pot on every second year using John Innes potting compost No. 3 until the plants are in 10-in (25-cm) pots and then feed regularly.

Stromanthe

In common with all members of the _Marantaceae_ family to which it belongs, _Stromanthe amabilis_ requires warm, shaded conditions in order to succeed. Shade from direct sunlight is particularly important, as plants quickly deteriorate when not protected. It is also of the utmost importance that the compost in which the plants are growing should have a high peat content, as the plants will inevitably do less well in soil that is heavy and badly aerated.

Stromanthes are at their most effective when grouped together with other plants where the attractively marked grey-green foliage is seen in contrast with other colours. They are ideal for larger bottle gardens and terrariums as the close, warm and moist conditions that prevail in such containers suit them admirably.

New plants may be made by rooting pieces of firm stem with two or three leaves attached, and these can be taken at almost any time of the year provided conditions are satisfactory. Ideally, cuttings should be put in small pots filled with clean, moist peat, which in turn should be placed in a sealed propagating case heated to a temperature of some 20°C (68°F). As with all forms of propagation a careful check should be kept for any signs of rotting or dead leaves, which should be removed immediately. Once well rooted the cuttings are then potted into slightly larger pots, several pieces being put in each pot as individual cuttings take much too long to grow up into attractive plants.

Acalypha wilkesiana musaica

Aphelandra squarrosa louisae

Difficult Indoor Plants

In the past many of the subjects in this section would have been referred to as 'stove plants', which meant that they required very hot greenhouse conditions in order to succeed – with recommended temperatures of 30°C (85°F) often being quoted as essential if plants were to prosper. Fortunately, the need to economize with heating in recent years has proved that many of the stove subjects will tolerate temperatures that are much lower than those recommended in older books on the subject. However, it must be added that tender plants will seldom do well in temperatures of less than 16°C (60°F) – they may well survive, but one would not expect to see much in the way of new growth. And new growth, seeing plants grow and prosper, is the principal reason for purchasing living plants as opposed to plastic or imitation ones.

The higher the temperature maintained indoors then the dryer the atmospheric conditions will become, and dry air conditions can be particularly harmful to many of the more delicate plants. Many pests, particularly red spider mites, will also thrive where the conditions are warm and dry. Therefore it is important to provide a moist material such as peat or moss into which plant pots can be plunged – keeping the plunging material moist will obviate the need for too frequent watering. It will also help to maintain a degree of moistness around the plants if the foliage is occasionally sprayed over with a light mist-type sprayer when conditions tend to be very warm.

Acalypha

This can be one of the most challenging of indoor plants for the householder who has little more than average conditions at his disposal. Oddly enough, when growing in moist and warm greenhouse conditions that appeal to it acalypha can be almost invasive in the way it produces new leaves. So it would seem natural that the indoor gardener should, as far as possible, endeavour to emulate the conditions of his more favoured greenhouse-owning neighbour, and that is to provide warm, moist and shaded conditions at all times for his plant. Not easy in the majority of homes, but much can be done to offset the dry atmospheric conditions that these plants so abhor by plunging the pots in larger containers that have been filled with moist peat. Increase by cuttings taken in late winter and spring and rooted in a propagator.

Dry conditions, besides being less conducive to healthy growth, will also provide an excellent breeding ground for red spider mites which will quickly reduce acalyphas to an untidy mess of dead and dying brown leaves. Discoloration of the foliage and browning of the leaf edges with a generally dry overall appearance to the plant is an indication of red spider attack.

Favoured with two common names, chenille plant and red-hot cat's tail, the principal attraction of *Acalypha hispida* is the tail-like flowers, red in colour, that are produced in quantity by mature plants. There are other kinds with highly coloured foliage that are especially decorative. These go by the common name of copperleaf and are forms of *A. wilkesiana* (syn. *A. tricolor*).

Aphelandra

If treated as a flowering plant that is purchased and enjoyed for its beauty over the fairly long summer-flowering period only, then the aphelandra is probably not one of the most difficult of plants to care for. In these circumstances the plants are best kept in good light with some protection from strong, direct sunlight, and in a reasonable temperature. It is also important, in any event, to ensure that aphelandra plants do not at any time dry out at their roots, as this will almost assuredly result in loss of leaves and general deterioration of the plant. It is also of the utmost importance that aphelandra plants are fed regularly from the time of purchase.

One good reason for aphelandra plants being difficult indoors is that they develop a strong and vigorous root system that requires ample nourishment in the way of regular fertilizing. Should you wish to keep plants from one season to the next then, as well as feeding, it will be essential to pot the plant on into a larger container immediately after flowering. A thin, or very peaty compost will be totally inadequate, so use either John Innes potting compost No. 2 or 3, depending on the size of the plant – the lower number for smaller plants. After flowering and prior to potting on remove the dead flowers by cutting the main stem of the plant back to a good pair of leaves – new growth will then develop from the leaf axils. Cuttings with two good pairs of leaves may be rooted in a heated propagator.

The varieties of *Aphelandra squarrosa* are the ones usually offered, notably *A. s. louisae* and *A. s.* Brockfeld.

84

Ardisia crispa

Varieties of *Caladium*

Ardisia

There is little chance of the ardisias ever getting into the top ten house plants – not because they are unattractive, but simply because there will never be a sufficient supply of this painfully slow-growing plant.

The leaves are glossy, waved at their edges and quite plentiful on plants that seldom attain a height of more than 4 ft (1·25 m). Besides the obvious decorative value of the glossy green foliage, masses of scarlet berries follow the white flowers. The berries are grouped in clusters and are the main attraction of the plant, particularly so as they remain colourful for much of the year and give the plant its common name of coral berry.

If obtainable, seed will not be difficult to raise in warm conditions but, having germinated, there will be a long delay before the plants reach maturity. Being slow growing there should be no anxiety to put plants into large pots where they will seldom do well. It is very much better with slow subjects to pot them gradually into slightly larger pots each year using John Innes potting compost No. 3. For example, when fully mature *Ardisia crispa* will only be about 4 ft (1·25 m) tall, by which time the ideal pot size will be one of about 7 in (18 cm) in diameter.

Established plants should have a light, airy position and at no time should the temperature be excessively hot. As ardisia is a naturally glossy leaved subject it will be found that regular cleaning of the foliage will greatly improve its appearance.

Caladium

Many of the plants grown as 'house plants' begin their lives in very distant parts of the world, either as seed, cuttings, or as tubers in the case of the caladium. It is often better for the tropical 'house' plants to be produced in their natural environment so that they make the maximum amount of vegetative growth, thereby providing a much greater amount of cutting material. Besides the quantity being greater, the quality is usually very much superior to stock that has been raised in the more unnatural environment of a greenhouse. The major difficulty lies in the cost of transporting them from their natural habitat and this is most often the reason for many plants appearing to be very expensive in comparison to their size.

Caladiums are examples of plants that are grown in the moist, swamp-like areas of the tropics before being shipped as tuberous roots to their various destinations around the world. Protecting the tubers from frost is most essential, and when starting plants into growth it is necessary to place them in very warm propagating beds that are heated to temperatures in the region of 25°C (77°F). The rooting medium is composed almost entirely of peat and this must be kept moist in order to encourage growth. Once plants have rooted the temperature can then be reduced, but should at no time fall below 16°C (60°F) – this is of particular importance indoors. Even when making the initial purchase it is important that the plant should be bought from a retailer with heated premises and then adequately protected on the journey from shop to home.

Caladiums are available in a large number of named varieties in a range of colours that embrace red, pink, green, and the white form that is almost translucent. The latter variety is *Caladium candidum,* the leaves of which have attractive green venation – a combination that makes a particularly striking plant.

Indoors it is important that all caladiums should enjoy the environment of an evenly heated room where the temperature does not drop below a minimum of 16°C (60°F). At all stages of growth the compost should be of a peaty nature and the mixture must at no time dry out while the plants are actively growing. When the foliage dies down naturally at the end of the summer the compost must then be allowed to dry out completely, and the tuber should be stored in a warm, dry place until the next cycle of growth is started during the following February.

85

Codiaeum reidii

Calathea insignis

Clianthus puniceus

Calathea

A challenge is ever worthwhile for many indoor plant growers, and almost all the calatheas will provide just this; anyone who is successful in growing them may well feel proud of their achievements. But it must be emphasized that the majority of the calatheas will require all the skill of the experienced grower.

They do at times oblige with a few flowers, but the principal attractions are the many shapes and colours of the leaves. All calatheas need warm temperatures of not less than 18°C (65°F) and shade from direct sunlight. Also moist conditions in the vicinity of the plant are almost as important as moisture at the roots themselves, but excessively wet compost must be guarded against, so an open peaty compost that drains freely is recommended. One of the most satisfactory ways of supplying the necessary conditions is to grow calatheas in bottle gardens or terrariums.

There is a range of interesting and colourful species all as difficult as each other. *Calathea makoyana* (also offered as *Maranta makoyana*) has oval leaves of extraordinary colouring and pattern which result in the common name of peacock plant. *C. insignis* has longer, more slender leaves in many shades of light and dark green and an attractive purple on the reverse, while *C. ornata* is even more distinctive with oval dark green leaves striped with pink which changes to white as the plant ages; once again the leaves are purple on the reverse. By contrast *C. picturata* has silver-grey leaves with a dark green margin and dull red reverse side.

Clianthus

There are a number of these more unusual plants that the keen plantsman may have difficulty in acquiring, but seed is often more easily obtained and can be an excellent means of building up a collection of the rarer plants. The seeds should be sown in the conventional manner, but it is essential that the temperature is adequate, and not less than 20°C (68°F) is recommended. When potting it is important to ensure that a free-draining compost is used, and that the pots are adequately provided with 'crocks' so that compost does not become totally saturated for long periods.

The fern-like foliage of the clianthus is attractive in itself, and there is the added bonus of exotic flowers that resemble large claws – hence lobster claw being one of the common names. Probably better suited to the heated garden room rather than average room conditions, the clianthus may be grown as a conventional pot plant, as a climbing plant against the wall or trellis, or as a hanging basket subject.

Good light is essential, and regular watering of plants that will dry out quickly in warm summer conditions is something that must not be neglected.

Clianthus formosus (syn. *C. dampieri*) has a weak root system and is often grafted on to *Colutea arborescens*. It is well worth looking for such grafted plants when acquiring a specimen. *C. puniceus* is a more vigorous variety which makes a good climbing shrub to a height of 12 ft (3·5 m). *C. puniceus* is summer flowering, *C. formosus* flowers from spring onwards.

Codiaeum

Better known as crotons, these tropical shrubs originate from Ceylon and are available in many riotous foliage colours – for sheer brilliance there are few plants that can compete with them. The discerning plantsman can build up quite a collection of these by keeping an eye open for the different sorts that are available in the plant shop or nursery. Sad to say although most are hybrids of *Codiaeum variegatum pictum* they are seldom offered as named varieties, but by visiting any botanic garden it should not be difficult to put names to the plants acquired. Even so it will be found that there is some confusion in the naming of these superb plants, and this is one reason for the grower's reluctance to put specific names to all the plants he may sell.

Although plants may be grown from seed, it is very much better to produce new stock by means of cuttings. Cuttings may be taken at almost any time of the year, but spring or summer is best when there is better light and it is easier to provide the relatively high temperature that is needed in order to be reasonably sure of success. Cuttings with firm leaves will do very much better than those taken with soft, new top growth. The actual size of the cutting is not of particular importance, as it will be found that cuttings a foot (30 cm) or more in length will root as readily as those of more conventional size provided the conditions are suitable. In this respect a temperature of some 20°C (68°F) is desirable, and the conditions should be moist, close and shaded. The severed end of the cutting should be treated with a rooting powder to encourage more rapid root de-

86

Codiaeum variegatum pictum hybrid

Dieffenbachia Pia

Dionaea muscipula

Dieffenbachia

Dionaea

velopment, and the potting medium should be clean peat with a little sand added. The sap of the croton should be kept away from clothing as it will make an indelible stain that no amount of cleaning will remove.

Loss of lower leaves is a common problem with crotons that are grown indoors, and this can often be traced to the plants becoming too dry at some time or other. Although it is important that the compost should not become soggy and waterlogged, it is equally important that it should at no time dry out, as loss of lower leaves will be the inevitable result.

Croton plants need regular feeding and it is preferable when potting to use a compost that is loam based, John Innes No. 3 being the most suitable for larger plants. Crocking the bottom of the pot is also necessary as this will ensure that surplus water drains freely from the pot, a most important requirement for all potted plants.

Good light is another requirement, and this will mean placing croton plants in the lightest possible window position, it will be entirely futile to attempt to use croton plants to brighten up a dark corner. The minimum temperature required is 16°C (60°F) and the plants will quickly suffer if it is allowed to drop below this. Keeping a careful watch for pests is essential and particular attention must be placed on the underside of leaves. Red spider is the most common pest of the croton when grown as a pot plant, and regular spraying of affected plants is the only answer – there are many insecticides for keeping red spider under control.

The dieffenbachias get their common name, dumb cane, from the fact that the sap is an irritant and can cause considerable unpleasantness if it gets into the mouth. They are plants that need warm, shaded and moist conditions although there are some, see page 80, which are not quite so demanding.

One of my favourites is *Dieffenbachia oerstedii*. The leaves are dark green, almost to the point of being black, but the interesting aspect is the beautiful ivory-white midribs. As dieffenbachias go the leaves and entire plant are comparatively small. By contrast one of the most majestic is *D. amoena*. This has dark green leaves which are subtly blended with light and dark green in the centre. Similar in appearance is *D. Tropic Snow* with much lighter variegation in the central part of the leaves.

Dieffenbachia Pia has very little green in the leaves and is one of the most difficult to care for. The overall colouring is creamy white with faint green speckling. This must have warm and moist conditions and does very much better if the plant pots are plunged to their rims in damp peat.

Cuttings about 3 in (8 cm) in length taken with an eye will not be difficult to root in warm and moist conditions. It is not necessary to have leaves attached – the bare stems are simply cut into sections and allowed to dry before being laid on their sides partly buried in moist peat. Because of the poisonous sap it is important to wash the hands thoroughly after taking the cuttings.

To be grown with any degree of success it is essential that *Dionaea muscipula*, Venus fly trap, must have warm and very close conditions – close to the point whereby the atmosphere surrounding the plant is at the point of total saturation. Indoors, or in the greenhouse, a separate plant case should be provided, and the pots in which the plants are growing should be plunged to their rims in wet sphagnum moss. Keeping the moss wet will help to increase the humidity level. Treated in this way some degree of success may be achieved but the inside of the glass container will have a permanent film of condensation which will make seeing the plants somewhat difficult!

The potting mixture could scarcely be given the name compost, as it should be composed almost entirely of sphagnum moss with just a little clean peat added to it. The great attraction of these plants is, of course, their ability to catch flies and other insects in their leaves – the slightest touch on the sensitive leaves will induce them to fold together, so trapping any unfortunate insect that may have been foolish enough to find its way on to them.

However, I must add that these are extremely difficult to care for even in greenhouses looked after by the expert, and they are almost impossible for the indoor gardener. They are, indeed, plants for the enthusiast who can offer them the environment of a heated glass cabinet.

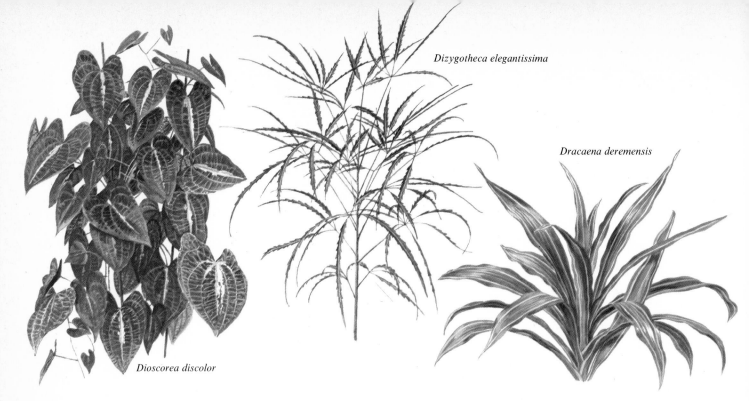

Dizygotheca elegantissima

Dracaena deremensis

Dioscorea discolor

Dioscorea

Grown for its attractive foliage *Dioscorea discolor*, variegated yam, is a quick growing deciduous climber that requires moist, shaded and warm conditions in order to succeed. It is best suited to the greenhouse or garden room, but will give much pleasure to the keen indoor plantsman who is seeking something a little more challenging on which to test his skill.

Plants are grown from potato-like tubers that are started into growth in early spring, and it is most essential that they should enjoy the warmest conditions – temperatures not less than 24°C (75°F) for preference. Growth will be quite rapid if tubers are plunged in boxes or pots filled with moist peat and kept at the temperature recommended, but it will be lamentably slow if the temperature is inadequate. When purchasing tubers it is important to ensure that the variegated yam is asked for as the green form is not at all attractive.

Once the tubers have produced a number of leaves the plants should be individually planted in pots filled with John Innes potting compost No. 3. A trellis or similar support will be needed for the growth to cling to as it develops. The plants die down naturally in the autumn, when the compost should be allowed to dry out before the tubers are stored in a warm, dry place for the winter in readiness for starting into growth again in fresh compost in the spring. The compost should be kept moist and fed while the plant is actively growing.

Dizygotheca

Dizygotheca elegantissima, false aralia, is one of the most graceful and delicate (in more senses than one) of all our indoor plants in its early years of development. The leaves are dark green in colour almost to the point of being black, and provide an excellent foil for other plants when placed in a group. Older foliage becomes coarse and less attractive as the plant ages, but this is not a problem that will greatly worry the average grower of house plants as it is not easy to keep plants for more than a year or two indoors. However, this does not imply that these plants are not well worth acquiring and enjoying for the time they are at their best.

For reasonable success, constant warmth, light shade and a watering programme that errs on the side of dry rather than wet conditions should be provided. Only established plants will need feeding, and when this is done it will be wise to apply a weak liquid fertilizer at frequent intervals as heavy doses will only damage the root system. Potting on should be undertaken in the spring and the compost must be open and well drained. A heavy lifeless compost will give roots little chance to develop as they should. In time, in ideal conditions, plants will develop into trees of considerable size. New plants can be raised from seed sown in the early part of the year.

Dracaena

As I mentioned earlier there are both easy and difficult members of the dracaena tribe; the easier kinds will be found on page 40 and some of the more difficult ones are described here.

Possibly the best known of all the dracaenas is *Dracaena terminalis* (syn. *Cordyline terminalis*) with its bright red, upright leaves which make it a very handsome and compact plant. Commonly named flaming dragontree it requires temperatures of not less than 16°C (60°F) and when watering it is advisable to allow the compost to dry out a little between each application. It is also advisable, wherever possible, to use rain water in preference to hard tap water. The growing position should be reasonably well lit, but away from strong sunlight. In any event, given all these requirements, this is a temporary rather than a permanent room plant.

Similar in colour though smaller, and needing the same treatment, is *D.* Rededge. This is a particularly fine plant for grouping with other subjects in trough and dish gardens.

One of the most majestic of plants is *D. massangeana*, which has broad, strap-like leaves of a mustard colour and grows to a height of some 7 ft (2·25 m) when the roots are confined to pots. Identical in its habit of growth is *D.m.* Victoria, which has brighter colouring and is more difficult to care for. New plants are propagated from stem sections, and the ability of stem sections to retain their essential reproductive qualities over many months from the time they are severed from the plant is quite

Ficus elastica doescheri

Dracaena terminalis

Ficus radicans variegata

Ficus

extraordinary. Stem sections several feet in length can be rooted by standing the piece upright in rooting compost, so that a beautiful palm-like effect is the result when the over-size cutting has rooted.

Dracaena deremensis and its many varieties are some of the most attractive of foliage plants, and will well reward the extra care and more agreeable growing conditions that they demand. Excessive watering and low temperatures are the principal enemies, and a combination of the two will almost surely be fatal. Mature plants of the taller dracaenas will often produce strong stems of flower, but these are seldom attractive and so are best removed.

Dracaena godseffiana has small, speckled green leaves carried on wiry stems and is not particularly decorative, but the much improved form *D. g.* Florida Beauty is well worth acquiring. The leaves are also speckled, but the colouring is cream to gold and most attractive.

In order to do well it is essential that the compost should be well drained and this is one reason for plants seeming to do much better when several are planted in shallow containers that have a number of drainage holes in the bottom. Established plants should be fed regularly during the summer months with a balanced liquid fertilizer. Pot on when plants have filled their existing pots with roots, using John Innes potting compost No. 2 or 3 depending on plant size. Adding a little extra peat to the John Innes will be beneficial. Generally low growing, in ideal conditions they will attain a height of 5 to 6 ft (1·5 to 2 m) in as many years.

The genus *Ficus* provides some of our most successful and popular indoor plants, a number of which have been described on pages 44 and 45. The following kinds are all variegated forms and, as is often the case with variegated plants, they fall at the difficult end of the scale, requiring some skill and good conditions if they are to be regarded as anything other than temporary inhabitants of the home.

Ficus elastica doescheri and *F. e. schryveriana* (page 44) are somewhat similar in appearance, but whereas *F. e. schryveriana* is not among the most difficult of plants to care for, the same cannot be said for *F. e. doescheri* which will try the skill of the most accomplished grower of plants. The leaves of the latter have the narrow drooping habit of *F. elastica*, which was one of the front runners when house plants were becoming popular some thirty years ago. In spite of its narrow leaves the variegation of *F. e. doescheri* is most attractive. However, it is among the most difficult of indoor plants to care for and in room conditions it is more usual to see it just about surviving rather than growing. The cream-coloured outer margins of the leaves have very little chlorophyll in them, so making these areas particularly susceptible to rotting and brown patches, usually as a result of root damage. Careful watering that errs on the side of dryness is most important, as is the need for reasonable warmth and a position that is light but not too sunny.

Equally difficult, but I think much more attractive, is *F. decora tricolor*, which has the larger, more rounded *decora*-type leaves

variegated in cream and sometimes flushed with pink, and beautiful upright habit of growth. Alas, as the heating of greenhouses becomes ever more costly the nurseryman tends to look more and more favourably on the plants that are most likely to give good results at the end of the day. So the difficult plants, of which only a small percentage are likely to be of good quality, are gradually being weeded out, so making them very scarce and in some cases unobtainable. This is certainly the case with *F. d. tricolor* which is seldom seen today, even at major flower shows.

Probably the smallest of the variegated ficus is *F. radicans variegata* which has attractive silver and green variegated leaves that are carried on stiff stems. By putting several cuttings direct into the growing pot rather than first into a propagating bed, this plant matures quite quickly in warm, moist and shaded greenhouse conditions, but in the dryer conditions that generally prevail in the average home *F. radicans* can be a very difficult plant. Indoors, terrariums and bottle gardens provide the nearest conditions to those of a greenhouse, and in such containers this particular plant does very much better. The more accomplished grower with near-perfect conditions, such as a warm greenhouse, may wish to experiment and provide a moss-covered support to which the growth can be trained. By keeping the moss moist very decorative columns of foliage can be formed.

Fittonia verschaffeltii

Medinilla magnifica

Pachystachys lutea

Fittonia

Of these, the red and silver foliaged sorts have been with us and proving very difficult to care for almost as long as potted plants have been in existence. *Fittonia argyroneura* has attractively silver-veined leaves, while *F. verschaffeltii* has leaves that are veined in a dull red. For both of these shaded conditions are most essential, and the temperature should not fall below 18°C (65°F). Moisture surrounding the plant is almost as important as water in the pot, so it is well to provide peat or moss as a plunging material into which plant pots can be buried to their rims. In a warm propagating case new plants can be raised from firm cuttings with two or three leaves attached.

Occasionally odd and almost inexplicable things happen in horticulture, and the appearance in recent years of the miniature form of the silver fittonia, *F. a. nana*, would seem to be something of a phenomenon. The leaves are quite miniature in comparison with the more usual form, and the markings are equally attractive. But the strange part of it all is that the newer form is very much easier to care for than the parent from which it would seem to have sprouted. The miniature form is likely to have a considerable future as a potted plant for use in dish and bottle gardens, and similar arrangements where less robust plants are required. A peaty compost is essential, as is the need for shade and careful watering.

Medinilla

With hard, woody stems and coarse unattractive leaves this plant would not seem to have much to justify its name of *Medinilla magnifica*. However, the sight of mature plants some 6 ft (2 m) in height heavily laden with pendulous pink flowers is enough to catch the breath of the most seasoned plantsman. Plants may be grown from cuttings rooted in heat but as they are slow to get under way they may seem to be disappointing in the first couple of years. It takes at least this length of time before they begin to produce flowers in any quantity.

Warm, evenly heated conditions are important, and medinilla will need some protection from bright sunlight. Careful watering is, possibly, the one most important requirement for success if the growing conditions are correct. Careful watering often depends on potting plants properly at the outset, as no amount of proper watering will avail if the compost is inferior and the pots have not been adequately provided with drainage. With the medinilla it will be necessary to put a good 2-in (5-cm) layer of crocks in the bottom of the pot before the compost is introduced – it will also help if some coarse peat is placed over the crocks below the compost.

Pachystachys

An apt common name can often give a reasonably ordinary sort of plant much more appeal; mind-your-own-business being a very good example. At a Chelsea Flower Show one of the most famous visitors looked at *Pachystachys lutea* for the first time and said it resembled a child's lollipop, so the common name of lollipop plant was a natural step. However, it would seem that the pachystachys needs something more than a good common name for it to make the grade as a popular flowering plant. The plant is, in fact, fine, but it takes unkindly to being packed in paper and boxes for despatch to markets and shops, so is better bought from the grower.

The leaves are not particularly attractive, but these are amply compensated for by the months of pleasure that will be derived from the rich yellow bracts that are borne on the ends of every stem and side growth. The bracts are similar in shape to those of the more common aphelandra, but are much more plentiful and appear over a much longer period.

Cuttings of non-flowering shoots taken early in the year will not be difficult to root in a heated propagating case and, once well rooted, they should be potted into rich compost as they soon lose their colour if there is not sufficient goodness in the compost. Other than that, keep the plants moist, shaded and warm – a minimum temperature of 16°C (60°F) should be the aim. Regular feeding is required and if the compost is allowed to dry out to the extent that the plant flags then some loss of leaves may be the result. Watch out for whitefly.

Scindapsus aureus Marble Queen

Selaginella affinis

Scindapsus

Members of the important *Araceae* family, scindapsus have leaves that are similar in shape to the more common *Philodendron scandens*. The leaves of the scindapsus will, however, be larger and altogether bolder than the smaller *P. scandens*, and the stems of the plant will be very much thicker. Many of the philodendrons will tolerate conditions that are much less favourable than the ideal of warm, moist and shaded, and will not suffer too much harm provided the adverse conditions prevail for only a short period. However, the scindapsus must have the suggested conditions, and the warmer and moister the atmosphere surrounding the plant then the better it is likely to do.

In the moist and warm conditions of a warm greenhouse these plants are perfect for growing in hanging baskets, or as plants trailing from pots suspended from the ceiling or attached to the wall. But it is not infrequently that plants are purchased with the thought in mind that they will cascade from pots and decorate the wall of the home that offers only average growing conditions. Frankly, in most instances it would be money ill spent, as plants of scindapsus seldom do well when grown in this fashion. It is very much better then to grow them more conventionally by allowing them to climb or be attached to a moist support that they will eventually cling to. Wet sphagnum moss wrapped around a stout cane will provide a moist foothold for the aerial roots that will naturally develop along the stem of these plants. If the moss is kept permanently moist by means of regular spraying with water it will be found that scindapsus plants will have a very much better chance of survival indoors – even so they will not be the easiest of plants to maintain in good condition.

The most common is *Scindapsus aureus*, which has yellow-variegated foliage that is most attractive in healthy plants. Variegated colouring always varies and is dependent on the quality of the parent stock from which cuttings are taken. Therefore, it is wise when purchasing to select the most colourful plants. Also available occasionally is *S*. Marble Queen with white-variegated leaves that contain only slight flecks of green in some types. Having little chlorophyll in their leaves they are particularly difficult to keep in good order, and will provide a challenge for the most able plant grower.

Scindapsus are propagated from single leaves with a piece of stem attached – these should be struck in moist peat in a warm propagating frame. A rooting powder should be used to encourage rooting and the area surrounding the cuttings must remain moist, but excessive wetting of the peat in which cuttings are inserted should be avoided. At all stages of potting an open peaty compost should be the order of the day, and plants should only be potted on when they have well filled their existing pots with roots.

Selaginella

Although some species of *Selaginella* tend to be more straggling in their habit of growth, the majority form beautiful clumps of fern-like foliage that are ideal for use in small dish gardens, terrariums and bottle gardens. In the closer and moister atmosphere of the latter they seem to grow very much better than when placed in isolation on the windowsill. One should aim to provide a temperature in the region of 16°C (60°F) or above to keep plants in good order. It will also be beneficial if the area surrounding the plant is kept moist.

New plants may be raised from cuttings of about 2 in (5 cm) in length placed in small pots filled with a mixture of peat and sphagnum moss. Varieties with smaller, more compact leaves can be propagated simply by placing small pieces of leaf on the surface of the suggested compost – when employing propagation methods of the latter kind it will be most essential to ensure that a propagating case is used, and that the surface of the compost is not allowed to dry out at any time. Otherwise, cuttings, being so small, shrivel and die before they have had a chance to produce roots of their own.

At all stages of potting a mix of sphagnum moss and peat should be used, and for preference shallow rather than very deep containers. These will not only be better for the plants but the plants will be very much more attractive in pots that are shallow and more in keeping with their appearance.

91

Cacti &
Succulents

T. C. Rochford

Distribution of Succulents

Although the only cacti growing in the wild which most of us see are round the shores of the Mediterranean, the species is exclusively American in its origins. Other succulents come from all five continents of the world and although the cactus family has established itself over nearly as wide a geographic area it is entirely a product of the New World. In prehistoric times, however, some species of cactus travelled and *Rhipsalis cassutha*, for example, has been growing in Africa for a considerable time. Pliny, too, knew about opuntias and this suggests that seeds must have crossed the Atlantic, possibly with birds on their migrations as both species have attractive berries. Within America itself the cactus family is most heavily concentrated in Mexico but there are also large numbers of species in Southern and Northern America.

In spite of this concentration of the cacti around the Equator the family is very tolerant in its requirements and representatives are found in sub-arctic regions in both north and south. Altitude too seems to make little difference and some species actually grow near the edge of the snow line. However, before pulling down your greenhouse and planting up your garden with these fascinating plants, I should point out that the air is very much less humid in these regions than in Britain and like many alpine plants cacti cannot cope with the cold damp weather that is so characteristic of a British winter.

Generally the more distantly spaced members of the family tend to be rarer in cultivation. *Pterocactus valentinii* is supposedly one of the most southern species as it is a native of Patagonia, and *Opuntia polyacantha* grows at 56° North in Canada near the Peace river. *Oreocereus trollii* can be found on mountain ranges to a height of some 13,000 ft (4,000 m) but opuntias, which are able to grow so far north, probably hold the record with *Opuntia floccosa* growing at a height of 17,000 ft (5,300 m) in some isolated cases. The most easterly species is *Monvillea insularis*.

Succulents other than cacti are far more generally distributed throughout the world occurring not in the true deserts such as the Gobi, the Sahara and the great central desert in Australia but in the semi-deserts. Succulents adopt their fleshy characteristics for reasons of water conservation and there are many species of coastal plant which can be considered as succulent, especially plants which are found in British tidal waters and whose succulence arises from the need to conserve fresh water within the plant as opposed to brine. The main families in which succulence occurs are the *Crassulaceae*, represented in Britain by sedums and sempervivums, the *Euphorbiaceae* represented in Britain by the largely non-succulent spurges, the *Aizoaceae*,

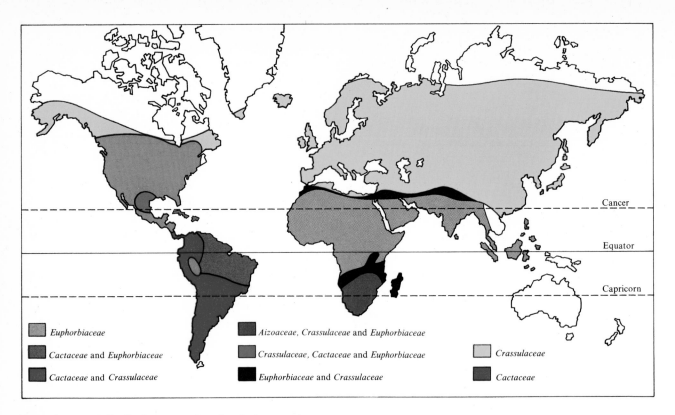

The main natural distribution areas of cacti and other succulents

which is largely represented in British gardens by the mesembryanthemums, although the Kaffir fig is naturalized in certain parts. The *Amaryllidaceae* and the *Liliaceae* also somewhat surprisingly produce succulent varieties, and the other major family is *Asclepiadaceae*, although there are no wild succulent members of these last three groups in Britain. Many other families have some succulents among them; the *Compositae* or dandelion family has some rather unexpected relatives, and well known house plants such as pelargoniums and tradescantias can also exhibit succulent relatives.

With such a wide variation it is not surprising that it is difficult to generalize about the distribution of succulents other than cacti, but, and this is being very general indeed, the most significant areas for the *Aizoaceae* and *Euphorbiaceae* are Southern Africa while the *Crassulaceae* have a very much more general distribution, some succulent species being found in nearly every major country. The succulent *Amaryllidaceae* and *Liliaceae* can be divided in turn into the agaves, which are largely American and West Indian in origin, and the somewhat similar aloes, which are natives of Southern Africa, together with their relatives haworthia and gasteria.

Distinguishing Features

The succulents have developed their strange forms in response to the challenge of their environment, and although the areas in which they grow are not totally devoid of water during the year, there are long periods of drought during which the water accumulated during the short but intense wet period must be carefully stored and used to best advantage. The original forebears of the cacti were probably leafy shrubs similar in appearance to pereskia, and although relatives of the opuntias have been found in fossil forms in deposits going back some fifty million years it is possible that they achieved some separate identity at a still earlier stage.

At this point it would be as well to draw the distinction between cacti and other succulents which is fundamental to the understanding of the different cultural requirements of each group of plants, and which is equally important to finding your way around this part of the book as the cacti have been put on pages 100 to 164 and the other succulents have been put on the pages that follow. The illustration shows some typical features of succulents. The spines are in fact the equivalent to leaves on conventional plants and have achieved their present shape through the need to reduce transpiration (the evaporation of the water from the plant bodies). They are divided into two groups, centrals, which are generally the larger ones and occur at the centre of the cluster, and radials, which radiate round the sides of the cluster. The spines arise from a felted or hairy base or pad which may also support hairs or bristles and which in certain families produces the flowers. The felting or hair is peculiar to the cacti and is one of the most important distinguishing features of the group. If your spiny unknown plant has no hair, look for it amongst the succulents in this book, if there is any hair present round the base of the spines at all, you must look for it amongst the cacti. Where this soft pad exists it is called the areole, and the presence of areoles distinguishes cacti from all other succulents. The stems have become globular, cylindrical or even flattened plant bodies and these may be characterized by the presence of tubercles or elongated points, or by ribs running up the sides of the plant. Some cacti, notably pereskias, have real leaves but still produce areoles on the stem between them. Opuntias, too, produce rudimentary leaves especially on the young growth although only a few species actually overwinter with their leaves. Many of the euphorbias, on the other hand, which have a superficial resemblance to cacti but lack the distinctive areoles, produce leaves which can persist for several seasons if given a moist humid environment.

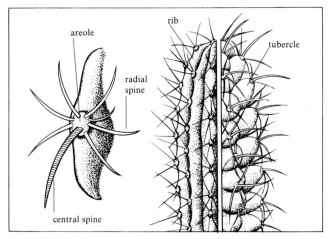

Some of the typical features of cacti. A close-up of an areole is shown on the left

Pests and Diseases

Cacti are particularly susceptible to diseases, especially fungal attacks through lack of hygiene in the soil or the greenhouse. One of the most disappointing things is to see a prize specimen suddenly keel over and die as a result of rot spreading out from the watery tissues round the central core of the plant. Three different types are common. *Pythium* is generally associated with the roots, and its presence should be suspected when sections of hitherto healthy root go brown and become easily detached from the main stock, accompanied by sudden rot or wilting. *Rhizoctonia* attacks the part of the stem which joins the root at soil level and for this reason it is as well to guard against water, in which fungal diseases thrive, lying for any length of time round this danger point. *Fusarium* is also sometimes found. The best method of avoiding this is the use of sterilized pots and composts, and the regular use of systemic fungicides. It may be a wise precaution to dip new

specimens in a solution of benomyl until the bubbles stop rising from the compost.

While fungal attacks are the most trying features of cactus collections, pests are more easily controlled and generally do less harm than they do to less tough house plants. Nearly all the standard household pests attack succulents. Ants, for example, can be a problem through their tunnelling in the soil, and also because they carry aphids around, a proprietary ant killer is the best cure. Mealy bug is by far the most common pest; malathion may be used to control it in most cases although care should be taken before spraying some crassulas and you should refer to the appropriate entry in this book, especially if their skin is greyish or felted at all. As an alternative to malathion a matchstick dipped in methylated spirits can be used for a spot kill. The treatment should be repeated at fourteen-day intervals until the infestation is clear. Red spider mite is normally found on cacti, euphorbias and mesembryanthemums. It is a difficult pest to kill and many chemicals which were effective a few years ago are no longer of any use as the mite is now resistant to them. A nicotine solution can be effective if sprayed on carefully, but it is probably best to use one of the systemic insecticides which act through the stem of the plant. Scale insects can be very troublesome pests. As their name implies they appear like small scales on the plant; the insect itself lives under this scale-like shell, which is generally impervious to chemicals, so routine spraying will be ineffective. If systemic insecticides do not solve the problem, then the insects will have to be removed with a pointed stick. Other common garden pests such as greenfly (aphids) are best killed with the normal proprietary insecticides.

Propagation

From seed. Most commercial growers raise their cacti from seed. This is not always a reliable means of propagation as cross hybridization occurs fairly readily between members of related genera and cacti are generally self-sterile so that it is necessary to have two separate plants in order for pollination to be effective. The seed should be harvested while the pod is still intact and stored in a small envelope in a sunny place, allowing it to ripen of its own accord. When the pod has burst open and the seeds are reasonably dry they should be separated from the husk of the berry in so far as is possible and mixed with a small quantity of dry sand. Seed trays are best prepared by filling with a mixture of two parts sterilized loam, one part of peat, one part of coarse sand and one part of fine grit or shingle. A little lime may also be added. The tray should be filled in such a way that there is a slight mound in the centre to assist drainage and the whole should then be dipped in

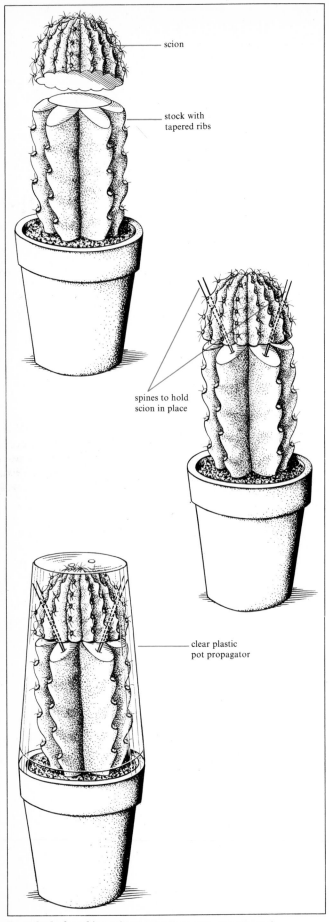

scion

stock with
tapered ribs

spines to hold
scion in place

clear plastic
pot propagator

**A method of grafting using a pot propagator to protect the
plant until union has taken place**

a solution of benomyl to assist in sterilization. The
seed–sand mixture should then be sprinkled lightly over
the surface and a sheet of glass placed on top. No water
should then be needed until the seedlings show through
after a period which varies from three days to three
weeks. Bottom heat is a useful asset and if a propagating
unit is available this is a great help. Watering should be
done often and lightly until the spines start to appear in
the case of cacti or until characterization starts in the
case of other succulents. Algae are the main problem
at this stage and one of the best cures is to spray with a
weak solution of copper sulphate at the rate of 1 cc per
litre. Seedlings of all kinds should be transplanted as
soon as they are big enough to handle and successive
transplants should be made until the plants are big
enough to go into a pot; this may not be until the end
of their second year of growth. There is some evidence
that parodias, which are very hard to raise from seed
even when given the best possible conditions, can be
more easily germinated if the seeded trays are kept in a
dark place such as an airing cupboard.

From cuttings. Although seed is the fastest way to build
up a large stock of a species it is a much slower process
than taking cuttings. Cuttings of all succulents should be
taken in the spring if possible as this is the time at
which the plantlet is best able to adjust to its new
environment and to develop a root system and start
growing. The autumn is another possible period since
roots may develop in time for growth in the spring.
Cuttings may be taken at most other times, although
the winter drought period does present some problems,
and offsets of certain cacti, such as *Notocactus ottonis*
and *Mammillaria zeilmanniana*, should be struck
regularly if possible as an insurance against the failure
of the parent plant due to fungal diseases.

When taking a cutting, particularly from cacti and
other succulents which have pronounced joints, avoid
putting the end of the broken-off joint into the rooting
mixture. Although the joint should be severed cleanly at
such a branching point, the cutting should then be cut
once more across the broadest part to enable as wide a
surface as possible to develop roots. In this way a large
healthy root system is formed. In the case of opuntias
and leaf cacti this is particularly important as both
species need considerable support from their root
systems as they attain some size. Some genera, notably
Kalanchoe, develop adventitious buds or plantlets on
the edges of the leaves. These subsequently detach
themselves and form their own clumps round the base
of the parent plant and can later be potted up and
grown on. In some species with adventitious buds,
miniature root systems may even be formed while the
plantlets are still attached to the main stem.

Cuttings are the most reliable means of increasing the

number of a particular species but they also tend to disfigure the original plant. They are the only means of increasing cristate or monstrose specimens which rarely flower in cultivation and which, even when they do, normally have to be a considerable age. Moreover cristate specimens will not necessarily come true from seed. Such varieties tend to do better when grafted as their own rootstocks are inadequate to support extensive growth, and grafting is not difficult provided sterilized tools are used and some form of propagation unit is available.

Grafting. The part to be grafted is normally called the scion and the rooted part which forms the base of the combined plant is generally called the stock. *Pereskia aculeata* is normally used as grafting stock for *Rhipsalis* and *Zygocactus* and other epiphytic hanging species, although staking may be required as extra support. Other varieties may be grafted on to *Trichocereus* species as this is a robust variety. *Hylocereus* and *Myrtillocactus* stocks although cheap are not entirely satisfactory as both species require higher winter temperatures if they are to survive unharmed, and this may not always benefit the scion.

The stock and scion should be prepared by slicing through the stem of each so as to leave a roughly equal surface area on each which can be bonded together fairly easily. The stock should then have the ribs tapered away so as to ensure that any condensation which accumulates round the grafting point will drain away. A light application of benomyl brushed over this point will help to prevent infection creeping in. The stock and scion should then be joined so that the central core of each is in contact and this should be secured by using one or two long cactus spines from any species. When the union is effected the cactus spines can then be withdrawn.

It is a good idea to surround the stock and scion with a small polythene bag, completely covering the union and fixed round the stem of the stock with an elastic band; this should be left in place for about three weeks, during which time the plant is best kept in a propagation unit, and after this period the bag can be taken off and the joint examined very carefully. If union has still not taken place the covering should be replaced for another three weeks, after which time if union has still not occurred the exercise is likely to have been a failure.

General Care of Succulents

Generally speaking succulents need normal watering throughout the summer months, during which period it can hardly become too hot for them provided a reasonable degree of air circulation is maintained. From September to March the true cacti should be dried out completely and will need low temperatures round the 7°C (45°F) level, while the succulents will need slightly higher temperatures. Before implementing these very general instructions the reader should consult the relevant section describing each species in detail as some have a completely different regime.

The most conspicuous features of the semi-desert environment are air, light, and warmth, and all three are essential for successful cultivation. It is not worth trying to grow succulents in a greenhouse if it is unheated or if it is overshadowed by tall trees; in the latter case the cacti will be reluctant to flower and the succulents will grow weak and long and leggy. Water should be given thoroughly: let the surface of the compost dry out and then allow three days for a $2\frac{1}{2}$-in (6-cm) pot or a week for a 4-in (10-cm) pot or bigger to elapse before plunging the entire pot in water and allowing it to stay there until the bubbles stop rising. Where this is not possible, as in the case of a large collection, do make sure that the plant is well watered. Failure to water thoroughly causes parts of the soil which remain dry to turn sour and this enables fungi and bacteria to take root there.

Although a common feature of flower shops and garden centres the cactus garden as commonly known to commercial horticulture should be avoided. Because of their somewhat different watering requirements, succulents other than cacti tend to need watering once every three weeks or so during the winter, thus cacti and other succulents generally make poor companions in the same bowl. The tendency to put chippings on top of the soil can also present problems as it prevents effective aeration of the soil. The best idea is to plant bowls of cacti or bowls of succulents and rely on rocks to provide the necessary variety in shape and texture where this cannot be achieved with the correct species.

Having outlined the chief botanical distinction between the cacti and other succulents, the main cultural differences are that cacti will generally tolerate lower winter temperatures and need considerably less water in this period than other succulents. There are, of course, exceptions to this as there are to any rule, but in the absence of information to the contrary cacti require a maximum temperature at nights of 7°C (45°F) in the winter and need to be kept completely dry between the end of September and mid-March. Other succulents generally prefer somewhat higher winter temperatures round the 10°C (50°F) level and consequently more regular watering, probably as often as once every four weeks. Do not stake cacti unless absolutely necessary as this tends to weaken them permanently, often an unstaked but floppy cactus or any other succulent will straighten itself and become stiffer with time.

Key to Arrangement of Plants in the Text

The arrangement of plants in this book is partly botanical and partly based on appearances. If you have a named plant the best idea is to look it up in the index and then refer to the appropriate page; but if, on the other hand, you have a plant without a name the following guide to the arrangement of genera in the book may assist you to find it.

First check whether the plant has a woolly or bristly pad below the thorns if it has any, or even, in the absence of any thorns, merely a woolly pad. If the plant does have areoles then it may be found between pages 100 and 164. If it lacks these it should be in the following pages.

The first group of cacti described on page 100 are easily distinguished by the presence of conspicuous and quite normal leaves. They are one of the most primitive groups of cactus and are called *Pereskieae*. [1]

The second group of cacti described between pages 101 and 107 are the prickly pear type, distinguished by the presence of glochids or easily detached and frequently somewhat painful bristles buried amongst the spine cushions. They are in turn subdivided into two distinct groups. Those more characteristic species with flat-jointed stems are illustrated and described between pages 101 and 105, [2] while those with round stems are dealt with on the following two pages.

The remainder of the family have been allocated to a very large group called *Cereanae*, which have neither leaves nor glochids and comprise the majority of cactus species. This large group is in turn divided into several sub-groups as follows.

First the candelabra-type or upright cylindrical cacti called the *Cereeae*, which is derived from the Greek word for a candle. These are illustrated on pages 108 to 118 and are distinguished by their generally somewhat thin cylindrical shape and a reluctance to flower when young [3]. *Wilcoxia schmollii* is a notable exception here which has pendulous stems, and *Carnegiea gigantea*, although one of the largest and most typically branched of the group when mature, has a somewhat rounded globular appearance when young.

The *Hylocereanae* are the more sprawling cacti, tending to be fast growers making adventitious roots which batten on to trees and rocks in the wild. They are somewhat freer flowering than the previous group and appreciate a little more warmth in winter. See pages 119 and 120. [4]

Then follow two groups of hedgehog cacti; the *Echinocereanae* (pages 121 to 128) are generally barrel shaped although some may become somewhat cylindrical, and are distinguished by the production of flower buds from the previous year's growth on the sides of the stems. They comprise some of the most easily flowered genera such as *Rebutia* and *Aylostera*. [5] The *Echinocactanae* (pages 129 to 147), on the other hand, produce their flowers at the top of the plant and the flowering areoles are unfolded with the non-flowering ones each year from the centre of the plant. [6]

The *Cactanae* consists of one genus *Melocactus*, page 148. The distinguishing feature of this group is the production of a large cephalium or woolly crown at the top of the plant just before flowering. These plants are all somewhat rare in cultivation and it is unlikely that an unnamed variety belongs to this group. Generally they require rather more warmth in winter. [7]

The previous groups have all been characterized by the production of flowers from the areoles, or spine clusters. The *Coryphanthanae* are tuberculate plants whose flowers are produced in the axils between the spines. I have included here the *Thelocacti* although they do not flower in this fashion because of their extreme resemblance to the *Coryphanthanae* and because of their general reluctance to flower when young. The *Coryphanthanae* are described on pages 149 to 160. [8]

The last two groups of cacti described are the *Epiphyllanae*, illustrated on pages 161 and 162, which produce mainly flat leaf-like stems, [9] and the *Rhipsalidanae* described on the following two pages which, with the exception of *Rhipsalidopsis rosea* (a bigeneric hybrid anyway) and *Rhipsalis houlletiana*, produce angled or cylindrical stems. [10]

The remaining succulents can be broadly classified according to their habit. Those which lack areoles and exude a milky sap when pierced are members of the *Euphorbiaceae* described on pages 165 to 169 (plants which have areoles and a milky sap are probably mammillarias described on pages 157 to 160). [11] The remaining succulents other than cacti have been subdivided into the 'living stone' group, having generally little or nothing in the way of stems and a pebble-like or chunky appearance. These are all members of the *Aizoaceae* and are described on pages 170 to 173. [12]

Pages 174 to 178 are devoted to those succulents which have little or no stems and form instead rosettes or clumps of leafy growth. [13]

In contrast, those succulents with upright, arched or hanging stems are described on pages 179 to 188 [14] and are drawn from a wide variety of genera, those with upright stems described at the beginning of the section and those with hanging stems described near the end.

Opposite. A guide to the identification of the groups of cacti and succulents which appear in this book. The types of plants are given in order left to right and top to bottom to correspond with the text on this page

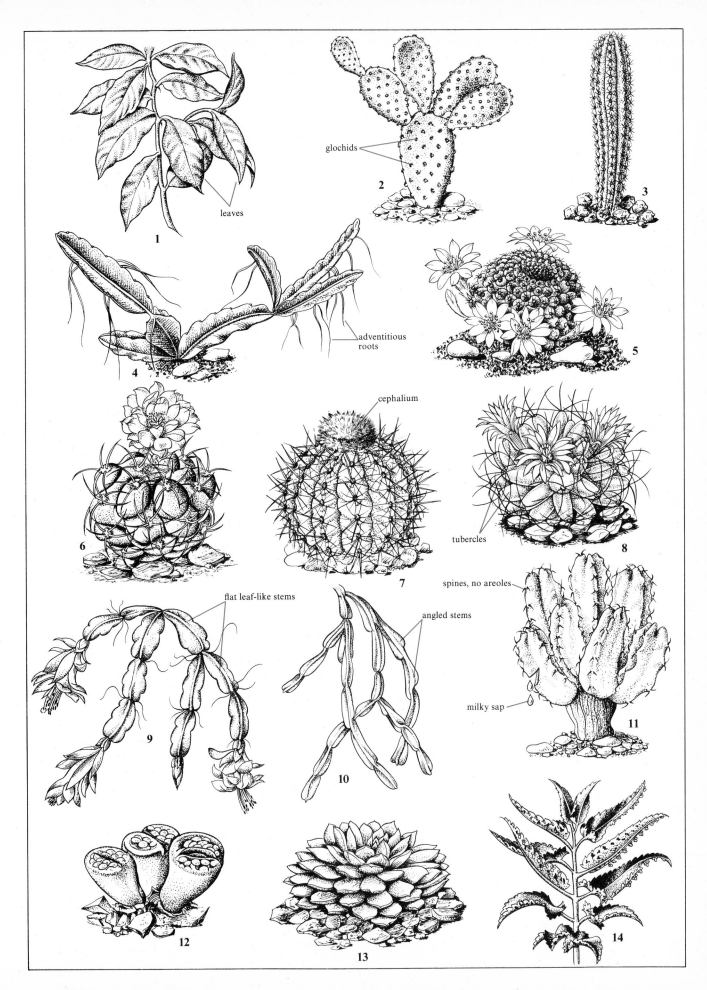

leaves

glochids

1

2

3

adventitious
roots

4

5

cephalium

tubercles

6

7

8

flat leaf-like stems

angled stems

spines, no areoles

milky sap

9

10

11

12

13

14

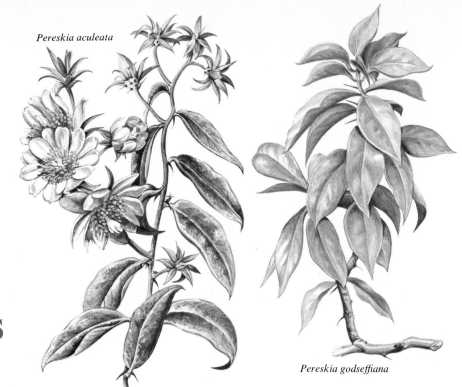

Pereskia aculeata

Pereskia godseffiana

True Cacti with Areoles

Pereskia

Pereskias are very like a dog rose in habit and might at first sight be mistaken for any plant species other than cacti. The give away is the presence of areoles below the leaves from which the stout and quite vicious spines emerge. They generally require more warmth than other cacti and will appreciate a different type of compost. A suitable mix would be four parts of medium loam or sterilized garden soil, six parts of medium peat and two parts of washed river sand. It is particularly important when using sand for cacti to make sure that it is fresh-water sand as salt-water sand can kill off the plants.

A minimum temperature through the winter of 10°C (50°F) is required if the plants are to maintain their appearance. If they are grown in the same greenhouse as conventional cacti, or rested on a north-facing bedroom windowsill as recommended when growing cacti indoors, they will drop many of their bottom leaves, and those that are grown for the foliage only, such as *Pereskia godseffiana*, will probably lose some of the top leaves as well. However, once the warmer weather returns and regular watering and feeding become possible again the plant will quickly produce fresh leaves.

Pereskias are not easy plants to raise from seed although nearly every flower will set in due course and it is best to propagate them by cuttings, which root very readily. Even the stems carrying buds will root and can produce a most attractive little flowering plant.

Pereskias ultimately make large sprawl-ing plants and will need support. If you have a greenhouse or conservatory with a sunny wall they will do best when planted out in the ground and allowed to sprawl naturally all over the wall. They can be trained up over the roof and when the pink flowers emerge are extremely attractive. They are also used extensively as grafting stock for other cacti, particularly the epiphytic types such as *Zygocactus* (the Christmas cactus) or *Schlumbergera* (the Whitsun cactus). For this purpose a stem about 18 in (45 cm) high is chosen and a vertical slit is made in the centre of it. The pads of the selected scion can then be inserted in the slit and the whole either bound round with an elastic band or pinned together with a long cactus spine.

There are three varieties commonly found in cultivation. *P. aculeata* is the most frequently seen and is a vigorous climbing shrub ultimately growing up to 30 ft (9 m) in height. The leaves are hardly succulent at all and each has a very prominent rib running down the centre. It is more spiny than other species having up to three brownish spines under each leaf. The spines also distinguish it from *P. grandiflora* in being hooked. The flowers have the great advantage of being scented, and the fruits, which are also ornamental, are yellow and spiny. *P. godseffiana* is regarded by many as a variety of *P. aculeata* and is distinguished by the reddish-gold colour of its leaves which are reminiscent of autumn foliage. *P. godseffiana* seldom flowers and is of a more bushy habit than *P. aculeata* although it is definitely less hardy, and makes a splendid pot plant. *P. grandiflora* has pink flowers and more oval leaves than *P. aculeata* and has long black spines on the older areoles, even though there are none on the newer growth.

Although I have recommended putting the plants against a sunny wall it is essential that they are given plenty of fresh air at the same time if the stems are to ripen sufficiently to produce flowers. Indoors they are probably best kept away from direct, unventilated sunshine as this can scorch the leaves, particularly those of *P. godseffiana*.

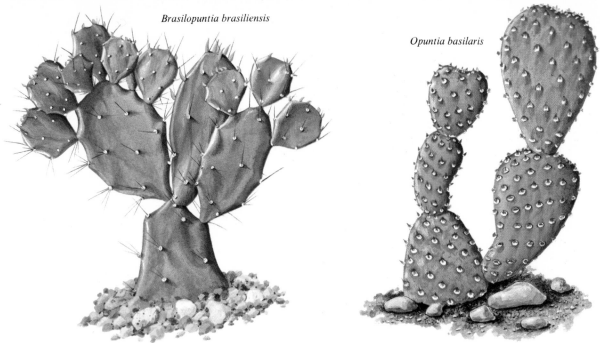

Brasilopuntia brasiliensis

Opuntia basilaris

Opuntia

Opuntias are probably the best known of all the different cacti genera and are more commonly known as prickly pears. The group has, in fact, been divided into more than ten genera and has been known to scientific literature since earliest times. The name opuntia derives from the supposed locality in Greece where it was first seen, but opuntias, although seen in great quantities all round the Mediterranean, are not native to that part of the world at all, and like all other cacti originated in the Americas.

Opuntias also have the distinction of having claimed Goethe's attention; he raised some from seed and made a considerable study of the plant, particularly of the cotyledon leaves, and embellished his notes with concise and accurate illustrations.

The name prickly pear derives from the use of the fruits as food. In order to remove the spines the fruits are roasted, and the skin together with the spines is then peeled off leaving the flesh exposed, something like a passion fruit.

Scientifically the genus is divided into quite a large number of subgenera but for the purposes of this book I propose to divide them into two groups: those that form fleshy pads, like the ones most commonly associated with the name, and those that are upright and cylindrical and which could easily be mistaken for some other type of cactus. The most important feature of opuntias which enables scientists and others to place them immediately is the presence of glochids. These are small

bristles which detach themselves very readily from the areoles and can pierce the skin and cause considerable irritation. Great care should, therefore, be exercised when handling the plants. If you do get some of these bristles in your fingers the best way to get rid of them is with one of the rubbery sorts of glue. This should be smeared over the affected area and then when it has hardened and become elastic it should be pulled off and the spines should come away with it. If there is no glue available soap and water can help.

Propagation is very easy and the pads root readily when detached and plunged in a mixture of peat and sand. Before attempting to root them it is best to cut off the bottom quarter of an inch (6 mm) in order to provide a larger area from which the roots can develop.

The two species illustrated are both quite distinctive. *Brasilopuntia brasiliensis* is a very attractive kind with small pads. The pads are of two different sorts, those nearest the main stem are circular but as they get further from the stem they become increasingly oblong or elliptical. The flowers are white but they are seldom produced on smaller plants, which grow fairly slowly.

Opuntia basilaris is commonly known as the beavertail cactus on account of the shape of the pads. It is not so commonly seen as the preceding species and is slightly delicate. It is particularly susceptible to fungal attacks during the autumn and winter and it is advisable to drench the plants before their winter rest with a systemic fungicide as a preventive measure.

It will probably also benefit from being kept slightly warmer during the winter if possible as this will help to keep the roots active and able to resist any attack. The thick joints are almost grey in colour but are tinged reddish round the edges. It is frequently spineless although there is the usual proliferation of yellowish-brown glochids in the recessed areoles. The flowers, like those of *B. brasiliensis,* are only produced on older plants and since this species is extremely slow growing flowering cannot be reliably expected on pot-grown specimens.

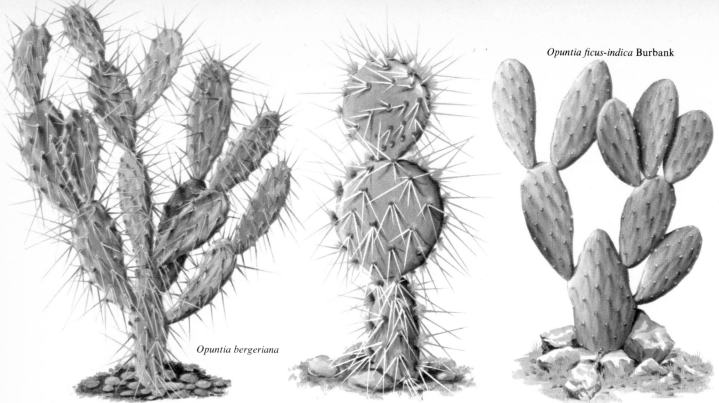

Opuntia ficus-indica Burbank

Opuntia bergeriana

Opuntia engelmannii

Opuntia (continued)

Opuntia bergeriana and *O. rafinsequei* are the two species most commonly seen round the Mediterranean and both of them have edible fruits. They are semi-hardy and will do well if planted out in a conservatory. *O. bergeriana* ultimately becomes a large tree-like plant and will eventually have spreading branches and occupy a lot of space. In order to encourage rapid growth and to enable the plant to reach the considerable size necessary for it to flower profusely it is best to plant it out in the ground if this is feasible. If this is not possible, it should be fed heavily during the summer months to encourage it to develop to the maximum size in the smallest possible pot without starving it unduly. When grown in pots, and as soon as they attain some size, these plants make very attractive additions to a patio or they can be spread round a swimming pool during the summer when the fresh air circulating through the branches will help to ripen the stems sufficiently to produce flowers the following year.

Opuntia bergeriana will ultimately develop a sizeable trunk and tends to become somewhat unsightly as the trunk is inevitably brown and appears to be pockmarked with woody-coloured scars. At first the pads are a refreshing pale green colour but as they age they gradually assume a bluish frosting. The spines are slightly bent over at the tip and in older specimens can grow up to 2 in (5 cm) in length. The flowers, when they are eventually produced, are profuse and orange in colour with a central green six-lobed stigma.

Opuntia engelmannii is almost the exact opposite of the preceding species and tends to sprawl around, branching freely so that it has a semi-prostrate habit although, of course, younger specimens in pots will have the usual upright appearance. For this reason it is best to let the plant graduate to a more saucer-shaped bowl or pot rather than restricting it to a conventional pot, or, best of all, to plant it out if possible in order to allow it to reach its full size and the shape which is characteristic to it. The joints are very thick and can be up to a foot (30 cm) in diameter in mature specimens; they tend to appear a little starved in colour but this is their natural appearance. As with *O. bergeriana*, the flowers are only produced on well established mature specimens, and planting out the cactus will enable it to reach flowering size more rapidly. The areoles are extremely pronounced, bulging conspicuously outwards from the surface of the pads, and like most opuntias they are filled with dirty looking greyish wool. The flowers are yellow on the outside and red on the inside and are up to 4 in (10 cm) in diameter. *O. engelmannii* is not really to be recommended to anyone who is either just starting a collection or who has only a small amount of space as it is neither particularly ornamental in itself nor characteristic of the mature plant while grown in a small pot.

Opuntia ficus-indica is the original prickly pear and has the finest of all fruits as far as edibility is concerned. The joints are elongated and up to 18 in (45 cm) in length and are much darker than either of the two preceding species. Like *O. basilaris* it is almost completely spineless and the areoles only have the usual whitish wool and straw-coloured bristles.

Nopalea coccinellifera is another very similar species which is useful as a host plant for the cochineal bug from which the food colouring is made. Like *O. ficus-indica* it is almost spineless but it does not grow so tall and has red flowers as opposed to the yellow ones of *O. ficus-indica*.

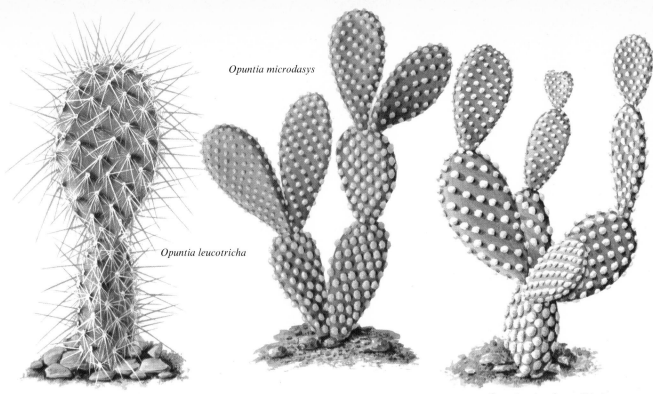

Opuntia microdasys

Opuntia leucotricha

Opuntia microdasys albispina

Opuntia leucotricha makes one of the best pot plants of all the opuntias which are commonly sold in the shops. The dark green pads make an excellent contrast to the long wispy white hairs or bristles that grow out of the areoles and surround the slender white spines. The joints are broadly oblong and can grow up to 7 in (18 cm) in length. This species has the advantage of being comparatively fast growing but the attractive yellow flowers are only produced on mature plants. In its wild state it can attain a height of 15 ft (4·5 m) or more with numerous spreading branches. A curious feature is the aromatic pulp that is produced from the seed. The plant is sometimes sold under the name of Aaron's beard.

Two other species with white spines are *O. amyclaea* and *O. spinulifera*, but the spines are less closely packed together on the joints than in the illustrated species and they are much less commonly seen in cultivation. *O. bella* is distinguishable by its brown hairs and the much thicker and stronger spines (the spines of *O. leucotricha* are very weak and can easily be broken or damaged in handling).

Opuntia microdasys as commercially available covers an extremely wide variety of forms with different shapes, sizes and colours. The three most commonly seen varieties are described here and on the next page. *O. microdasys* itself is frequently a low, creeping shrub in its native habitat but in cultivation it is normally upright, the prostrate habit, as with so many other natural phenomena, coming only with old age. The joints are either oblong or roughly round in shape, can grow a little over 5 in (13 cm) in length and are normally spineless. The absence of spines, however, should not be regarded as *carte blanche* to handle the plant without respect as, in common with all other species of *Opuntia*, it is the glochids round the base of the spine which detach themselves so easily when touched and adhere to the skin causing grave irritation. The species is commercially grown on account of its prominent closely set areoles which are densely packed with straw-coloured, yellow or brown glochids. Flowers can be produced on plants of six years of age or more and will ultimately be carried in great quantity; they are a magnificent pure yellow lightly suffused with red.

As mentioned earlier there are a great many variations on the basic species and one of the most commonly seen is *O. m. albispina* which is sold in the United States as polka dots, a name aptly describing its appearance. The joints are a very much darker green, more akin to *O. leucotricha*, and the glochids are pure white. There are some varieties of *O. m. albispina* coming on the market now which lose their glochids less readily and there is also a variety labelled *O. m. alba* whose areoles are set slightly further apart.

The opuntias illustrated above and on the next page are particularly susceptible to a type of brown rust-coloured spotting which can be observed on the plants during the late winter or early spring. The discoloration is not in itself harmful and no sprays need be applied. It appears to be caused by the plants being allowed to become excessively cold and damp during the winter and the best way to prevent it is to grow them slightly warmer, if this is at all possible. In a greenhouse with limited possibilities for temperature differentials, the best idea is to place plants which are likely to be affected in this way nearer to the sources of heat with which the greenhouse is provided. Care must be taken, on the other hand, not to allow the plants to become desiccated or shrivelled and the first signs of this occurring should be followed by watering the following morning.

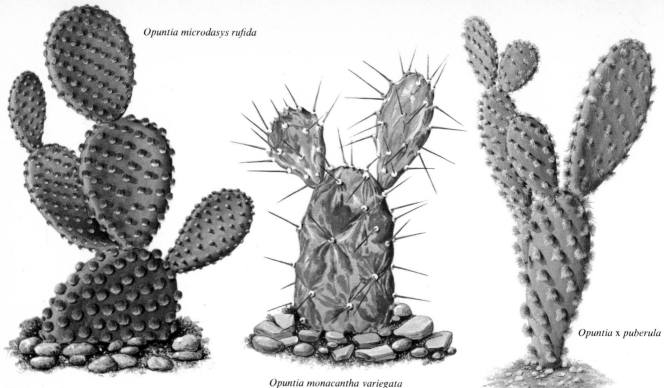

Opuntia microdasys rufida

Opuntia monacantha variegata

Opuntia x puberula

Opuntia (continued)

Opuntia microdasys rufida is very similar to both the preceding species but differs in having reddish-brown glochids instead of the straw-coloured ones of *O. microdasys* and the white ones of *O. m. albispina*. The joints are paler green than in the preceding species and a little darker than those of the true species. In addition to the one illustrated there is a variety which is sometimes seen called *O. m. rufida minor*. This is probably not a true relative of *O. microdasys* as the joints are slightly cylindrical in shape instead of being flat, but it shares the spreading prostrate habit of the others. *O. rufida* is, on the other hand, a completely different species and is more erect than *O. microdasys*. As a plant this species grows to far greater size than *O. microdasys* and the joints are more rounded in shape and a more greyish green in colour. Rudimentary leaves are frequently produced, sometimes up to 2½ in (6·5 cm) in length and often with a reddish tip. The flowers are yellow or orange but, as with most opuntias, are only produced on older plants. Although not commonly available it is a good grower.

Opuntia monacantha and *O. vulgaris* are frequently confused with one another and some authorities even consider that they are the same plant. To make the confusion worse the name *O. vulgaris* is frequently given to other opuntias, ranging from the upright *O. ficus-indica* illustrated and discussed on page 102, to a low creeping species which is probably *O. compressa*, thus belying the botanists claim that Latin names do enable the purchaser to know exactly what he is buying. The distinguishing feature of *O. monacantha* is supposed to be its single spine but it is not uncommon for parts of the trunk of mature specimens to have ten or more spines and most joints normally have up to two sprouting from each areole. The plant is upright and can attain a height of 7 ft (2·25 m) or more in its native state. The joints are usually oblong in shape but can be more rounded so that they are almost oval, however, they always narrow markedly at the base. The skin is dark green and very glossy and the flowers, when produced, are bright yellow. The areoles are fairly distant from each other and the glochids are less troublesome than those of many other species and brownish in colour.

There is an interesting though somewhat delicate variety of *O. monacantha* known as *O. m. variegata*. As its name implies this plant is variegated and the young growth is often suffused with pink. It is a very weak grower, however, and seldom reaches any great size in cultivation. The spines are much more brittle than in the true species.

Another species often confused with *O. monacantha* is *Nopalea coccinellifera*; this latter plant is, however, usually spineless. Both species are widely used in their native habitat as host plants for the cochineal bug from which the dye of the same name is made.

Opuntia puberula is another species where considerable confusion exists over the exact species to which the name refers. The true *O. puberula* is a low, often creeping plant, which is seldom seen in cultivation to any great extent, whose correct name is *O. de-cumbens*. The variety more commonly offered as *O. puberula* should, in fact, be sold as *O. x puberula*, the cross indicating that it is not a species at all but a hybrid. The parentage of this variety is not known for certain but most authors seem agreed that it is a hybrid between the *O. microdasys* described earlier and *O. cantabrigiensis*. The hybrid differs from *O. microdasys* in having more distantly spaced areoles, but it is much hardier and this it derives from its other parent which to this day can be found growing outside the glasshouses in the Cambridge Botanic Gardens.

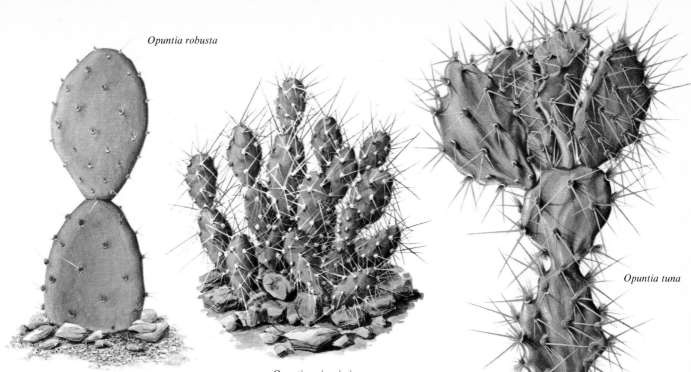

Opuntia robusta

Opuntia spinosissima

Opuntia tuna

Opuntia robusta is one of the largest jointed species available to the amateur and is as vigorous and upright as its name suggests. It develops many branches and the pads will ultimately grow to a foot (30 cm) or more in diameter. They are also extremely thick and of a bluish-green shade. Although in its wild state the species usually produces between eight and twelve very stout spines varying in colour, even on the same plant, from a deep brown to a pale yellow, the specimens grown in greenhouses in pots are usually spineless. The plant will also not attain its full-size pads unless it is planted out in the soil. The flowers, which only appear on older specimens, are yellow, occasionally tinged red on the outside. The fruit is deep red in colour and this distinguishes it from a similar species called *O. guerrana* which has greenish-white fruits and is not so commonly found in cultivation. *O. robusta* is very widely cultivated for its edible fruits.

Opuntia spinosissima is typical of another erect-growing group of prickly pears, which, however, may need staking when cultivated. The stems of this group of cacti are hardly jointed at all, and the pads appear to elongate with age rather than to make fresh ears. *O. spinosissima* is densely covered with areoles, which are in turn packed with brownish glochids and vicious spreading spines up to 3½ in (9 cm) in length. The body of the plant is a dull green, and because of the unusual growth habit of the plant the joints can be up to three times as long as they are wide. The flowers, which are produced only on mature specimens, are at first yellow but turn red as they grow older.

Opuntia tuna is another plant which although it grows erect in its native state frequently needs some support in the greenhouse. It is a fast-growing variety and therefore ideal for the beginner or for someone with ample space at their disposal. It can attain a height of 12 ft (3·5 m) and the dark green joints are elliptical in shape with large areoles from which two to four, or occasionally more, spines emerge. The glochids and spines are both yellow as are the flowers, which are produced only on adult specimens.

It is worth appending at this point a short note on the staking of cacti. Sticks are not, of course, normally available to a plant in its natural state and the upright-growing varieties should not require sticks if grown properly in cultivation. Generally speaking if a plant starts to flop about and if both it and its roots have reached a fair size, it is probably better to pot it on to enable the roots to have greater access to and draw up sufficient food to support the plant in a vertical condition. If the plant has not got sufficient roots to justify potting on, then, except in cases where I specifically recommend staking, it is probable that there is something amiss with the plant and the best bet is probably to cut the plant back to some upright joints and allow it to start again and to grow up more strongly.

Before leaving this section on flat-jointed opuntias, I would also like to mention the phenomenon of cristation. This occurs naturally even in several English wild plants such as the thistle and normally indicates a thickening of the stem. In cacti, which are virtually all stem, this can cause the plant to assume incredibly bizarre and convoluted shapes, which are of a generally crested appearance as the name implies. The growth of the plant is otherwise in no way inhibited and such plants are often greatly prized by collectors. Occasionally a quite normal plant will throw out a cristate branch and when this occurs it is often a good idea to remove the affected section, making a clean cut with a knife, and then to graft it back on to *Cereus* stock, following the instructions given for grafting on page 97. There is a slightly similar form known as a monstrose variety, in which the plant retains its cylindrical appearance but loses its regular structure. Cristate varieties are normally indicated by the presence of the word *'cristata'* after the name of the plant, and monstrose varieties by the addition of the word *'monstrosa'*.

105

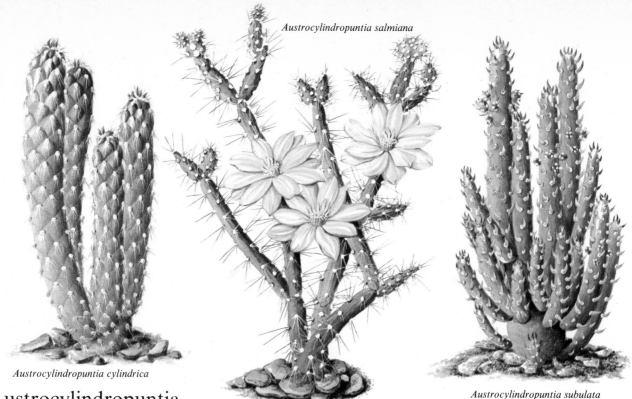

Austrocylindropuntia salmiana

Austrocylindropuntia cylindrica

Austrocylindropuntia subulata

Austrocylindropuntia

We come now to a group of opuntias which are characterized by having rounded or oval stems as opposed to the flat-jointed ones discussed earlier. Here again considerable confusion exists between botanical and commercial names. Most growers, probably as a result of having long runs of printed labels in the past, sell the plants under the generic name *Opuntia*. Botanists seem to prefer to call them *Cylindropuntia* or, even worse, *Austrocylindropuntia*; thus for example *Opuntia subulata* is, in fact, probably the same plant as the one described in this book as *Austrocylindropuntia subulata*.

The name *Austrocylindropuntia* is given to a group of plants coming from South America, and is derived from the Latin *australis* meaning south, as in Australia. *Austrocylindropuntia cylindrica* is a slightly branched upright plant with cylindrical stems covered in wart-like tubercles from which the areoles emerge. As the trunk of the plant becomes older so these tubercles disappear leaving it smooth. The joints are flattened at the apex, looking somewhat as though they had been hit rather too hard with a mallet, and long leaves are produced at the tips of the young shoots which fall off naturally the following winter, if not earlier. The areoles are set down quite deeply in the tubercles and are filled with white wool, and have some long hairs hanging down from them. Although greenhouse-grown specimens are often spineless, the wild variety has two or three spines growing out of each areole. The flowers are very small and inconspicuous and are seldom seen on cultivated specimens. The plant grows at some considerable height in Ecuador and Peru, and will tolerate fairly low temperatures if the air can be kept very dry. It will not, however, tolerate a damp cold such as we normally get in Britain in the winter. This particular variety is also often sold in both cristate and monstrose forms, and the former can make a very handsome plant indeed.

Austrocylindropuntia salmiana is probably the most worthwhile of all the opuntias for the amateur. It is a delicate shrub and flowers can be induced on four-year-old specimens with no great difficulty. It comes from Brazil, Paraguay and Northern Argentina. The plants are all sterile and this means they cannot be raised from seed, but this is no great hardship as the cuttings root readily and grow quickly into fair-sized plants. Plants grown in a good soil with plenty of natural light should not need staking, but may be pruned regularly to prevent them becoming top heavy; however, on a windowsill in a city the plant may become straggly and need staking if it is to retain its attractive appearance. The stems are normally purplish and this in itself does not indicate lack of water, but great care should be taken to prevent the plants drying out as the weak slender branches can desiccate very quickly in the summer and also in the winter if allowed to stay in too warm an environment. The flowers are the main attraction of this species and are similar to those of a dog rose. The colour is very variable, most commonly yellow, but there is also a white variety, and some of the white ones are occasionally tinged pink.

Austrocylindropuntia subulata is another excellent species for the beginner but may be confusing since it can adopt one of two different habits. The more commonly seen type is the branching one, throwing up from the base a cluster of thick fleshy joints tipped with very long succulent leaves which, unlike other species, may persist for several years before finally falling off. The younger areoles are sometimes completely spineless but often have up to two slender weak straw-coloured spines. Later the older areoles on the trunk develop up to eight spines or more in a cluster. The branches start at right angles to the stem but as they grow they soon become upright giving the plant its traditional clump appearance. The young pads root easily. There is also a form with a simple erect stem, rather similar to *A. cylindrica* but lacking the long white hair. The flowers, which are very small, are orange or greenish yellow; they are rarely produced in cultivation and were for a long time unknown. The species was also for a long time thought to be a pereskia but was transferred to its correct genus in 1883 by Dr George Engelmann after whom *Opuntia engelmannii*, illustrated and described on page 102, was named.

Austrocylindropuntia vestita

Cylindropuntia leptocaulis

Cylindropuntia tunicata

Cylindropuntia

Austrocylindropuntia vestita comes from Bolivia where it grows in the hills round La Paz. The roots are very fibrous and the plant is intolerant of overwatering or poor soil hygiene. The stems are very branched and weak and the plant forms small clumps in its native state. The joints of imported specimens may be quite short, but greenhouse-grown plants, with better soil and more fertilizer round their roots, tend to produce lusher, longer joints; however, even the greenhouse varieties retain the fragile nature of the originals and the cylindrical joints can be damaged very easily by careless handling. The areoles have short wool in them, spines, and some long hairs which give the plant a very decorative appearance. Very small leaves are also produced although these fall quite naturally once water is withdrawn in the winter. The flowers are small, produced only on well established plants, and are followed by bright red fruits. These persist for some time on the plant and subsequently produce up to five rather spiny joints each, after which they fall off and re-establish themselves as new plants on the ground. There is also a cristate form of this plant quite readily available and this makes an extremely decorative addition to a collection as well as being considerably less fragile than the true species.

Cylindropuntia leptocaulis is another species where great differences can occur in shape. As most commonly offered it is a bushy compact plant, but there are also some forms which have short, definite trunks up to $3\frac{1}{2}$ in (9 cm) in diameter. The stems or side branches, like those of the preceding species, are slender, but become a little thicker with age. They are easily detached from the main stem but if this happens they can be rooted with the same ease. The areoles have white wool set into them but no long hairs. The most conspicuous feature of the plant is the long, white, usually solitary spines up to 2 in (5 cm) in length. These are covered in papery sheaths which can become detached as the spines mature on the plant. There is considerable diversity of appearance in the length of the spines and the character of the spine sheaths, but this may have something to do with the very wide area where the plant grows wild, ranging as it does from the Southern United States to Puebla in Mexico.

Cylindropuntia tunicata also has very conspicuous papery sheaths round its spines and like the preceding species is very variable in habit, coming from the Highlands of Mexico, Ecuador, Northern Chile and Peru. As most commonly seen in Britain it forms a prostrate much-branched clump, but forms are available in which it grows upright to some considerable size and develops numerous lateral branches. The joints are very brittle but they rarely attain their full size in cultivation; the spines, however, usually develop well. Although very ornamental the spines are vicious and great care should be taken in handling the plant. In view of its normally prostrate habit it is best grown in a seed tray or wide shallow pan as this delays the evil day on which it has to be repotted since this is not a job to be undertaken lightly. Other species with similar papery spines are *C. imbricata*, which differs in being far more upright in habit; *C. bigelovii* and *C. ciribe*, which are bushier plants, the former more densely armed with spines than the latter; and *C. alcahes* and *C. fulgida*, the latter with joints which are very readily detached and brownish spines, and the former having more persistent joints with white spines.

Generally this last group of plants is unsuitable for the amateur or for those with only limited space available, since although they are fairly tolerant of poor conditions the dense covering of vicious spines makes them difficult to handle, and the spreading nature of their growth makes it awkward to get at other plants in cramped conditions without hurting oneself.

Carnegiea gigantea

Cereus forbesii

The Cereanae

The *Cereanae* are a group of candelabra-type cacti falling within a very large sub-group of the cactus family known collectively as the *Cereeae*. Seventy-five per cent of all cactus species belong to the *Cereeae* and a great diversity of forms and flowers is exhibited within it. The *Cereanae* have mainly spine-bearing areoles, ribbed stems, and produce their flowers and spines from the same areoles. They produce several joints and are normally erect, bushy or arching, as opposed to the *Hylocereanae* which are more vine like and sprawl around producing aerial roots at intervals. Many of the typical branching .characteristics of the group do not appear until the plants are well established, a particularly good example being the national flower of Arizona, the saguaro, which when purchased is normally a small dumpy little plant that takes a long time to achieve any resemblance of its natural shape as it is very slow growing. As a group they flower only when they have reached a fair size; it is unusual, for example, for *Cereus peruvianus* to flower when less than 2 or 3 ft (60 cm or 1 m) tall. For potting compost use a sandy well drained loam and be sure to give them a cool dry environment in winter, generally a temperature of 6 to 8°C (43 to 46°F) is adequate, although some kinds, notably *Lemaireocereus* will appreciate another 3°C (5°F). As a group they are also fairly easily raised from seed, and cuttings taken by slicing off the tops of the stems root readily in most cases, as well as causing the parent plants to start branching.

Carnegiea

Carnegiea gigantea is one of earliest recorded species of cactus and is so impressive in its natural habitat in Arizona, Southern California and Mexico that it has been adopted as the national emblem of Arizona. It is commonly known by the Indian name of saguaro but it is also sometimes referred to in the literature as pitahaya. Parts of the plant are used to make building materials and the fruit is made into a sort of broth by the Indians. It is extremely slow growing and very unlikely to flower in cultivation. Commercially available specimens have a somewhat globular appearance and the normal upright shape only begins to be apparent in plants of six years of age or more. The stems are mid-green with about eleven ribs carrying areoles about half an inch (1 cm) apart supporting eleven or more radial spines and four or five central spines. All the spines are of a somewhat brownish colour but the central spines become paler as they grow older.

Cereus

While *Carnegiea gigantea* can really only be recommended to the beginner on account of its national and historical associations, *Cereus forbesii* can be strongly recommended for its horticultural appeal. It is also known as *C. validus*, is a native of Argentina and is easily raised from seed. Moreover it starts forming branches when quite young and even pot-grown plants have an attractive and typical appearance. The branches have a slight bluish sheen when young which fades quite naturally with age and each branch has four to six ribs somewhat compressed. The areoles are set in slight notches along the flattened edges of the ribs, fairly close together, and support up to five short radial spines and usually a solitary central spine (although occasionally even as many as three) which is much stouter than the radials and nearly 6½ in (16 cm) in length on mature specimens. It is distinguished from *C. peruvianus* by having fewer ribs (*C. peruvianus* has between six and nine in mature specimens) and from *C. jamacaru* by its closer areoles and red flowers. [*C. jamacaru* has green flowers and areoles nearly an inch (2·5 cm) apart.] Such extensive cross hybridization has occurred between all three species as to make it very difficult to assign a given plant to a particular species, especially when they are very young, and the above guide lines are only very general. Few varieties are named correctly when bought, as the process of differentiating between them is almost impossible when the plants are young and before they have developed their full complement of ribs.

Cereus peruvianus

Cereus jamacaru

Eulychnia floresii

Eulychnia

Cereus jamacaru is one of the commonest and most spectacular of all the upright cacti. Many plants offered for sale as *C. peruvianus* are, in fact, *C. jamacaru* and the difference between them is in the number of ribs. *C. jamacaru* has four to six ribs while *C. peruvianus* has six to nine, although the count should only be made on plants of three years of age or more. If you have young specimens it is probably best to label them merely as *Cereus sp.* until the plants are large enough to hazard an identification.

Cereus jamacaru is found native in Brazil, although it has been used extensively as a hedging plant throughout the West Indies. It is a very large plant in its native state often growing to 30 ft (9 m) in height or more and the name 'jamacaru' is supposed to be the Indian name of the plant. The trunk can be up to 2 ft (60 cm) in diameter and is frequently used to make boxes and picture frames. The young shoots of the plant are also occasionally used during very dry periods to feed the cattle. The young shoots are normally quite blue although as they grow older this bloom fades naturally, just as in *C. forbesii*. The ribs are fairly pronounced when young and, like the preceding species, are wavy along the edges with areoles recessed into them. The spines vary greatly from plant to plant but are yellowish in colour. The flowers are only produced on fairly large specimens and they are nocturnal and pollinated by moths.

Similar species are *C. stenogonus* and *C. xanthocarpus*. The former sometimes has glaucous-blue young shoots but the latter never does. For those who want to try cook-ing the fruits there is quite an important distinction between the two. The fruits of *C. xanthocarpus* are quite tasty but those of *C. stenogonus* are rather unpleasant; they are yellow and reddish orange in colour respectively.

As has been already said *C. peruvianus* is not nearly as common in fact as the number of plants labelled as such would lead you to believe; the distinguishing feature is the greater number of ribs (up to nine and not less than six). There are two very attractive monstrose varieties of this plant known as *C. p. monstrosus* and *C. p. monstrosus minor*. The former is frequently seen in collections but is very slow growing indeed, neverthe-less mature specimens make a splendid showpiece for a collection. As if to make the problem with the names more difficult *C. peruvianus* is not, in fact, a native of Peru at all but comes from South-eastern South America.

Cereus aethiops and *C. azureus* are both similar when grown in pots. They differ from each other in the shape of their ribs, the latter having more wavy ribs than the former. They differ from *C. peruvianus* in their much lower habit, although they all have the magnificent bluish flock on the young growth, the latter, as its name sug-gests, being particularly attractive in this respect.

Eulychnia floresii is probably more correctly called *E. iquiquensis*. The generic name is derived from the Greek word meaning a torch and the plant is a native of Chile. The spines of this species are particularly im-pressive on the young growth although they fall off as the plant ages leaving a virtually spineless trunk. They are used as fire logs in South America where they dominate the landscape in many parts. *E. floresii* is an upright columnar plant attaining a height of over 20 ft (6 m) in its native Chile, branches are formed near the base and the stems are dark green with ten to fifteen low broad ribs almost hidden behind the prac-tically adjacent areoles. The areoles are full of tufts of whitish wool which hides the numerous short radial spines. The central spines are very variable but most cultivated specimens have a solitary central spine, of a rather handsome grey colour with a darker tip, up to 5 in (13 cm) or so in length on mature plants and normally over 2 in (5 cm) even on quite young plants.

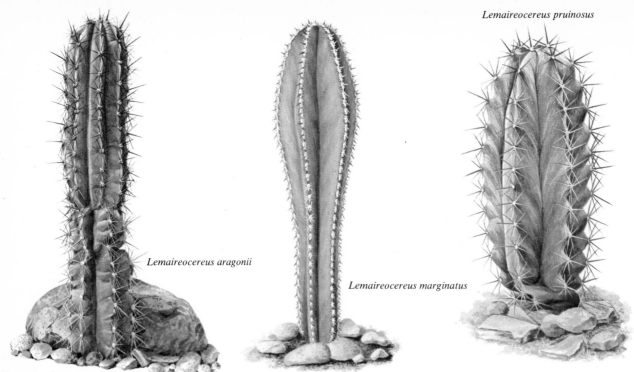

Lemaireocereus pruinosus

Lemaireocereus aragonii

Lemaireocereus marginatus

Lemaireocereus

Lemaireocereus are, on the whole, difficult plants for beginners and require rather more warmth in the winter than most other cacti and succulents. They appear to be extremely susceptible to rhizoctonia, the fungus which attacks the soft collar of a plant's stem where the main body of the plant meets the compost. Systemic fungicides such as benomyl can give some help here and it may be a good idea to drench the plant with a solution of water and benomyl in the proportions recommended by the manufacturers with the last two waterings being given in September. *Lemaireocerei* generally form tall, branching clumps in their native habitat although *Lemaireocereus humilis* forms a dense low-growing thicket. The flowers are only produced on older plants and, with the possible exception of *L.thurberi* (the organ pipe cactus), are generally rather slow growing.

Lemaireocereus aragonii is one of the most handsome species whose dark green stems bear pronounced glaucous bands at the point where each year's fresh growth has been made. The ribs are very large and form a feature of the plant being between six and eight in number. It is, unfortunately, rather slow growing in cultivation which is curious since, in its native Costa Rica, the plant is extensively used as a hedging plant. In order to preserve the glaucous tinting of the stems it is best to apply water to the roots from underneath, either standing the pot in a saucer of water if this is possible, or growing it on a bed of sand which can be moistened as necessary. Not only does this help to preserve the bluish tinge of the plant

but it also helps to prevent the occurrence of the collar rot caused by rhizoctonia and mentioned earlier.

Lemaireocereus marginatus is now frequently referred to as *Marginatocereus marginatus* but it is included here because many nurserymen still sell it under the older name. It is widely planted in Mexico (where it is also native) on account of its very decorative stems. The dark green slender stems with five or six ribs are highlighted by the areoles which are so closely set together as to appear almost continuous down the side of the ribs, and which are filled with brilliant white wool. The young growth is made even more spectacular by the red tinge on the juvenile spines. Like the preceding species this plant is widely used as a hedge and because of its upright habit it makes an almost impenetrable barrier when mature. It is slightly faster growing than the preceding species, but similar care should be exercised when watering it, and it needs a warm dry atmosphere during winter.

Lemaireocereus pruinosus is another plant frequently found but it appears to be more delicate than the others and more difficult to overwinter. It has five or six very pronounced ribs with few spines on them, the areoles are closely set, and the young growth near the apex of the plant has a dense hoary grey frosting. *L. eburneus* is also sometimes sold as *L. griseus* and is similar to the preceding species but has between eight and ten ribs and rather less 'frosting' on the young growth. The fruits, which are, of course, only produced on much older plants, are delicious and it is consequently

widely grown throughout South America. The plant has other values besides its fruit. It is used in Curaçao for hedging and in Venezuela it is used by the Indians in the construction of their houses, in rather the same fashion as lath and plaster were formerly used in Britain, the split open sections of the stem forming the laths to which the mortar and tiles could subsequently be attached. The branches are also thick and fleshy enough to be used as a vegetable in Curaçao.

Other species of *Lemaireocereus* frequently offered for sale are *L. chichipe*, whose areoles are set deep into the ribs, as opposed to *L. pruinosus* where the areoles are borne on top of the ribs, and *L. chende* which is similar but has between seven and nine ribs, whereas *L. pruinosus* has between nine and twelve.

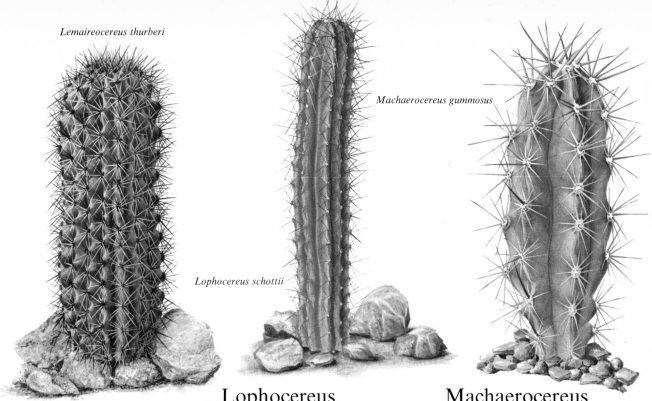

Lemaireocereus thurberi

Machaerocereus gummosus

Lophocereus schottii

Lophocereus

Machaerocereus

Lemaireocereus thurberi, commonly known as the organ pipe cactus, belongs to a group of *Lemaireocerei* with dark brown or even black felt in the areoles, as opposed to the previous ones which all had light-coloured felt. It is also distinguished by having many more ribs, between twelve and seventeen in number, giving it a very different appearance from the other. In its wild state in Southern Arizona, Sonora and lower California it forms a large clump branching from the base, and this unusual branching habit persists even in pot-grown specimens making this an excellent addition to a collection and particularly suitable for show work. The numerous ribs are rather low and separated by narrow intervals with closely set areoles barely half an inch (1 cm) apart borne on the edges. The areoles become filled with a sort of waxy substance as the plants mature; this is quite natural and in no way detracts from the growth of the plant. It has numerous spines which practically cover the entire body of the plant.

Lophocereus schottii is the only representative of its particular genus and, like *Lemaireocereus thurberi*, it branches from the base rather than from part of the way up the stem. The Greek name is derived from the word meaning a crest and alludes to the crop of bristles found on the flowering stems; however, this is unlikely to be a feature of pot-grown plants in this country as they require a warm sunny position. The stems of the plant form a large clump when mature with up to a hundred erect stems over 20 ft (6 m) in height. The ribs usually number between five and seven but sometimes there are as many as nine; they are separated from one another by broad intervals round the rather sickly looking greenish-yellow stems. The areoles tend to be small with little or no felt in cultivated specimens and bearing up to seven short radial spines and two central ones. The dense bristles which have been mentioned as being produced only on the flowering stems of the plant, are very much longer and can be over 2 in (5 cm) in length. Some imported specimens may have these spines present.

This cactus grows in very dry areas of Western Mexico and Southern Arizona where it survives because of the dense clumps it forms which provide a little shade to conserve any moisture that is available. There is an unusual and handsome monstrose form in which the ribs have been completely superseded by large tubercles, and a form with fasciated growth is offered under the name of *Cereus mickleyi*. It should be kept on the dry side in cultivation.

Machaerocereus eruca, the creeping devil cactus, is an extremely impressive prostrate sprawling cactus whose stems bend over, root into the ground and then grow up again into the air. Because of this sprawling habit and because it is at any rate none too common in cultivation it has not been illustrated here. The name is derived from the Greek for a dagger and is a particularly apt reference to the shape of the spines, which are very sharp. When cultivated it tends to be grown upright but it is able to pass over or round obstacles in its natural state where, because the base of the plant dies off with age and fresh roots are formed where the branches touch the soil, it gives the appearance of walking like a huge caterpillar across the desert. For the amateur who wishes to have a representative of this remarkable genus I recommend *M. gummosus* which does not sprawl around quite so much and whose initial stems are at least erect. It usually has eight ribs which are low and somewhat flattened and along the edges of which the areoles are borne nearly an inch (2·5 cm) apart. The stout spines are similar to those of *M. eruca* in that the centre spine is flattened into a dagger shape in the middle of between eight and twelve radial spines.

The plant is common in lower California and is easily raised from seed. In spite of the fruit being a local delicacy the body of the plant is poisonous and the battered stems are thrown into streams by the natives in order to kill the fish.

Monvillea haagei cristata

Myrtillocactus geometrizans

Myrtillocactus schenkii

Monvillea

Monvilleas are robust fast-growing species provided they are given plenty of sunshine in the summer and about the same amount of warmth in the winter as *Lemaireocereus*. There are about eight species of which only two are frequently offered commercially. The hardiest of these is undoubtedly *Monvillea haagei* (sometimes referred to as *haageana*). This forms an erect or climbing shrub, occasionally needing staking as it becomes older. The stems are very slender, often less than an inch (2·5 cm) thick, and tinted purple. The best idea, if space permits, is to plant it out in the greenhouse and allow it to develop into a sort of thicket on its own. The shoots are surrounded by four to six prominently notched ribs and the areoles, which support a number of grey spines, are arranged in these notches at intervals of about an inch (2·5 cm). *M. cavendishii* is similar but has more ribs, sometimes up to ten in number, borne on greenish stems. The stems are less deeply notched and the areoles are not so far apart, often less than half an inch (1 cm). It is comparatively free flowering, especially if planted out in borders in the greenhouse, and the white blooms are produced right through the summer in succession from April to September.

Monvillea insularis, although not commercially available, is interesting because it is the most easterly occurring cactus known. *M. spegazzinii* is sometimes offered as a grafted plant and is similar to *M. haagei* but has the bluish stems heavily marbled with white; it is sometimes for this reason sold as *Cereus marmoratus*.

Myrtillocactus

Myrtillocactus geometrizans is a large, vigorous and handsome cactus frequently and perhaps inadvisably used as grafting stock for species with less well-developed root systems. It has the advantage of forming pronounced branches even on quite young plants, and the stems, which are bluish green, develop bands with age showing where each year's growth has occurred. The stems carry five or six ribs, which on most cultivated specimens are so broad as to give the plant a sort of pentagonal-shaped stem. The areoles are just over an inch (2·5 cm) apart with a few short radial spines flattened against the sides of the stem. The central spines are very different being long, black and flattened and contribute greatly to the appeal of the plant. It is very common in Mexico where it is grown for its edible fruits known as garrambullas. These, if they are produced on your own specimens, should be left out in the sun to dry like raisins, which they look like and for which they can be safely used as a substitute.

Although this particular species is greatly valued as a grafting stock because of its vigorous growth, I cannot recommend it. Plants in cultivation tend to develop a hard scaly spot on the stems which I have been unable to associate with a pest or disease and which appears to do the plant no harm but renders it unsightly. It is possible that this brown marking, like that referred to in the section on opuntias, is brought on and encouraged by the cold damp winters in this country, and certainly growing the plants a little warmer at, say, 10°C (50°F)

seems to discourage these spots from appearing. It is a pity to spoil an otherwise impressive cristate specimen which has been grafted on to such a stock by allowing these spots to develop and the more experienced amateur is recommended to regraft on to a different species, such as *Pachycereus pringlei* illustrated on the opposite page.

Myrtillocactus schenkii has dark olive-green stems and shorter central spines. The areoles are filled with blackish-brown felt and get further apart as the plant grows older. *M. cochal* is another species occasionally found in shops which differs from both the preceding species in normally having no central spine at all.

Nyctocereus serpentinus

Pachycereus pringlei

Pachycereus pecten-aboriginum

Nyctocereus

Nyctocereus serpentinus is best trained up a stick in cultivation, although in its natural state in Mexico it sprawls everywhere over houses and walls. The upright stems of cultivated specimens are produced from a clump and can grow up to 9 ft (3 m) or more in length. They are an inch (2·5 cm) or so in diameter and light green in colour, surrounded by ten to thirteen low ribs densely covered by the areoles which bear about twelve spines, dark brown at the tips and becoming whiter towards the base. There is a certain amount of felt in the areole and also some wool. It is fairly free flowering for a cereus and blooms may be found on plants of six years of age or more. As with many of the clambering plants it will benefit from being planted out, particularly if a spot can be found against a south-facing conservatory or greenhouse wall. During the summer it is tolerant of fairly intensive heat which is probably a factor in encouraging it to flower. If grown in a pot it is a good idea to stand it up on a greenhouse shelf if this is available in the winter as it continues to appreciate all the light it can get. If plants are being grown in the home then it is better to grow them during the winter on a south-facing windowsill rather than on the north-facing one recommended for most other varieties of cactus during the resting period.

Pachycereus

As mentioned earlier the *Pachycereus* species are noted for their particularly strong vigorous growth and for this reason they have been used extensively, where appropriate, as grafting stock for other cacti with weaker root systems which are unable to support themselves. The name is derived from the Greek for fat and alludes to the thickness of the stems of the plants. *Pachycereus pringlei* is a native of Northwestern Mexico and Southern California where it is one of the dominant features of the landscape. It is possible that in former times vast forests of this plant covered the region but there are now only limited areas of forest left. The plant is extremely important economically and is used to make laths, walking sticks and firewood. The seeds are used by the Yaqui Indians to make a kind of flour which they then bake into the traditional tamales of the area. In most collections where this cactus has been grown from seed and kept under glass all its life the plant is only a semblance of its wild parent. However, it is still extremely attractive and the robust greyish stems are thickly covered with spines, sometimes tipped with black, which sprout from the densely set areoles on the eleven to fifteen ribs that surround the stems. The ribs themselves are flattened and the areoles are so close as almost to touch each other, and in addition to the twenty-odd radial spines have a filling of brown felt. On younger parts of the plant the spines may sometimes be completely black, but as the plant matures the bases of the spines become paler.

Pachycereus pecten-aboriginum is named after its spiny fruits. The Latin phrase *pecten aboriginum* means native's comb and the very spiny fruits are supposed to have given rise to this description although I do not know of any record of their actual use as such being observed. The plant is considerably smaller than *P. pringlei* and has fewer ribs, normally only ten or eleven. The areoles have a great deal of greyish wool in them (flowering areoles have brownish wool but will seldom be found on home-grown plants) and the spines are rather fewer in number than those of *P. pringlei*, seldom exceeding twelve. On the other hand the central spines are similar, being of a light grey colour and generally tipped darker. The long yellow bristles which give the plant its name are only produced on the fruits, and these in turn are only produced by older plants.

In addition to the varieties described there is a species called *P. columna trajani* which resembles *P. pecten-aboriginum*, and *P. chrysomallus* (sometimes referred to as *Backebergia* or *Mitrocereus chrysomallus*) is also another member of the family which is a worthwhile if less-often-seen addition to a collection. This latter species is distinguished by the dense yellow wool produced on the flowering parts of the plant, particularly round the ovaries, but it is also valuable for its attractive yellow spines which are produced on younger plants.

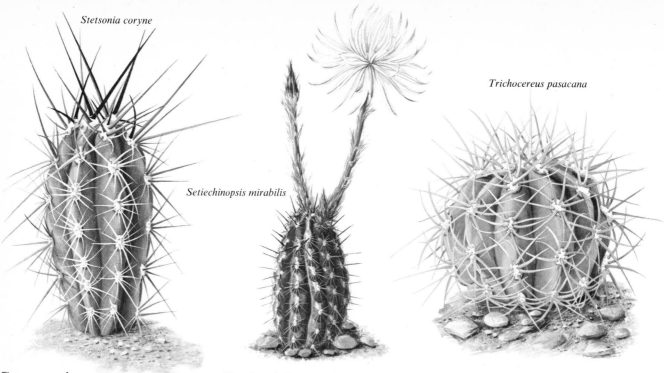

Stetsonia coryne

Setiechinopsis mirabilis

Trichocereus pasacana

Stetsonia

Stetsonia coryne is a very spiny tree-like cactus forming dense groups of columns in North-western Argentina where it is an essential feature of the landscape. In the wild it is a massive plant but because it is fairly slow growing it makes an excellent pot plant as well. The stems are pale green and even young plants quickly develop fairly thick ones; they are surrounded by eight or nine ribs and these are marked by a sort of triangular-shaped notch above the areoles, which are spaced down the sides of the ribs at intervals of three-quarters of an inch (2 cm). The areoles support seven to nine radial spines of varying length, and the white flowers are only produced on well established plants, and seldom, if ever, on pot-grown specimens.

There is a somewhat similar species called *Escontria chiotilla* which is sometimes confused with *Stetsonia coryne*. One of the major botanical differences between them lies in the structure of the scales of the ovary, but as this is unlikely to be a feature of pot-grown specimens in the hands of the beginner we must look for other distinguishing features. *E. chiotilla* is generally smaller in habit and has seven to eight ribs and more radial spines, between ten and fifteen in number. The Latin name derives from the fruit which the Indians of Southern Mexico call chiotilla and which tastes a little like a gooseberry when dried.

Setiechinopsis

Setiechinopsis mirabilis is currently included in the *Cereeae* but may, in fact, only temporarily be there. It is at any rate sufficiently similar in habit for us to treat it in this section of the book. The plant bodies are very slender and of a curious purplish colour. They seldom exceed three-quarters of an inch (2 cm) in diameter and it is difficult to grow them to any great height. This is not in itself a drawback as they flower freely, even in the second year of growth, and can be raised very readily from seed. The ribs number eleven and are very low, barely conspicuous under the thick covering of bristly, weak, black and white spines. The presence of flowers is indicated in the early summer as the areoles begin to push out dense tufts of black hair and the long tube-like flower stems emerge. The actual flower is white and very slightly scented. Once the bud becomes apparent you must take the plant around with you if you wish to see it flower as this opens at about 9 p.m. and is dead by midnight; moreover it develops very quickly and the petals may not be distinguishable even just before it opens. The plants die down very easily and become desiccated, and some authors suggest that this is encouraged if too many flowers are allowed to set seed in any given year. At any event it is extremely advisable to save the seed as and when it is produced to guard against the eventuality of the plant dying off.

Trichocereus

Trichocereus pasacana, on the other hand, is one of the giant species of cacti and comes from valleys high in the hills of Argentina and Bolivia where it can grow up to 30 ft (9 m) in height and looks a little like the saguaro. It occasionally branches from the base but it is more usual for the branches to be formed some way up the stem of older plants. The stems are surrounded by between twenty and thirty-eight low somewhat flattened ribs and the large areoles are densely spaced along the edges, sometimes being so close together as to touch one another. On pot-grown specimens the spines are extremely variable in size and number, but are generally stiff and yellow. The plant is named after the fruit which the Indians call pasacana and the woody trunks, which become virtually spineless with age, are used as timber in the building of corrals and huts.

Trichocereus pasacana makes excellent grafting stock because of its robust growth and broad stems which enable the graft to take place over a large area of both stock and scion. Also as it is fairly easy to obtain specimens of the plant there should be no difficulty in finding a replacement for a plant which has been used in this fashion. In its native Argentina it grows on exposed cliffs and hillsides and thus it is fairly tolerant of low temperatures in the winter and appreciates a certain amount of dryness at all times.

114

Eriocereus jusbertii

Trichocereus werdemannianus

Trichocereus spachianus

Eriocereus

Trichocereus spachianus and *T. santiaguensis* are, in fact, the same species although the former is the more correct name. It is columnar in growth but older plants will eventually form branches near the base of the stem. The stems themselves are mid-green and as they mature they become almost yellowish, giving the appearance of a golden trunk. The number of ribs is extremely variable although most cultivated specimens seem to have between ten and fifteen. The size of the ribs varies too from plant to plant, some having very shallow, barely visible ridges and others having prominent, quite conspicuous ones. The spines are at first pale yellow but as they mature they turn brown and ultimately become quite white. The radials are normally nine in number but they can be very much more numerous on some varieties. They surround a solitary central spine which is a little longer. The white nocturnal flowers are only produced on much older plants.

Trichocereus werdemannianus is another extremely variable species produced probably as the result of natural cross hydridization as there is little prospect of pot-grown plants flowering. The plant bodies of this species are at first globular but elongate from the third or fourth year onwards to assume a more characteristic habit. There are about eleven ribs surrounding the pale green plant bodies although there are some forms with more ribs and stouter spines which are probably related to *T. chiloensis*. The spines, as with *T. spachianus*, are extremely variable – the plants with stouter

spines probably being forms of *T. chiloensis*. The most important distinguishing feature of *T. werdemannianus* is the comparative closeness of the white areoles.

As already mentioned *T. chiloensis* is very similar and several forms of it have been given Latin names. *T. c. eburneus* has white spines while those of *T. c. spinosissimus* are brown and are bent backwards so they point upwards round the sides of the stems. In *T. c. panhoplites* the spines are very nearly black in colour.

Plants with very slender almost needle-like spines are probably more closely related to *T. poco*, especially where they are dark brown when young and form a dense covering round the ribs of the plant.

Of all the upright cereus, the *Eriocerei* are some of the most rewarding to grow. They are vigorous plants and for this reason are frequently used as grafting stock for varieties which do not do well on their own roots. *Eriocereus jusbertii* can be induced to flower when only five years old at a height of about 2 or 3 ft (60 to 90 cm). The stems are dark green with a tinge of purple in them and are surrounded by between four and six ribs in commercial specimens. There is a curious difference between imported plants raised from seed and those which are struck as cuttings, the former adopting their characteristic upright habit only later in life whereas plants taken from cuttings start growing upright straightaway.

In addition to flowering freely *E. jusbertii* also has the advantage that the spines are quite small, being produced together with a certain amount of wool in the areoles, which are set on the sides of the ribs at intervals of just under an inch (2·5 cm). The flowers are very large and worth waiting for, greenish yellow in colour and over 6 in (15 cm) in length.

Eriocereus martinii is another variety which is frequently used for grafting but is not so floriferous as the previous species. It differs in having the areoles set upon quite prominent tubercles and in having much longer spines. There is some confusion in the trade between harrisia and eriocereus, both names being used more or less indiscriminately to describe the same plants, although they appear to be two quite different genera in the wild.

115

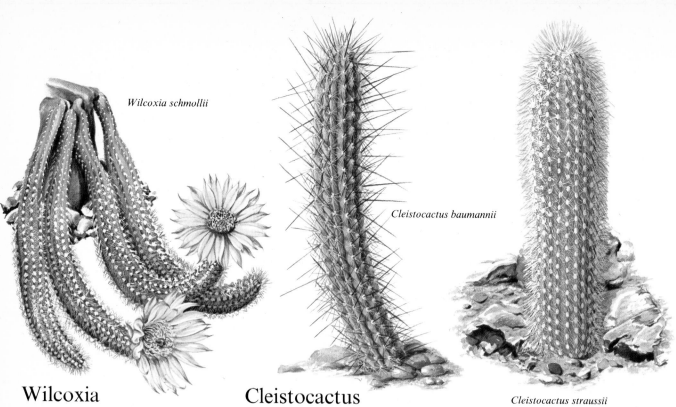

Wilcoxia schmollii

Cleistocactus baumannii

Cleistocactus straussii

Wilcoxia

Cleistocactus

Wilcoxia schmollii is a most unusual cactus which can easily be distinguished by its extraordinary dahlia-like root system. It produces a series of tubers below the ground and has weak sprawling shoots which may need staking. *W. schmollii* is normally sold as a grafted plant since its tuberous roots are more suited to the open sandy soils of the areas of Texas and Mexico in which it is native, and under cultivation it tends to develop somewhat thicker stems. The stems are very dark green, almost purple, and as they grow older the basal part becomes yellowish. The stems are up to half an inch (1 cm) thick and carry eight to ten low flattened ribs with fairly dense areoles which support some weak bristly spines, the radial ones numerous and white and the central ones solitary and black, and a large number of hairs which appear to be extensions of the spines. The hairs seem to grow more densely as the plant gets older.

In spite of its apparent need to be grafted it is an excellent plant for the amateur and when quite young produces a most attractive pink flower with a green-lobed stigma. It was probably partly on account of this green-lobed stigma, which is a feature of the *Echinocerei,* that is was originally called *Echinocereus tuberosus senilis.*

Wilcoxia poselgeri, although quite capable of being grown on its own roots, is a rather weaker and generally more slender plant. It becomes completely spineless with age and the ribs are almost inconspicuous and normally number about eight. It definitely needs staking, even if grafted, but if it can be kept growing well it will flower freely.

Cleistocactus baumannii is a native of Uruguay, Paraguay and Argentina where it forms branching clumps of upright stems up to 6 ft (2 m) in height. It is faster growing than the following species and distinguished from it by the very much less dense covering of spines and by their yellow colour. The stems themselves are dark green with twelve to sixteen low obtuse ribs. The areoles are densely packed along the edges of the ribs, and are often practically touching one another. In addition to the twenty-odd spines that come out of each areole there is a quantity of dark brown, almost black, felt. The flowers of this variety, like those of the following one, do not really open and the name is derived from the Greek word meaning shut. They can be produced on a specimen which is 2 ft (60 cm) or more in height with no great difficulty and this makes it a valuable addition to the collection, particularly as the flowers are a good red colour and contrast well with the yellowish spines.

Many of the plants which are currently offered for sale as *C. straussii* are, in fact, a variety of this known as *C. s. jujuyensis.* Like the preceding species it forms clumps from the base of the plant but young plants do not send up fresh stems as readily as *C. baumannii* does. The stems are not as dark as the preceding species being more of a mid-green and are slightly thicker with many more ribs, often up to twenty-five in number. The spines are inconspicuous and are almost hidden amongst the long white hairs which are produced with the spines from the almost adjacent areoles. The

species is particularly pleasing in that one can run one's fingers up and down the lower parts of the stem with impunity, so it is an attractive plant to handle as well as to look at. Sometimes up to four central spines are produced on the young growth near the top of the plant, these are frequently yellow but some forms of the plant have pure white spines. *C. s. jujuyensis* differs from the illustrated species in having fewer hairs and rather longer spines, moreover the spines are more perceptible and are a much darker yellow, sometimes even brown.

Cleistocactus smaragdiflorus is another species often found in the shops. This has only twelve to fourteen ribs, and more erect spines which are densely packed round the stem. The main botanical difference between this latter species and *C. baumannii* is the shape of the flower tube; the latter having a curved one and the former having a straight one. Faced with a choice between the two I would generally recommend *C. baumannii* as being the faster growing and more readily flowered.

116

Haageocereus chosicensis

Cephalocereus palmeri

Cephalocereus senilis

Haageocereus

Haageocereus comprises a number of very attractive species which are chiefly remarkable for their highly coloured spines. The varieties available can be divided into two categories depending on the thickness and coarseness of the spines. Of the group with slender spines *Haageocereus chosicensis* is by far the most common species in cultivation today, and is distinguished by its strongly coloured yellowish spines from the other variety which is often seen – *H. versicolor*. The Latin name of the latter refers to the rainbow-like markings on the spines. The plant forms columns with slender stems each surrounded by about sixteen dark green low ribs and the spines, which range in colour from reddish brown through to orange, are produced in large numbers from the closely set areoles, the central spines pointing slightly upwards. In their natural state in Peru the species belonging to this genus form plants about 4 ft (1·25 m) high. Plants imported from the wild may have quite different coloured spines from home-grown plants of the same species.

The second group of *Haageocereus* is characterized by coarser spines and one of the main types found in shops – *H. acranthus* – was once probably called *Binghamia acrantha*. This species has thicker stems, up to 3 in (8 cm) in diameter, and fewer ribs, normally not exceeding fourteen in number. These species also tend to produce yellowish hair at the areoles as well as the spines. Some varieties have spines with a slight purple shade to them, most notably *H. olovinskyanus*.

Cephalocereus

Cephalocereus palmeri is, to my mind, a more rewarding cephalocereus to grow than the more frequently found *C. senilis* which is illustrated beside it. It is considerably faster growing and the stems with their many fewer ribs, numbering seven to nine, are more clearly visible, while the bluish tinge of the young growth can also be observed. In Eastern Mexico, where it grows wild, this species attains a height of nearly 20 ft (6 m) and carries numerous branches. The most pronounced feature of the plant is the abundance of long white hairs produced all the way down the ribs from the areoles, which are well hidden by the hairs and normally set fairly closely together, often only half an inch (1 cm) apart. Beneath the hairs there are about ten radial spines. As the plant matures and grows taller the hairs at the base will start to disappear.

Other varieties of *Cephalocereus* which are similar to the species illustrated are *C. sartorianus*, which differs in having fewer spines on the younger growth, seldom more than eight in number, and in having more distantly spaced areoles, and *C. leucocephalus* which has up to twelve ribs and long wool. *C. chrysacanthus* is distinguished by its yellow spines.

Cephalocereus senilis is well known as the old man cactus, and fulfils one of the commonest prejudices against cacti in that it is immensely slow growing; however, it is a popular species on account of the long white flowing hairs that completely cover the numerous low ribs and closely set areoles. In city areas where the plant may be exposed to soot and grease in the atmosphere it is a good idea to wash the long hairs occasionally in a mild solution made of soap flakes and water. The hairs can then be combed out and the plant stood in a sunny location to dry, otherwise the hairs can become very matted and thoroughly unsightly. As stated earlier the plant is very slow growing and it is unlikely that cultivated specimens will ever flower. Specimens may be encouraged to grow a little faster by grafting them and such plants are often sold in the shops. Unlike most other cacti, *C. senilis* does not develop the slightly woody trunks and this makes it especially prone to attacks of basal rot fungi such as rhizoctonia; grafting on to a stronger-growing rootstock such as *Trichocereus* will help to avoid this.

A similar species with shorter hairs and longer spines is *C. hoppenstedtii*, now frequently sold as *Haseltonia hoppenstedtii*.

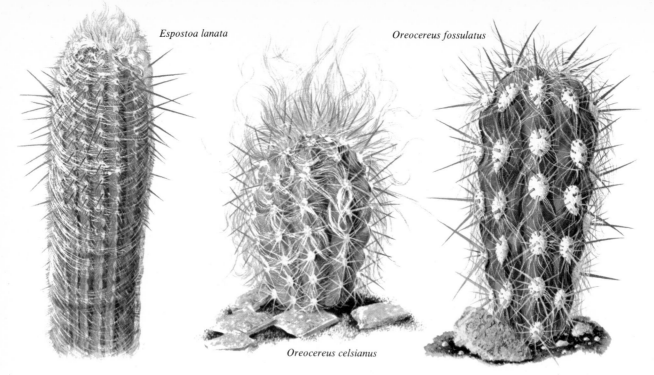

Espostoa lanata

Oreocereus fossulatus

Oreocereus celsianus

Espostoa

Espostoa lanata can at first be mistaken by the amateur for *Cephalocereus senilis* and is often loosely referred to as an old man cactus as well. It differs primarily in having quite sharp and well pronounced central spines, especially near the top of the stem, whereas *C. senilis* is almost completely spineless. It grows wild in the northern part of Peru where it forms a large tree with numerous spreading branches. Cultivated specimens are fairly slow growing. The species has between twenty and twenty-five low rounded ribs with closely set areoles which support a large number of radial spines largely concealed by the long white hairs. These hairs tend to wrap themselves horizontally round the stem, and even in quite young plants form a dense tangled tuft of wool on top. They are further characterized by the presence of a solitary central spine, yellowish brown in colour, which can be felt quite distinctly if the plant is grasped in the hand. Within the overall name there are two distinct varieties commonly offered for sale on a commercial scale. *E. lanata* has ribs which are to some extent visible beneath the hairs and can be quite easily counted, whereas the variety *E. l. sericata* is very much more densely covered with a tangled mass of hairs. These plants should not be washed.

The two species discussed so far both have dark green bodies, but there are also forms with almost black or purplish plant bodies even more densely covered by long hairs which may be referred to *E. melanostele*, sometimes now called *Pseudoespostoa melanostele*.

Oreocereus

Although some authors feel that *Oreocereus celsianus* and *O. fossulatus* are, in fact, the same species there are two quite separate forms that can be distinguished in cultivation and they are listed here for convenience as two distinct species. *O. celsianus* forms an upright columnar plant whose branches sprout from near the base when the plant gets older. The stems are mid- to grey-green with between nine and seventeen prominent ribs which are heavily rounded and conspicuously notched above each areole. The radial spines are completely hidden beneath the dense covering of hair surrounding the stems but the central spines, up to four in number, protrude through the hairs and can be seen quite clearly.

Oreocereus fossulatus, on the other hand, is an altogether sturdier plant with darker green stems with nine to fourteen prominent ribs and much deeper notches above the areoles than the preceding species. The spines are generally thicker and more vicious than those of *O. celsianus* with eleven radials and up to four centrals, which start as a sort of brownish colour and become much paler with age. The main difference lies in the distance from one another of the areoles. Those of *O. celsianus* are fairly close, seldom more than half an inch (1 cm) apart, while those of *O. fossulatus* are normally three-quarters of an inch (2 cm) apart with conspicuous white felting inside them and fewer hairs which are less matted and tangled in appearance.

There is also a species sometimes seen known as *O. trollii* which has fewer ribs than either of the preceding species and a rounder stem at the base.

The reason that cacti develop the very long white hairs that are characteristic of the last few species described is to reduce the amount of transpiration that takes place. Transpiration in plants is similar to perspiration in humans, but for a cactus it is essential that this process is reduced to the absolute minimum in order to conserve the maximum amount of water for the plant's own use. The long white hairs not only reflect the rays of the sun away from the stems of the plant and help to keep the plant cooler in this fashion, but whatever water is transpired from the plant is gathered on the hairs and runs down them to be reabsorbed by the soil below and eventually by the roots. In their native state cacti with these white hairs tend to grow on exposed hillsides where the sun falls directly on them, and their refreshing white appearance is best maintained in this country by giving them a position either in the home or the greenhouse where they can get as much sunlight as possible. Otherwise their requirements are simple and the only variety that can give any trouble in cultivation is *Cephalocereus senilis*, which for this reason is often grafted.

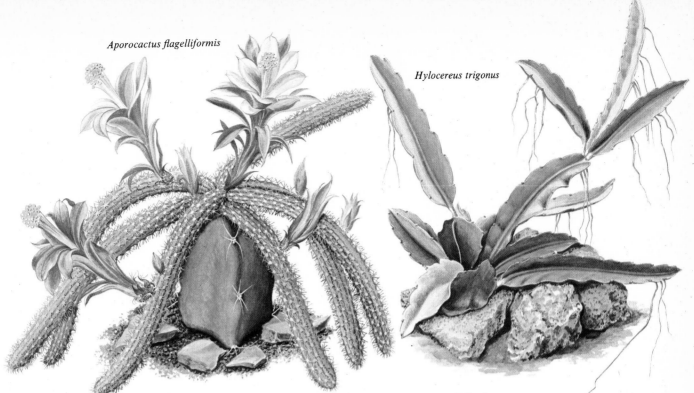

Aporocactus flagelliformis

Hylocereus trigonus

The Hylocereanae

The *Hylocereanae* are climbing or sprawling plants whose older stems frequently develop aerial roots which support them in the wild. As a group they come from Mexico, Northern and Southern America and the West Indies and their appearance is broadly similar to one another. Their name in Greek means forest cereus and this is a reference to their preferred environment in the wild. With the exception of aporocactus and its hybrids they generally benefit from staking and it is a good idea to grow them up a mossed stake which is kept moist. A mossed stake is fairly easily made by binding pieces of sphagnum moss round a reasonably stout cane with P.V.C.-covered wire.

Hylocerei which climb may also be grown against the wall of a greenhouse or conservatory and can even be trained, if required, like a fruit tree. Generally this planting out encourages them to grow very freely and can help to induce early flowering in many cases. It is also important to give these forest cereus a more humid condition in summer, similar to that required for rhipsalis (page 163), and a warmer position in winter. This may not be so essential when the plants are bedded out but when grown in pots it is a good idea to bring them into the house in the winter rather than to leave them with all the other cacti in the greenhouse. Pot-grown specimens will also benefit from the addition of some beech leafmould to the normal sandy soil that suits cereus as this gives it more texture and enables the plant to grow more freely.

Aporocactus

The true *Aporocactus flagelliformis*, or rat's-tail cactus, makes a most attractive hanging plant and can be brought to flower even when comparatively young. It is sensible to graft this variety on to a stock such as *Hylocereus undatus* as the long tails have a habit of dying back to the base and this ultimately can cause the whole plant to rot off. Somewhat similar to *A. flagelliformis* but far less often seen is *A. conzattii*. This latter species can develop aerial roots and closer areoles [seldom more than a quarter of an inch (6 mm) apart] as opposed to *A. flagelliformis* which has areoles seldom less than a quarter of an inch (6 mm) apart. There is also a bigeneric hybrid between *Heliocereus* and *A. flagelliformis* sometimes sold as *A. mallisonii*, but probably more correctly called *Heliaporus smithii*, which is distinguished by its much larger flowers.

Hylocereus

Hylocereus trigonus is a generally unremarkable plant whose main popularity lies in its use (together with *H. undatus*) as grafting stock as already referred to. But while the use of these grafting stocks may be of great use to the grower, since both grow profusely, their generally higher temperature and humidity requirements make them, to my mind, unsuitable stocks for most desert types of cactus. The main distinction between the two species lies in the margins of the stems, those of *H. undatus* being horny while those of *H. trigonus* are not. In the wild the sharply three-angled stems can grow up to 30 ft (9 m) in length sprawling over rocks and other bushes. The margins of the species are very wavy and the areoles, which carry about eight short spines, are borne on the crests of the undulations. Because of their sprawling habit they are not really suitable for collections with only limited space available and they also need to be some size before they will flower.

Deamia testudo

Selenicereus grandiflorus

Deamia

One of the most elusive of all cactus species is *Deamia testudo* – named after the botanist Charles Deam who discovered it. Although a great rarity this cactus has always been a favourite and is worth striving for even though it may take years to find one. Like all the members of this group of cacti it is a sprawling plant clambering over rocks and encircling trees in its native habitat in Guatemala.

The stems are generally five angled although younger stems may have fewer joints at first and they are at first upright but become more pendulous with age. It seems to prefer a shallow pot and grows well on a shelf exposed to the sunlight where the branches have ample room to hang down. The areoles are fairly close, and are produced on slightly raised points on the edges of the ribs. The stems are mid-green and the wings or ribs are tall and very narrow. Fresh joints are formed each year at the growing tip of the previous year's growth and the spreading habit which evolves gives the plant its similarity to the tortoise and hence its Latin name. This likeness becomes even more pronounced in the wild state when the plant has been allowed to dry out and become somewhat shrivelled and colourless. The spines are irregularly arranged, generally about eight in number with one central spine longer than the others. They are pale brown in colour becoming increasingly grey with age, and the areoles produce a small quantity of pale felt. The flowers are bell shaped and greenish white in colour but are only produced on plants of some considerable size.

Selenicereus

Selenicerei derive their botanical name from two Greek words meaning moon and candle. They do best when planted out in a bed and grown up a sunny wall in the greenhouse or conservatory as this allows them to adopt the normal sprawling habit which they have in the wild. *Selenicereus grandiflorus* is undoubtedly the finest representative of the genus with enormous flowers reportedly up to 15 in (38 cm) in diameter which are white and heavily scented and are produced at night. Its English name, queen of the night, sums up admirably its appeal to botanists and amateurs alike.

In habit it is a much-branched climbing or sprawling plant which if not grown up against a wall will undoubtedly need some staking or training round a hoop. The pale green stems become purple with age or drought and bear between five and seven low ribs. The spines are produced on closely set areoles barely half an inch (1 cm) apart, and are at first yellow but become increasingly grey with age and arise from a pad of golden wool in the areole. Like the spines, however, this wool becomes paler with age.

Selenicereus grandiflorus is reputedly less hardy than *S. pteranthus*, often known in this country as the princess of the night on account of its somewhat smaller flowers. The main distinction between the two species lies in the stems, those of the latter being rather more angled than ribbed.

In spite of their sprawling habit both the preceding species are somewhat slow growing and take a considerable time to reach flowering size. Those with less time and patience may prefer *S. boeckmannii*, which is faster growing although it has less spectacular flowers. This species is considered by some authorities to be a hybrid between the two just described and is generally similar in colour and appearance to *S. grandiflorus*, but the spines are whitish rather than yellow and the areoles are very much more closely set on the five to seven low ribs surrounding the stems. It flowers somewhat more freely than the preceding species, even when quite young.

Another strange member of this group of climbing or sprawling cacti is *Cryptocereus anthonyanus*, which at first sight could easily be mistaken for an epiphyllum. The stems are completely flat and tend to hang down making the plant a good subject for a hanging basket. The areoles are buried deep in the notches of the saw-edged stems and are practically invisible on the mature stems although they are a little more conspicuous on the younger growth where they may be accompanied by some wool and a few bristles. The most important distinguishing feature of this species is the presence of adventitious or aerial roots which are formed along the mid-rib at irregular intervals and this is not a feature of epiphyllums. The stems are pale green and the younger growth is prominently tinged with red at the sides.

Aylostera deminuta

Aylostera spegazziniana

The Echinocereanae

The *Echinocereanae* are a group of clump-forming cacti which generally have short stumpy bodies. They are distinguished for practical purposes as a group by the presence of ribs on the stems, although these may be arranged spirally as in the rebutias, and especially by the way they produce their flowers from areoles on the sides of the stems, normally on the previous year's growth. This differentiates them from the *Echinocactanae* which produce their flowers at the top of the stem on the new year's growth.

Generally speaking the *Echinocereanae* include some of the best flowering species for the beginner, giving the lie completely to the idea that one must wait several years to obtain flowers on cacti. *Rebutia kupperiana* will flower well when only two years old from seed, when the plant is less than 1½ in (4 cm) in diameter. They are generally early flowering varieties and they should be kept perfectly dry and as cool as possible, without actually freezing them, between September 23rd and March 23rd in our climate. In the spring water should be withheld from rebutias until the small red buds are visible round the base of the stem; even then it is advisable to wait a week or two and allow the buds to develop slightly as premature watering will encourage the production of vegetative rather than flowering growth. The rebutias, I find, tend to give an excellent guide to the watering requirements of other members of the group and these should be watered at the same time as the rebutias.

Aylostera

Aylostera deminuta is extremely typical of the group and flowers when three years old or occasionally even younger. The dark green plant bodies grow up 3 or 4 in (8 or 10 cm) in height in cultivation, are broadly club shaped and are surrounded by about thirteen spirally arranged rows of flattened conical tubercles or warts which are, in fact, the rudimentary ribs of the species. The areoles produce small white radial spines between eight and ten in number with a little brownish felt in between them and the occasional central spine. The fiery-orange flowers are the most important feature of the plant, they are over half an inch (1 cm) across and are produced in great abundance during May from the sides of the plant bodies. A large clump in flower is one of the finest sights of any collection, and the large number of flowers produced on older plants ensures a continuity of bloom throughout the whole month.

Similar species with club-shaped bodies are *A. fiebrigii,* which is slightly smaller but has more numerous ribs and is much more densely covered with radial spines, and *A. pseudodeminuscula,* which has almost purple flowers and a glossy texture to the stems.

Aylostera spegazziniana, on the other hand, forms cylindrical plant bodies which are not nearly so flattened on top as those of the preceding species. The tubercles are arranged spirally in eleven to thirteen rows round the glossy green plant bodies, and from these are produced areoles which are almost spineless at first, but later carry a few very short, rather bristly spines and the occasional central spine. A characteristic feature of the plant is the presence of a little brown wool in the areoles. The flowers also differ slightly from the preceding species in being more crimson than orange and rather larger in size, often over 1½ in (4 cm) in diameter.

Although it is possible to propagate aylosteras by cuttings, breaking off the clump-forming stems near the base and rooting them, it is more satisfactory to raise them from seed which germinates easily if the instructions on seed raising on page 95 are followed. For this latter course two separate plants are required and it may be necessary to divide the first clump in order to obtain this. Most cacti are self-sterile, meaning that cross pollination is required between two different plants of the same species in order to produce viable seed.

Chamaecereus silvestrii

Echinocereus enneacanthus

Echinocereus fitchii

Chamaecereus

Echinocereus

One of the most frequently grown cacti in this country is *Chamaecereus silvestrii*; yet it is also one of those most frequently grown badly. This is a great pity since when grown well the plant flowers freely and is extremely tolerant of neglect, doing well on a bright south-facing windowsill. It is a native of Western Argentina and forms a dense matted clump of short stumpy peanut-shaped branches up to half an inch (1 cm) thick and 3 or 4 in (8 or 10 cm) long. They detach extremely easily but root readily and it is a good idea to keep some plants coming on behind as reserves as there is a tendency for the centre of the clump to die off sometimes. The branches have fairly prominent low ribs, usually eight in number, and the spines are produced along the edges of these from the closely set areoles, which also have a few short hairs. The close setting of the areoles gives the plant the appearance of being well covered with the bristly spines.

It is essential to treat the plant as described in the introduction to this section if it is to reward one with flowers during May and June. These are produced from the sides of the stems, generally from the longer more pendulous stems rather than the short stumpy almost upright ones in the centre of the plant. Water given in too great a quantity or too soon before the flowers are developed will merely cause the production of more vegetative growth. There is also a curious form with yellow bodies known as *C. s. luteus* which has to be grown as a grafted specimen.

Echinocereus enneacanthus is still frequently sold as *Cereus enneacanthus*. It is a shy flowerer in cultivation and for this reason is not recommended for those who want a showy display. It is a native of Texas and Southern Mexico and makes a more or less upright plant which quickly forms clumps round its base. For this reason it is as well to grow it in a shallow pan similar to that recommended for stapelias (page 186). The stems are quite thick, frequently up to 2 in (5 cm) in diameter, and are a pale rather chlorotic-looking green. These are surrounded by seven to ten quite prominent ribs, on which the areoles are set on slightly raised wart-like protuberances which are rounded at the edges. The spines are straw like and yellowish at first, becoming white later. The Greek specific name literally means nine spines, but most cultivated specimens have anything between seven and nine radial spines and at least one, and occasionally two, central spines. As mentioned earlier it is a shy flowerer but when flowers are produced they are large and deep pink in colour. It is possible to make a sort of strawberry jam from the fruits which is said to be very fine.

Echinocereus fitchii is one of the best flowering cacti available. The stems are very variable in habit and colour but generally branch from the base of older plants. They are surrounded by between twelve and twenty-three ribs and completely covered by a network of bristly radial spines. The flowers are very spectacular, frequently 2 in (5 cm) or more across and a vivid fluorescent pink with the green stigma

in the centre that is characteristic of this genus. As good drainage is essential this species generally requires a rather more sandy soil than most other cacti. I find it is very difficult to grow a plant to any size as it is susceptible to any sort of fungal attack that is going. However, this need not be a problem if seed is saved as the plants grow very readily in this way and flowers can be produced on plants of three years of age or more with little difficulty. If using a standard cactus compost it is probably as well to add a third as much sand by volume to the original mix, or alternatively granulated polystyrene may be used if this is available. Like all cacti which make rather slight root systems it is important not to overpot as this will result in almost immediate death if the plant becomes waterlogged.

Echinocereus salm-dyckianus

Echinocereus rigidissimus

Echinocereus stramineus

Echinocereus rigidissimus is frequently confused with *E. pectinatus* and to make the confusion doubly confounded the *E. pectinatus* of horticulture is frequently more correctly botanically referred to *E. rigidissimus*. It is similar to *E. fitchii*, described on the opposite page, but is generally very much smaller. The stems are usually solitary and tend to be rather low, although in the native habitat they may attain a height of nearly a foot (30 cm). They are mid-green in colour and have about twenty low obtuse ribs. The radial spines are produced in great profusion, up to twenty or more at each areole, and because they spread widely they appear to cover the stems of the plant completely, giving the plant its rather geometric appearance by being practically joined together at the tips which are adjacent to one another. It is not as free flowering as *E. fitchii* but the flowers when they are produced are similar.

It is probable that many of the forms of *E. fitchii* offered for sale are, in fact, hybrids with *E. rigidissimus* as it is not uncommon to find plants described as the former with the extra 'ridge' formed by the touching ribs of the latter. Similarly, as mentioned above, many forms of *E. pectinatus* are referable to the illustrated species. The true *E. pectinatus* has two or three central spines, whereas the true *E. rigidissimus* has none.

Although *E. enneacanthus* is sometimes referred to as the strawberry cactus, it is more usual to hear *E. salm-dyckianus* called by this common name. It is not easy to get hold of plants of this species but it is worth trying hard to do so as they make excellent pot plants The stems branch readily from the base and the branches can be rooted easily; they are light green in colour and have seven fairly prominent ribs arranged at regular intervals around them. The young areoles, which are closely set together on the sides of the ribs, produce yellow felt when young but this later turns brown. The spines are a dull greyish yellow and comprise nine radials and up to three centrals. The main attraction is the orange flower; this is difficult to obtain on younger plants but since they are fast growing one does not have to wait long until the plants are large enough to flower readily. When it is produced it contrasts well with the pale green stems.

This species, because of its clump-forming habit and shallow rooting system, really does best in a three-quarter pot or pan, as this allows it to spread around to the maximum and enables the air to circulate round the centre of the clump encouraging the ripening of the stems to assist flowering.

Rather similar in appearance but branching far less freely is *E. stramineus*. This has slightly thicker stems up to $2\frac{1}{2}$ in (6·5 cm) in diameter and is a more erect plant than the preceding species. The stems, like those of *E. salm-dyckianus*, are pale green in colour but with many more ribs, normally between nine and thirteen in number, surmounted by the same rounded warts which characterized *E. enneacanthus*. The spines, as the name suggests, are weak, rather bristly and straw like in appearance, at first brownish in colour but becoming white with age. The central spines are very prominent and up to $3\frac{1}{2}$ in (9 cm) long in wild specimens although seldom attaining quite this size in cultivation, and the radials number between seven and ten. Cultivated specimens generally have white radial spines from the start. The flowers, which are a spectacular purple, are seldom produced on cultivated specimens unless these are quite old.

Echinocereus viridiflorus

Echinopsis eyriesii

Echinopsis tubiflora

Echinocereus (*continued*)

Echinocereus viridiflorus is an extremely variable species in cultivation although it is probable that much of the variation is due to hybridization rather than natural mutation, but it is, as its name suggests, characterized by its curious green flowers. In habit it is dwarf, more or less erect, and branches freely from the base to form a good clump. The stems are green and the ribs, which are usually twelve in number, are arranged spirally round the stems. This is a distinguishing feature from the other *Echinocerei* described in the book. The young spines are red at first, turning yellow as they age. They number about fifteen and are very small. Wild plants have a central spine but this is only occasionally found in cultivated specimens and seldom, if ever, on grafted plants.

It is usually fairly easy to spot the young flower buds on *Echinocerei* as large quantities of wool are produced from the flowering areoles before the flowers actually emerge. Any unusual growths from the upper part of the stem are likely to be buds and if possible it is a good idea to withhold water until this woolliness is apparent. If no wool has materialized by the end of April, however, it is better to water the plant as prolonged drought will cause it to shrivel up and it may never recover.

Echinopsis

Echinopsis, Echinocactus and *Echinocereus* all derive their names from the Greek word *echinos,* meaning a hedgehog. While it is true that very many cacti give the appearance and the feel of hedgehogs I think the name is most appropriately ascribed to the genus *Echinopsis,* which not only seldom produces flowers, but when it does do so, produces them in the evening. Most species of *Echinopsis* will benefit from being left outside during the summer although they should not be exposed to full sunlight; the north-facing slope of a rock garden, if available, is ideal. They also require a maximum temperature of 7°C (45°F) during the winter if they are to flower the following summer as too much warmth or too much water will merely encourage the production of large numbers of offsets but little in the way of flowering growth. Given the correct treatment echinopsis should flower within their fourth year from seed but they are not the easiest of cacti in which to induce flowering. *Echinopsis eyriesii* as a true species is somewhat rare in cultivation and most of the varieties described as this are either *E. multiplex* or hybrids of this with *E. eyriesii.* The true species has eleven to twelve pronounced ribs and very small reddish-brown spines which become a darker brown with age; the areoles are tightly filled with greyish wool. It is very fast growing because of its tendency to produce vegetative rather than floriferous sideshoots, and these may easily be rooted if broken off. The flowers, which are difficult to obtain unless the instructions above are followed, are white and fragrant.

Echinopsis tubiflora has much more prominent spines than the preceding species and these are borne on white woolly areoles on the edges of the twelve conspicuous ribs. The spines are black and can grow up to half an inch (1 cm) in length. Like *E. eyriesii* this has been extensively hybridized and these crossed varieties are distinguished by the absence of the black spines, whose dark coloration has been restricted to the tips of the young spines. This species flowers fairly readily for an echinopsis and as the name suggests the flowers are more funnel shaped, hardly seeming to open properly.

Another spiny species, seemingly somewhere between *E. eyriesii* and *E. tubiflora,* is *E. oxygona,* which has pale rose-pink flowers. One of the most fragrant of all the *Echinopsis* species is *E. turbinata,* which has white flowers.

Echinopsis multiplex

Echinopsis rhodotricha

Lobivia haageana

Lobivia

Echinopsis multiplex is an extremely prolific plant producing very numerous offsets that make its chances of flowering extremely remote. Really harsh treatment and an extended period of drought and low temperatures are required in order to induce flowering. It is one of the most commonly seen plants on cottage windowsills and tolerates total neglect and bright sunlight without demur. I have known plants go for several months in summer in full sunlight without water and without showing any ill effects.

Grown properly and induced to flower it makes a very ornamental addition to any collection since the blooms, like those of *E. turbinata,* mentioned on the opposite page, are strongly scented. The spherical habit of the plant is often hidden under the numerous offsets which, if they are produced too copiously, will cause the main plant body to become more club shaped. It normally attains a height of 6 in (15 cm) but can spread to a foot (30 cm) or more in diameter by means of the numerous offsets. The stems are very pale green, giving it the permanent appearance of being hungry, but it should not be fed as it will only respond by producing more and more offsets rather than flowers. It is distinguished from most of the species so far described by having many more ribs, between twelve and fourteen on the true species. The areoles are armed with ten radial spines, yellowish in colour but tipped with a dark point, and about four much darker central spines which are bent slightly over. The flowers, when they are produced, are white,

fragrant, and borne at the end of long tubes.

Echinopsis rhodotricha might not at first be thought to be a member of this genus as it looks far more like a cereus in its young stages. It is extremely variable in habit, partly as the result of hybridization, and is very reluctant to flower even on older plants. The similarity to a cereus is further accentuated by its normally unbranched habit, although older plants will develop branches from the base. It is taller than any of the previously described species, often attaining a height of more than 2 ft (60 cm) in time, and the dark or occasionally mid-green stems are surrounded by up to thirteen straight ribs. The radial spines are curved and vary between four and seven in number; their colour too is extremely variable, all shades between brown and white being found. Similarly with the central spines it is hard to lay down the rule, sometimes there are none at all and sometimes they are quite long.

Lobivia is an excellent group of plants for collectors and the name is an anagram of Bolivia, their native country. Like other members of this group of cacti the flowers are produced from the sides of the plant about two-thirds of the way up the stem, and the first indication of their presence is the appearance of woolly buds in the base of the areoles. Ideally, water should only be given when these appear and have been identified, but on no account should it be withheld after the end of April. If no woolly buds are apparent by then it may be necessary to abandon all hope of obtaining flowers that summer.

Lobivia haageana is one of the prettiest of all lobivia species. The plant bodies are upright and cylindrical and can attain a height of 12 in (30 cm) where it grows on the frontiers between Bolivia and the Argentine. The ribs are numerous, between twenty and twenty-two in number, and are arranged spirally up the sides of the stems. The areoles have some grey wool in them and about fourteen radial spines, but the most prominent feature consists of the four long black (when young) central spines that protrude from each areole. The flowers are produced fairly freely on three-year-old plants and are pale yellow in colour, and in shape similar to an inverted bell on the end of a short tube.

Lobivia densispina hybrid

Lobivia jajoiana

Lobivia famatimensis

Lobivia *(continued)*

Lobivia densispina is probably more correctly known as *L. famatimensis densispina*; however, it is so commonly sold under the former name that I have decided to include it as such. The true *L. famatimensis* is illustrated beside it for reference.

As its name implies it is easily recognized by the very dense covering of spines that almost completely obscures the glossy dark green plant bodies. It seldom attains any great height, even in its native habitat in Southern Bolivia. In cultivation mature specimens are normally about 4 in (10 cm) tall by 2 in (5 cm) in diameter and for this reason it is sensible not to overpot it as this can cause a lot of water to collect round the part of the stem which meets the soil. The cultivated specimens are very variable in their more specific characteristics such as the number of ribs and spines, and this is due to the almost inevitable hybridization that occurs between the variety and the true species.

The variety illustrated is much more floriferous than the true species and the large yellow flowers are produced freely on plants of only two years of age. The flowers have a satin sheen about them that gives them an almost fluorescent appearance.

Lobivia famatimensis is also sometimes referred to as *L. pectinifera* and differs in having many more ribs, normally twenty or more, and purplish plant bodies, rather than the darker green ones of the preceding species. As mentioned earlier, horticultural varieties provide a great diversity of form partly due to hybridization and partly due to the naturally occurring mutations of the species. It is far less densely covered in spines than the variety *densispina*, and the cultivated forms exhibit a very wide variety of flower colour ranging through the spectrum from red to orange and yellow to white.

Although there is a very rare white-flowered variety of *L. famatimensis* called, appropriately enough, *L. f. albiflora*, most of the white-flowered specimens are the result of hybridization rather than naturally occurring mutation. There are also lobivias with greenish flowers, a not unusual colour for cacti, notably *L. chlorogona*.

Lobivia f. leucomalla resembles *L. f. densispina* in having a dense covering of greyish spines, but differs in its almost miniature flowers which are more like those of *Pseudolobivia aurea* described on the opposite page.

Lobivia jajoiana is typical of a group of lobivias characterized by hooked spines. It is rather less floriferous than the species so far described but when it does flower the unusual colouring of the throat, which is almost black, more than makes up for this. The plant bodies are almost spherical in shape and are surrounded by about fourteen very prominent ribs. The sides of the ribs are marked with slight furrows and these raise up the areoles giving the plants a slightly tuberculate appearance. The areoles themselves are filled with greyish wool and have short, unremarkable radial spines and up to three central spines, the longest of which can grow to 2 in (5 cm) in length and has a conspicuous and somewhat vicious hook at the end. On the true species the flowers are a bright crimson, but some forms occur with more wine-coloured flowers; however, they all have the magnificent dark throat referred to earlier. Yellow-flowered varieties of this species are referable to *L. j. nigrostoma* and there is also a variety with more rounded petals called *L. j. fleischeriana*.

Another species with hooked spines is *L. wrightiana*. This has very much more rounded ribs and is generally smaller than the species illustrated. The spines are far less numerous and do not cover the stems to nearly the same extent as they do in *L. jajoiana*; the hooked spines also tend to rise more vertically than they do in the latter species, even on the sides of the stems.

Pseudolobivia aurea

Rebutia haagei

Pseudolobivia kratochvilleana

Pseudolobivia

Pseudolobivias are very close relatives of the *Lobivia* genus and many of the species are frequently sold under either name. *Pseudolobivia aurea* is by far the most common of the varieties sold and flowers readily given the right conditions. The plant bodies are almost spherical at first but as the plant matures they tend to elongate, ultimately giving the stems a more club-shaped appearance. It is a native of Argentina where it can attain a height of 5 in (13 cm) or so and the pale green stems are surrounded by up to fifteen prominent and sharply angled ribs. The radial spines vary in number between six and ten and are grey or occasionally purplish with a darker tip. Up to four central spines are produced from the areoles and on mature plants these can attain a length of an inch (2·5 cm), although younger plants tend to have much shorter central spines. The yellow flowers are the most rewarding feature of the plant and are plentifully produced during the early summer. A great deal of variation from the illustrated species will be observed in cultivated plants sold under this name due to the extensive hybridization that has occurred between this species and *Lobivia famatimensis*.

The pseudolobivias are botanically somewhere between *Echinopsis* and *Lobivia*; whereas the preceding species was more closely related to *Lobivia* the next species is more closely related to *Echinopsis*, and is often sold under that name.

Pseudolobivia kratochvilleana makes a globular or at first hemispherical plant up to 4 in (10 cm) in height with pale stems surrounded by fifteen or more narrow ribs. The radial spines, like those of echinopsis, are weak and number ten. One or two much more stout central spines are produced and these can attain a length of 1 in (2·5 cm). The flowers are white and are produced at the end of very long tubular stems which sprout from the side of the plant. They open in the evening and are occasionally lightly suffused with pink.

Rebutia

Rebutias are without doubt the most rewarding of all cacti to grow. They are undemanding plants which flower readily, by and large, even when very young. They are very closely related to the aylosteras described earlier and may be easily raised from seed. Because of their popularity they have been extensively hybridized with one another so as to make practical identification of cultivated material almost impossible. I propose to divide them into two groups; the quite clearly distinguishable ones, which because they are more shy flowerers tend not to be so extensively hybridized; and the very free-flowering varieties such as *Rebutia minuscula*, *R. marsoneri* and *R. violaciflora* which have been so extensively crossed with one another as to make it very difficult to obtain the true species any longer.

Rebutia haagei has in the past been known by a great many names and is still commonly referred to by nurserymen as *Mediolobivia pygmaea*, which is also extensively used as a synonym for *R. pygmaea* described overleaf. The confusion is made even worse by the former naming of *R. pygmaea* as *Pseudolobivia haagei*.

Rebutia haagei itself is a small species forming clumps with a thick fleshy root. The plant bodies are roughly oval in shape and the spines, which are almost transparent in colour, are rather longer than those of *R. pygmaea* being generally over a tenth of an inch (2·5 mm) in length. The flowers are somewhat more salmon coloured than those of *R. pygmaea*.

Rebutia pygmaea

Rebutia senilis

Rebutia violaciflora

Rebutia (continued)

Rebutia pygmaea is, as its name suggests, a very dwarf-growing species which is sometimes offered for sale as *Mediolobivia pygmaea*. The plant bodies are single when young but later form small clumps rising up from a prominent thick fleshy root. It is a native of Northern Argentina and even there it seldom exceeds 1½ in (4 cm) in height with stems less than an inch (2·5 cm) in diameter. Like all *Rebutia* species the dark green stems do not have ribs but instead there is a succession of tubercles arranged round them in spiral rows. The spines are very small indeed in cultivated specimens, normally less than a tenth of an inch (2·5 mm) in length. They are white and number about ten and are bent close back on to the stem; there are no central spines. In spite of its diminutive size it is quite free flowering, as is *R. kupperiana*, another miniature rebutia, and the flowers are a splendid carmine-red with rounded petals.

Somewhat similar but slightly taller and with more pointed petals of a rich golden hue is *R. schmiedeana*. The rows of tubercles here are more prominent and the stems grow to a height of 3 in (8 cm).

Rebutia senilis is easy to distinguish on account of the numerous silky spines or bristles which almost completely cover the plant. *R. senilis* is a great producer of offsets and consequently tends to be a shy flowerer. It is important for this reason to withhold water until the reddish buds appear at the base of the plant or at the bases of the branches and offsets that form round it. The plant bodies of *R. senilis*, although globular at first, will become more cylin-

drical with age, especially as the offsets form round the base and tend to force the growth in an upwards direction. The true species has pale red flowers but such extensive inter-hybridization has occurred that it is possible to find plants with all the outward appearances of *R. senilis* and orange, yellow or even white flowers. Some of these varieties have been given names but in so far as commercial use is concerned most of the different coloured forms are more probably the result of crossing with other *Rebutia* species. *R. s. dasyphrissa* has very much more enlarged tubercles.

Forms of *R. senilis* with seemingly yellow spines and bristles are probably hybrids with *R. chrysacantha*. It is fairly simple to check whether a yellow-flowered form is this latter species or merely the hybrid by saving the seed – *R. chrysacantha* is one of the very few forms of cacti which is self-fertile. That is to say no additional plants are required for pollination and for viable seed to be produced.

Rebutia violaciflora, R. minuscula and *R. marsoneri* as has already been stated are difficult to find as true species. Most of the flowering rebutias offered for sale in the shops are the result of extensive hybridization between these three distinct species. *R. marsoneri* itself is the only one with yellow flowers and small greenish plant bodies. Plants lacking the silky hairs of *R. senilis* but producing yellow flowers are probably more closely affiliated to *R. marsoneri*.

Rebutia violaciflora, as its name suggests, has curious deep purple flowers and rather

low plant bodies similar to those of *R. marsoneri*. It differs from *R. minuscula* in having twenty-five or more rows of spirally arranged tubercles, whereas the latter species has only about twenty. Of course there is every possible range of hybrids between them, and this range of variations extends to the number of spines. The true *R. violaciflora* has three to five central spines and the true *R. minuscula* has one, although even in the true species the spine coloration is variable. *R. minuscula* is probably the most free-flowering species of all and individual plants can have as many as twenty flowers open at the same time, the bright red of their petals forming a sort of circular ring of fire round the mid-green plant bodies.

Rebutias have been found growing at very high altitudes and although they may be exposed to considerable cold in the wild they are always dry. For this reason they respond better than any other cactus to a period of drought. Generally speaking the longer the period of drought to which rebutias are subjected during the cool winter months the greater the profusion of flowers. As mentioned in the introduction to this section they act as a sort of watering gauge for the whole collection and water should not be applied to any of them until the red buds are visible round the base of the plant bodies. Early watering or warm winter temperatures will merely result in the production of large non-flowering clumps.

128

Acanthocalycium violaceum

Ariocarpus fissuratus

The Echinocactanae

The *Echinocactanae* which are described in the following pages are characterized by the way in which the flowers are produced from the new year's growth at the top of the plant, rather than from the sides as in the preceding group. They include some of the strangest members of the cactus family, such as *Lophophora williamsii*, the peyote cactus, from which mescalin is prepared, and *Ariocarpus* species which appear to be completely dead.

Water should be given early in April and no attempt should be made to wait for the emergence of buds. Instead, as the new growth develops from the centre at the top of the plant and the spines begin to open out from the areoles, much bushier patches of wool or felt in the areoles will be seen where flower buds have been initiated during the winter resting period. For this reason members of this group generally flower later than those of the *Echinocereanae* and are to be highly prized on this account. One notable exception to this generalization is *Parodia chrysacanthion* which is one of the earliest flowering of all the cultivated specimens other than the epiphytic cacti.

Their requirements are similar to those of most other terrestrial cacti but the specialist grower with time to differentiate between the differing needs of individual groups of plants would be advised to add a little more peat to the soils normally used for these in contrast to the preceding group which tended to need more sandy soils.

Acanthocalycium

Acanthocalycium violaceum is an excellent, undemanding plant which flowers regularly once it has attained an age of four years or so. The plant bodies make an almost perfect hemisphere and sit flat on the ground rather than developing a stem. The ribs are extremely prominent and number about sixteen. The areoles are produced at approximately half-inch (1-cm) intervals on the raised sharp edges of the ribs and from these a number of spreading pale yellow brown-tipped radial spines are produced. The central spines are bent upwards and give the plant a somewhat ferocious appearance.

The flowers are produced between May and August, although cultivated specimens will seldom carry them continuously over this period. They are a deep mauve in colour and contrast well with the pale green plant bodies and yellowish spines. The Greek name is derived from *acanthos* meaning spine and *calyx* meaning cup; the stems on which the flowers are produced are densely covered in short spiny scales which are the distinguishing feature of plants of this genus.

Ariocarpus

Ariocarpus fissuratus is not really recommended for the beginner. It is inordinately slow growing and looks as though it is completely dead. It needs an extremely well-drained soil as it has a fleshy tap root which rots easily and it is often wise to start younger plants by grafting them before planting them out. I recommend the inclusion of some crushed bricks in the potting medium as this encourages the water to drain quickly. Although giving every appearance of being dead, between June and September they will reward their owners with a succession of pale pink flowers produced from amongst the woolly hairs at the top of the plant between the 'leaves', which have a deep fissure running longitudinally down the centre filled with more felting.

Haage recommends that no water at all is applied to the soil in which the plant is grown. Instead it should be potted up in a mixture of crushed bricks and loam and the pot placed in an outer container filled with a conventional compost. Water should then be applied to the outer container only. Care should be taken to avoid pouring water over the woolly centres. If it remains there, especially at night, it can cause damping off to start which will not only prejudice the formation of flowers but may also spread to the centre of the plant and encourage fungal attacks.

There are several other species of *Ariocarpus* but they are all broadly similar in appearance and cultural requirements and are all comparatively rare in cultivation.

Astrophytum asterias

Astrophytum myriostigma

Astrophytum capricorne

Astrophytum

One of the more curious genera of cacti is the bishop's cap cacti, so called because the bodies of the plants resemble a bishop's mitre. They are extremely geometrical in appearance but are not difficult to cultivate once established. *Astrophytum myriostigma*, indeed, is one of the varieties which is most easily raised from seed.

The species illustrated above, *A. asterias*, is somewhat uncommon. Although it may be easily raised from seed it is the growing on that presents problems as it is very slow growing and if grown in a conventional seed tray with other seedling cacti it may damp off or be overcome by algae where this is a problem. The best idea is to allow the seed to develop normally until it is big enough to handle, the plantlet can then be removed and grafted carefully on to *Trichocereus* stock, or if warm conditions are available for the winter it can be put on to one of the faster-growing stocks such as *Hylocereus* or *Myrtillocactus*. Although it is quite often offered for sale as a grafted specimen, after about three years when the plant is established it will grow slowly but adequately on its own roots.

The plant bodies are hemispherical and surrounded by eight ribs which are very broad, so broad in fact that the furrows between them are the only indication of their existence. The stem is mid-green and spineless and the white woolly areoles are produced like small tufts of hair at regular intervals down the sides of the ribs. It is not difficult to obtain flowers especially from grafted specimens, and although small they are an attractive yellow, showing up well against the contrasting darker stems.

Astrophytum capricorne, in contrast to the previous species, is heavily protected by spines. However, the spines are not nearly as vicious as they appear being weak and somewhat bristly in texture. Like *A. asterias* it is very slow growing, often producing only two new sets of areoles each year. The specific name is derived from the Latin words for goat and horn as the reflexed curving spines are supposed to bear a superficial resemblance to the horns of a goat. The ribs are prominent and the plant bodies themselves are pale green to greyish green. The areoles are in depressions on the edges of the ribs and spaced up to an inch (2·5 cm) apart on the true species. In mature specimens of the true species the spines fall off as they grow older, but there are very many different forms of this plant and these tend to have many more spines which often grow long and thread themselves into an intricate tracery round the plant bodies. The species flowers even when quite young, producing splendid yellow blooms, but most of the cultivated forms which have been bred for their spines tend to flower less freely.

The type species to which the name bishop's cap most obviously applies is *A. myriostigma*. This is another completely spineless cactus and the geometrically shaped ribs, normally five in number but ranging from four to six, are densely covered with white mealy spots which give the plant bodies a grey appearance. The areoles themselves are somewhat inconspicuous and appear as little more than depressions on the sides of the ribs with a slight filling of felt. The flowers, as in both the preceding species, are yellow in colour and are produced at the top of the stem as the new areoles unfold between April and September.

There are several cultivated varieties of this plant; one, *A. m. quadricostatum*, retains the four-sided structure of the seedlings even when mature, and another has almost completely green plant bodies on which the mealy spots have been relegated to the extreme edges of the ribs.

Astrophytums need a sunny situation and a prolonged period of drought and low temperatures in the winter if they are to be at their best during the summer and produce a good show of flowers. Care should be taken not to overwater them as they develop a long fleshy tap root similar to that of ariocarpus.

Astrophytum ornatum hybrid

Echinofossulocactus hastatus

Echinocactus grusonii

Echinocactus

Echinofossulocactus

Astrophytum ornatum is a shy flowerer although it makes up for this by having ornamentally banded stems as shown in the illustration. The true species is fairly well armed but there are a number of hybrids between *A. ornatum* and *A. myriostigma* which have sought to blend the ornamental bodies of the former with the free-flowering habits of the latter. However, they are generally poorly armed and the oblique bands of woolly hairs that cross the sides of the ribs are not nearly so pronounced.

The plant bodies are broadly cylindrical and the plant grows upwards rather than outwards as in *A. myriostigma*, ultimately attaining a height of a foot (30 cm) in its native habitat in central Mexico. The stems are dark green with five ribs when young which increase to eight with age. These ribs are prominent and have oblique bands of white mealy spots down the sides and often produce a few hairs as well. The spines are variable in number, with between five and eleven radials which are yellowish when young and become brown with age. The areoles are about half an inch (1 cm) apart and the younger ones have some felt in them which disappears with age.

Astrophytum ornatum is a shy flowerer and will seldom bloom when less than five years old. Plants which flower when younger are probably the hybrids referred to above and also probably lack the very prominent banding of the species, tending to have more continuous bands and less obvious patches of stem.

Rather unkindly referred to by many as mother-in-law's armchair, but more charitably known as the golden barrel cactus, *Echinocactus grusonii* is one of the best known of all cacti. Young plants raised from seed normally lack the appearance of the mature plant having much more coarsely spaced, somewhat tuberculate areoles and less distinct ribs, the latter developing with age. This is partly because the areoles are quite distant from one another and this prevents the true shape of the ribs becoming apparent until the areoles are numerous enough to form a continuous band.

The bodies are globular and cultivated plants are normally solitary although occasionally the crown will split and a branched appearance can result. Ultimately they attain a height of over 4 ft (1·25 m) but since this height is usually matched by an equivalent width they are unlikely to reach this size when cultivated in pots. The stems are light green, and mature plants can have up to twenty-five prominent ribs. They can be easily raised from seed and grow quickly at first but later, as they tend to fill in with more ribs, growth becomes slower. The spines are straw yellow at first becoming stouter and whiter with age. Younger plants have fairly weak spines but on mature specimens the central spines are really quite vicious. The flowers are yellow but they are seldom, if ever, produced on pot-grown specimens as the plant has to attain some size before it is able to flower.

The Latin name for the species illustrated above is *Echinofossulocactus*, although rather sadly many now think it should be called *Stenocactus*. The former name is far more descriptive and refers to the appearance of the plant which is reminiscent of a cross between a hedgehog and a ploughed field. The ribs are very numerous and are deeply waved forming an irregular pattern round the sides of the stem. *Echinofossulocactus hastatus* has up to thirty of these low lacy ribs surrounding the low, almost spherical, pale green plant bodies. Ultimately the plant will attain a diameter of over a foot (30 cm) but it is extremely slow growing. The areoles are well spaced from one another and support five or six straw-coloured radial spines and a solitary central spine over an inch (2·5 cm) in length.

The pale yellow flowers are quite freely produced in succession from early spring till midsummer on specimens of four years of age or more.

Echinofossulocactus lancifer

Echinofossulocactus zacatecasensis

Echinomastus macdowellii

Echinofossulocactus (continued)

Like the species described on the previous page, *Echinofossulocactus lancifer,* commonly sold as *Stenocactus lancifer,* is characterized by the presence of deep wavy furrows between the prominent ribs which run up the sides of the stem. It is about the same height as *E. hastatus* but is a darker green in colour, with grey rather than yellowish spines on the distant areoles. The flowers, which are large and pink in colour, are produced fairly freely on plants between three and four years of age during the late spring and summer.

An attractive species which is not commonly seen in collections is *E. vaupelianus*; this has an undoubted value on account of the magnificent white spines which surround the solitary black central spine. The areoles are much denser than on the preceding species and this gives the white radial spines the appearance of being interwoven in one another.

A similar contrast can be seen in *E. violaciflorus* where the central spines are brown in colour. As its name implies the flowers are cream tinged with purple and freely produced during the late spring.

Possibly the longest spined member of this group is *E. ochoterenaus* with magnificent purplish flowers up to an inch (2·5 cm) in diameter and densely interwoven spines surrounding the dark plant bodies.

All *Echinofossulocacti* will benefit from the addition of extra sand or leafmould to the potting compost in order to keep it well drained but open. If leafmould is not available coarser peat than usual must be used and water must be withheld altogether during the winter as the plants are otherwise susceptible to fungal infections, particularly in colder damp weather.

Echinofossulocactus zacatecasensis, in spite of its unmanageable name, is really a must for every collector. The pale green stems with the characteristically wavy ribs carry slightly woolly areoles with between eight and twelve white radial spines and three brown central spines, rather longer than the radials. The flowers, which are freely produced on plants of four years of age or more, are white with pale pink tips to the petals.

Echinofossulocactus multicostatus also has very numerous ribs and some species are reported with nearly a hundred in their wild state. However, it is an unreliable flowerer, the differences between one specimen in a collection and another in this respect being probably due to the presence of hybrids among the true species. It is one of the most typical of all the members of this genus and the somewhat distant areoles enable the wavy ridges which interlock closely with one another to be seen clearly.

Echinomastus

Echinomastus macdowellii is a variable plant, at first globular, which gives it a superficial similarity to the mammillarias, but later it becomes more elongated and attains a height of about 6 in (15 cm) in cultivation, although it is somewhat slow growing. The stems are almost completely covered by the dense white radial spines that are produced from the close areoles and can be as many as twenty in number. Although dense they are bristly rather than sharp and serve to reflect the sun's rays away from the plant and preserve a layer of humidity between the spines and the skin of the plant rather than to ward off predators. The central spines, three or four in number, are similarly weak and bristly and are at first a pale yellowish colour but they become white and later grey with age. Some nurserymen grow this plant as a flowering one, including it in collections for this purpose; however, I have never found it an easy plant to flower when young and the pink blooms are, in my experience, only produced on plants of six years of age or more.

Echinomastus intertextus is also occasionally seen in collections. The white flowers are sometimes distorted in shape because of the densely interlocking spines which seem to be a feature of this particular genus.

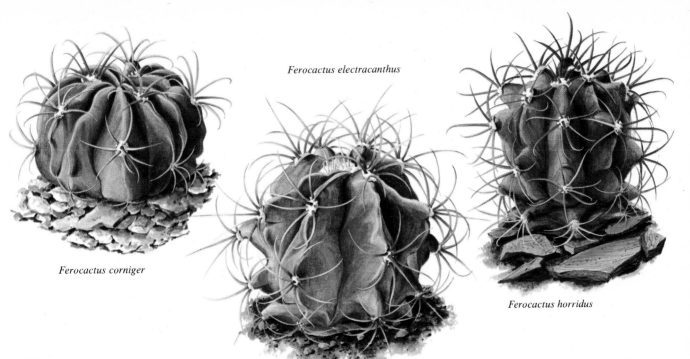

Ferocactus electracanthus

Ferocactus corniger

Ferocactus horridus

Ferocactus

Ferocacti are distinguished by their conspicuous and stout spines. They are a menace in their habitat as they can become lodged in the hooves of horses and the hooked central spines of certain species make it difficult to dislodge them. They are easy cacti to care for preferring a bright situation with plenty of air. Good air circulation helps to prevent the appearance of a black sooty fungus on the areoles which thrives in close damp conditions on this family. They generally make large plants although they may take their time in doing so and they will not normally produce flowers until they have attained a considerable size.

Ferocactus corniger and *F. latispinus* are synonyms although the wide variety of features in the same species makes it possible to find plants with certain superficial dissimilarities. The very broad flat central spines with their prominent red colouring have earned this plant the name of devil's tongue. In habit it is globular and solitary attaining a height of about a foot (30 cm) in cultivation although imported specimens may be considerably larger. The plant bodies themselves are greyish to olive green in colour and are surrounded by eight or so ribs when young and more, up to twenty in number, as the plant grows older. The ribs themselves are quite prominent and there are deep folds between them with the edges ending in a sharp ridge. The areoles are deeply recessed into notches at intervals of about an inch (2·5 cm) down the sides of the ribs and, in addition to a small amount of brownish felting which turns grey with

age, they produce about eight radial spines, some of which are stout and sharp and others smaller, finer and more bristly. Although older plants normally produce four central spines, young cultivated specimens may only make three. They are at first deep red and this colour persists, although waning with age, for about two years, after which the lower centrals become first brownish and then grey. The lowest central spine is the one which gives the species its common name and invariably points slightly downwards at the tip. There is a similar variety with prominent hooked yellow central spines which is known as *F. macrodiscus*.

Ferocactus electracanthus is one of the species in which the notches between the areoles are so pronounced as to make the plant somewhat tuberculate in appearance. In colour the stems are greyish green and the areoles, which are produced at intervals of between 1 and 1½ in (2·5 and 4 cm), have a certain amount of pale felting in them. There are seven or so rather thin spreading and slightly recurved radial spines, darker at the base becoming straw coloured nearer the tip, and a much longer central spine prominently banded. It may be that the *F. electracanthus* of horticulture and *F. melocactiformis* (otherwise sometimes known as *F. histrix*) are, in fact, the same species, in any event they are very similar.

In *F. horridus* the tuberculate appearance of the spines has been carried to an extreme with young plants appearing to have a more or less normal central stem from which the tubercles arise. Young plants have about

eight ribs which although fairly broad and flat in between the areoles are very pronounced at the tubercles. They are grey or blue-green in colour and the lower part of the stem and the skin immediately beside the areoles are frequently tinged with red. The areoles appear to have a small cap of thick brownish-grey felt on top which spills over the edge and round the sides to some extent. There are about six or seven radial spines and at least two of these are generally completely white and rather longer than the others. The remainder are at first reddish in colour gradually turning yellow from the tip downwards as they mature until the lower spines are almost completely pale yellow in colour.

The central spine is only very slightly bent and is of the same colour as the majority of the radials, like them turning pale yellow from the tip downwards. It is a robust plant although rather slow growing and makes an interesting contrast to some of the other species in this group.

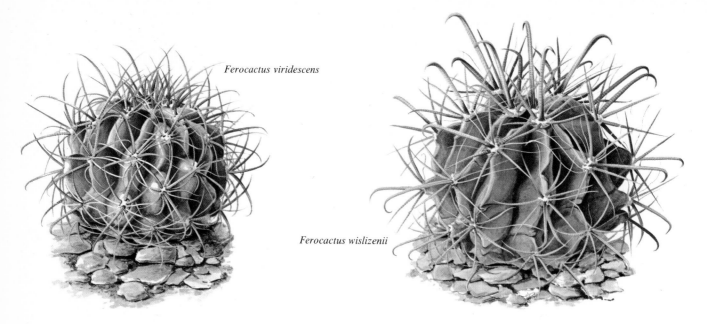

Ferocactus viridescens

Ferocactus wislizenii

Ferocactus (continued)

Ferocactus ingens is possibly more correctly known as *Echinocactus ingens*. Although only producing five ribs at first these will increase with age, extra rows appearing as the centre unfolds each spring. The ribs are broad but sharp near the base giving the younger plants a distinctly five-sided appearance, but nearer the top they become less broad and a more marked division between the ribs can be seen. The plant bodies are bluish green and the areoles, which are borne on conspicuous tubercles, are about three-quarters of an inch (2 cm) apart in the young plants. They are so woolly when young that the whole upper surface of the plant is completely covered in a brownish mat of hair through which the spines protrude, but as the areoles grow older the amount of wool in them lessens. The spines are stout, at first purple in colour and almost black near the base but becoming an attractive grey colour which eventually fades to a dirty cream. There are six radial spines of which the uppermost is considerably longer than the others and the lower is generally shorter. The central spines point directly outwards from the plant and are unhooked.

This species is a very slow grower indeed but is able to withstand long periods of drought or other forms of neglect. It should be kept as dry as possible during the winter although it will take average watering during the summer months. Flowering size is only achieved after many years have gone by, and the average collector is unlikely to flower a specimen raised in cultivation.

Ferocactus viridescens, like *F. wislizenii*

illustrated beside it, is distinguished by having more ribs than any of the preceding species even when it is quite young. The plant bodies are globular and solitary, dark glossy green in colour and with about thirteen or so broad but clearly defined ribs. It makes a good plant for the amateur wishing to have at least one representative of the genus in a collection because it will flower when younger than the others, but may still take ten or more years from seed before it is large enough to flower reliably. Once it has become established, however, it will produce quite a succession of flowers during the flowering season.

The spines are very variable in the specimens I have seen and it is probable that like so many of the members of this family much depends on whether the plant is an imported specimen or one which has been raised from seed in this country. There are seldom fewer than nine radial spines and these are at first red becoming brownish yellow with age. The centrals vary between three and four on most plants, although younger specimens may only have a solitary one.

Generally the *Ferocacti* make globular plants, one important exception to this is *F. stainesii* which ultimately becomes a large columnar plant with numerous sharp somewhat wavy ribs. It is distinguished by the long bristly hairs which are in reality modified radial spines.

Ferocactus wislizenii itself is generally globular in cultivation, although wild forms may become rather taller than broad with age eventually attaining a height of some

2 ft (60 cm) and making it one of the largest *Ferocacti*. The body is dark green but full sunlight and a little drought may turn it paler giving it a reddish tinge round the base. It is possible, in fact, that this species, like *F. viridescens,* prefers a slightly more shaded location. Young plants quickly develop about thirteen sharply divided strongly notched ribs and the areoles, which are produced at intervals of an inch (2·5 cm) or so, are quite prominently borne on the top of small tubercles. Although mature specimens may have numerous radials most plants for sale in the shops tend to have about seven somewhat bristly radials several of which are white and thin from the start. The remainder of the radials and the four centrals start off dark brown and become gradually paler as the plant grows older. The lowest central spine on each areole is turned sharply downwards giving it a hooked appearance.

Other giant *Ferocacti* are *F. acanthodes*, where the spine colour persists for very much longer but the plant is slower growing, and *F. emoryi* which has very pronounced tuberculate ribs like those of *F. horridus* but much redder spines.

Gymnocalycium gibbosum

Gymnocalycium damsii

Gymnocalycium denudatum

Gymnocalycium

The *Gymnocalycium* group which is illustrated above and on the following two pages is one of the most rewarding genera for the amateur, as most species flower reliably and continuously over a long period. They will benefit from being placed out on the rock garden during the summer if space in the greenhouse is at a premium and, at any event, should be given an airy position on a shelf or near the door of the greenhouse as this will help to ripen the areoles. The presence of flowers can be detected fairly early on during the growing season when small buds appear in the areoles just above the spines. These appear at first on those nearer the centre of the plant but as the season advances all the areoles down to about a third of the height of the plant will probably produce buds in many cases. The botanical name is derived from two Greek words meaning naked calyx and refers to the absence of spines on the perianth tube.

Gymnocalycium damsii as sold by nurserymen is a very variable specimen having characteristics belonging broadly to both the true species and *G. mihanovichii*, and it is certain that extensive hybridization has occurred between these two species making it difficult for collectors to be sure of obtaining the type unless they buy from a specialist. The plants sold by nurserymen as *G. damsii* have low globular plant bodies which produce small offsets from the areoles. They seldom attain any great height in cultivation and are mid-green in colour with ten broad rounded ribs. These ribs have a slight chin below each areole and they do not normally carry the diagonal

bands which are associated with *G. mihanovichii*. The flowers are extremely variable, ranging from pink through white to green. Those with green flowers are more closely related to *G. mihanovichii*, those with white flowers are more true to type, and those with pinkish flowers have yet another species mixed in with them.

Gymnocalycium denudatum not only has a naked calyx but also a great paucity of spines on the stems. It is referred to occasionally as the spider cactus because of the somewhat spidery appearance of the few spines it has got. The plants have about five ribs, occasionally more in cultivated specimens. It makes a taller plant than the preceding species, ultimately attaining a height of 4 in (10 cm) even when cultivated. The bodies are a dark green and the ribs are broad and much rounded at the edges. The weak spines are yellowish in colour and there is usually no central spine at all. The flowers, which are green on the outside and pale green within, are produced fairly freely. Because of its lack of spines and consequent difficulty in protecting its surface against direct sunlight this species will benefit from a little shade during the hottest part of the spring and summer.

Gymnocalycium gibbosum is extremely typical of the group called chin cacti. The plant bodies, which are normally solitary, are at first globular but become cylindrical with age, a feature which is quite distinctive. The general colour of the stems is bluish green and the ribs, which number between twelve and fourteen, are straight and prominently notched into chin-like tubercles

which give this group of plants its common name. The flowers are white, often suffused with pink, but the plant has to be well established and up to 3 in (8 cm) in diameter or so before it can be relied upon to produce them.

As with *G. damsii*, there is a great deal of variation in this species and this extends both to the spine formation and to the colour of the flowers. The climate in which it grows in Southern Argentina is cool and moist and like the preceding species it does not enjoy very hot summer temperatures; because of its normal environment it is suited to growing in Britain but is nevertheless a very slow-growing species compared with other members of this genus.

Gymnocalycium andreae is another plant with bluish-green plant bodies but it branches readily and the bodies are permanently globular, not elongating with age. The flowers are a pale yellow colour inside, a colour which is also found in the rare *G. leeanum*.

Gymnocalycium mihanovichii friedrichii

Gymnocalycium mihanovichii Hibotan

Gymnocalycium multiflorum

Gymnocalycium (*continued*)

Gymnocalycium mihanovichii has already been referred to under *G. damsii*. It forms small clumps by producing offsets at the sides of the plant from the areoles, and it is a low-growing variety normally only attaining a height of 3 in (8 cm). The stems are olive green in colour and the true species is characterized by paler bands running between the areoles. The ribs, which are normally eight in number, are broad and deeply notched with areoles about half an inch (1 cm) apart and five or six radial spines but no centrals. The flowers are a greenish-yellow colour and the true species has a faint red coloration near the edge of the petals.

Gymnocalycium m. friedrichii is altogether a much smaller plant and the plant bodies are curious in that they lack almost completely any trace of green colouring, being instead suffused with a brownish-purple coloration. The ribs are more sharply angled than those of the true species and the lateral banding of paler colours is more prominent. The spines are very much scarcer than those of the species and this is due to a large extent to the lack of chlorophyll. The flowers, which are seldom produced on cultivated specimens, are pink in colour and similar to those of *G. lafaldense*.

Hibotan varieties of *G. mihanovichii* are those in which the production of the green chlorophyll pigmentation has been stopped almost completely. It is not uncommon for both *G. mihanovichii* and *G. quehlianum* to produce variegated patches on one of their ribs. If the central growing area of the plant is then removed carefully with an apple

corer the growing point may be induced to form an offset which will have the same coloration. Once the offset is formed it must be grafted on to another species as it lacks the means of supporting itself by photosynthesis.

It is possible to buy plants of this variety which have already been grafted and the production of different coloured forms has become something of a cult in Japan. Four distinct colour varieties are available – red, by far the most common and the most satisfactory, pink, yellow and white. The red ones will produce rudimentary flowers and although these will reach the normal size as buds they are unlikely to open properly into full flower. As the plants mature further offsets will be produced from the areoles of coloured plants and these may be grafted on to fresh stocks in their turn. The coloration frequently disappears near the growing point where it becomes green, this can be reduced to some extent by giving the plant a brighter position but some green pigmentation must occur if the plant is to grow at all.

Gymnocalycium multiflorum, in spite of its name, is not one of the most reliable flowerers of the genus. The spines are arranged like spiders' legs in two parallel rows on either side of the areoles and are normally between six and ten in number. The areoles are more or less distant from one another and carried on the broad ribs, which number up to fifteen on mature specimens and surround the plant bodies. It is possible that some hybridization has occurred with other less free-flowering varie-

ties of *Gymnocalycium* and this may account for the variable ease with which cultivated specimens may be flowered, although once the plant has attained a diameter of about 3 in (8 cm) it seems that it may be flowered fairly freely.

Gymnocalycium ourselianum is somewhat similar in appearance but has fewer spines, seldom more than seven in number, and the flowers are rather fuller giving it the appearance of being semi-double. There may, however, be some confusion between *G. multiflorum* and *G. ourselianum*.

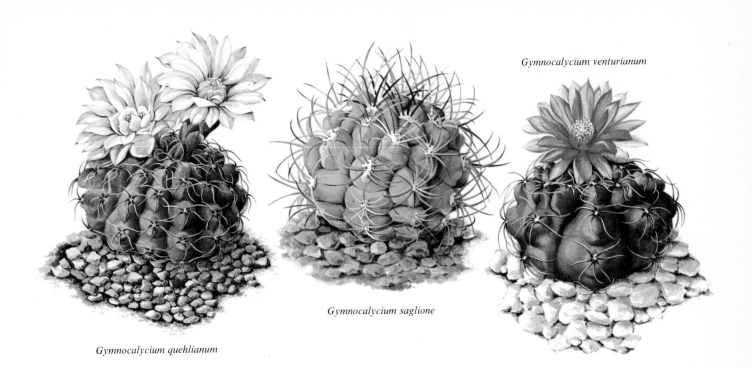

Gymnocalycium venturianum

Gymnocalycium saglione

Gymnocalycium quehlianum

Gymnocalycium quehlianum, like *G. damsii*, deserves a place in every collection, particularly as it is one of the earliest cacti to flower during the season and the flowers are produced right through the summer into the late autumn. The plant bodies are a bluish grey in colour and very much flattened, seldom exceeding 2½ in (6·5 cm) in height. They are surrounded by ten low ribs which are prominently divided up into the chins or tubercles so typical of this group of plants. The spines, which are normally only five in number, are flattened back against the plant bodies and are produced from more or less well-spaced areoles which carry a little wool alongside the spines.

Although a reliable flowerer it is subject to curious attacks of brown discoloration in the winter and particular care must be taken not to allow the plant to shrivel through overwintering in too warm an environment. I can offer no cure for these brown patches, which appear on the plant unpredictably and frequently with little ill-effect. It is possible that they are the symptoms of a virus or bacterial infection which is harmless as long as it is not allowed to get out of hand; but a certain amount of bronzing on the plants, particularly if the plants are grown in good light during the summer, is quite normal. The brown discoloration normally only manifests itself during the late autumn.

Gymnocalycium platense has plant bodies of similar colour and appearance when young but develops a much less squashed and more globular habit with age. The flowers of both species are white but those of *G. quehlianum* have a magnificent deep red throat and are produced on longer tubes. Once again it is probable that hybridization has occurred here amongst commercially produced plants as there is a great deal of variation in *G. quehlianum* in shape.

Gymnocalycium saglione is a species best grown for its attractive spines rather than for any hope of flowers. It is a native of North-western Argentina and very slow growing. It is occasionally grafted and this makes a very much larger, more robust plant, which ultimately attains a size of nearly a foot (30 cm) in diameter. The tubercles in this species have become so prominent that it is difficult to distinguish it from a mammillaria and the ribs are not at all clear, particularly as the areoles are very large and occupy nearly all the outer surface of the tubercle. When young the spines have a magnificent, almost black, coloration but as they mature this turns to red and subsequently fades to a greyish colour nearer the base of the stem. The colour of the spines can reputedly be maintained by overhead watering, but if this is tried it should be done early in the morning so that no puddles remain in the growing tip which might act as magnifying glasses for the sun's rays and scorch the plant's growing point. As mentioned earlier, the pink flowers are only produced on older specimens and the plants are even more difficult than most gymnocalyciums to raise from seed.

Gymnocalycium venturianum and *G. bal-dianum* are probably the same species and are distinguished from all other gymnocalyciums by the magnificent red flowers which are freely produced even on younger specimens. The ribs are at first fairly prominent with a conspicuous edge but this becomes flatter with age. The habit is at first hemispherical and the plant body looks slightly squashed but ultimately it develops a more globular shape. The spines are few and curved, grey at the tip becoming darker near the base, and the plant bodies are a greyish blue-green in colour. The areoles are divided from one another by deep V-shaped notches and the lower part of the tubercle has the characteristic chin-like appearance of other members of the genus.

Leuchtenbergia principis

Hamatocactus setispinus

Lophophora williamsii

Hamatocactus

The three varieties illustrated on this page are so diverse in form that it is difficult to believe that they are all basically of the same subtribe, let alone of the same family. *Hamatocactus setispinus* unlike the other two is a fairly common species and makes an excellent addition to the collection producing flowers through from midsummer until the drying-out period is begun in late autumn. The plant bodies are generally dark green and spherical although in the autumn as drying out commences they can become much paler and may even be suffused with a reddish-purple tinge, particularly on the side which gets the most sunshine. There are generally thirteen deeply divided ribs which can even be somewhat wavy in a manner reminiscent of *Echinofossulocacti*. The areoles are closely spaced, about half an inch (1 cm) or so apart, and are borne on pronounced pimples or tubercles on the edges of the ribs which consequently appear to be sharply notched between them. The radials are somewhat variable in number, generally twelve, at first reddish but becoming pale white or straw coloured with age and during the winter, the colour persisting longest in the upper three. The centrals are somewhat variable on cultivated specimens. Flowers are very freely produced even on quite young plants and are a magnificent yellow in colour often 2 in (5 cm) or so in diameter and in many horticultural specimens have a red throat.

There is another species called *H. hamatacanthus* which has larger spines, the central one being flattened on the upper surface and the areoles being borne on much more pronounced tubercles.

Leuchtenbergia

Leuchtenbergia principis is a great rarity whose tubercles have become so prominent as to dominate the entire plant giving it the appearance of the grass on the pampas amongst which it grows. It is rather rare on account of its very slow growth and the difficulty with which it is kept alive during the English winter when it has a distinct tendency to suffer from fungal attacks. For this reason young plants are frequently grafted on to somewhat hardier stock and then re-established on their own roots when they are of a fair size.

The tubercles themselves are bluish green and are prominently three sided with thin papery spines produced at the tips. It is quite normal for the older tubercles to dry up and fall off giving the plant the appearance of having a short trunk. The flowers are very spectacular, pale yellow, produced amongst the upper spines, but only on well established specimens normally of nine years of age or more. During the summer it should be stood in the brightest position possible, on a shelf in the greenhouse if this is available, and during the winter it needs only quite normal temperatures. It seems to do well in a rather more open compost than that used for most cacti and I recommend adding more peat for this purpose.

Lophophora

Mescalin is distilled from the plant bodies of *Lophophora williamsii* to which the Yaqui Indians ascribe almost divine powers. Its rounded spineless plant bodies taper into a thick tap root and it benefits from the addition of some crushed brick to the compost to ensure adequate drainage at all times. A curious feature of the plant is the way in which the hairs in the areoles are tufted up into small points. The areoles are in turn produced on tubercles which are so flattened as to be barely recognizable as such. The drug is obtained from the dried body of the plant which is sliced and dried before use.

In spite of its poisonous nature and its rarity it makes a good plant for the average collection since it flowers quite readily and the buttons or offsets can be grafted on to rather stronger stock in order to multiply it up. Buttons are normally produced in the fourth or fifth year and seem to do better when grafted than when grown on their own roots. The flowers, which are produced in the woolly top of the plant, are small and pinkish and are borne in succession throughout the summer.

Malacocarpus erinaceus

Matucana aurantiaca

Neoporteria subgibbosa

Malacocarpus

There are several species of *Malacocarpus* in cultivation but *Malacocarpus erinaceus* is one of the more common ones. The plant bodies are at first hemispherical but later they become more erect and start to form woody stems. This phenomenon in no way detracts from the growing ability of the plant and is formed in the wild state as a protective skin. Generally they are extremely slow growing, although once they have reached a size of 2 to 3 in (5 to 8 cm) in diameter they will flower freely, producing the flowers from a thick woolly mat called a cephalium at the top of the plant.

The plants are sometimes sold under the name of *Wigginsia* which is probably more correct. *M. erinaceus* has dark green plant bodies which grow to a height of about 4 in (10 cm) in time. These are surrounded by between fifteen and twenty broad prominent ribs with the areoles standing up between the notches on them. The radial spines are variable in cultivated specimens but are normally eight in number, greyer near the base of the plant and brownish at the top where they are younger. There is a single central spine of the same colour as the radials and the areoles when young have a considerable amount of white wool in them which forms the cephalium. The yellow flowers are produced from June onwards and their presence can be detected by the dense woolly buds on top of the plant.

Malacocarpus sellowii is a similar species but it has longer spines and is rather more greyish green than dark green. The flowers are yellow and the stigmas in the centre of the flowers are bright red.

Matucana

When young and not in flower *Matucana aurantiaca* is unremarkable in appearance and for this reason is often not sold on a commercial scale. However, when it does flower it is most rewarding. It is a native of Peru and the Latin name – *Matucana* – is in fact the name of the town on the cliffs beside which the species was first discovered. The plant is similar to the *Malacocarpus* species illustrated on this page in size and growth habits, being generally rather slow and seldom flowering before it is five years old or more and has attained a diameter of nearly 3 in (8 cm). The spines consist of about ten radials and up to three longer central spines which are considerably more prominent at the base of the plant and round the sides than on the top – the centre of which appears to be almost unarmed. It is a late flowerer like malacocarpus and flowers may only appear in September in Britain. When they are produced they are orange and seldom open fully, being more tubular in appearance than daisy like.

Both *M. aurantiaca* and the original species *M. haynei*, which is far more densely surrounded with spines and has reddish flowers, prefer an open compost with plenty of sand for drainage and a minimum temperature of about 4°C (40°F) in the winter. Since neither appears to form clumps propagation is best carried out by means of seed which germinates readily, although, of course, two plants are required to produce it.

Neoporteria

Neoporteria subgibbosa cannot be classified as a free-flowering cactus but its easy culture and attractive appearance make it a worthwhile addition to the collection. Although young plants are almost orbicular in shape they elongate with age. It is a native of Chile where it seems to grow in coastal areas. The bright green plant bodies are surrounded by about twenty ribs which are sharply notched and almost tuberculate in appearance. The areoles are borne close together on the sides of the ribs and have up to thirty spines, sometimes over an inch (2·5 cm) in length. In the type species these are normally yellowish in colour, but there is a most attractive variety called *N. s. nigrispina* with almost black spines which is reputedly freer flowering. The areoles are fairly densely packed with wool and the flowers when they appear are produced amongst the spines at the top of the plant and are pale pink in colour.

Neoporteria nidus is a species with brownish-red stems surrounded by very dense spines. It is sometimes sold as *Echinocactus senilis*. *Neoporteria napina* is a curious species, also from the coastal regions of Chile, with yellow flowers and such minute black spines that the plant appears to be almost completely spineless. During its resting period this latter species, like the South African mesembryanthemums, contracts its thick fleshy turnip-like root to such an extent that it practically sinks below the ground.

Neoporteria villosa

Notocactus apricus

Notocactus concinnus

Neoporteria *(continued)*

Neoporteria villosa unlike the species described on the previous page is a fairly reliable flowerer once it has reached a height of 2 to 3 in (5 to 8 cm). Like other members of this genus it is a native of Chile and starts as a hemispherical plant body which later becomes elongated and eventually reaches a height of over 4 in (10 cm). The plant bodies are normally tinged with red but this tint may disappear during dull summers or if the plant is shaded from direct sunlight. It has fewer ribs than *N. subgibbosa*, normally only about thirteen in number, but like the latter species the areoles are closely packed and filled with a considerable amount of white wool. The most prominent feature is, of course, the abundance of dense numerous yellowish radial spines which pale with age.

The species is free flowering, producing a ring of flowers round the apex of the plant often as frequently as twice a year – first in the early spring and then again in the late autumn. For this reason it should not be dried out too soon and should be rested only from December through to February. By allowing it to become dormant too soon the chances of flowers being produced so freely can be jeopardized.

Neoporteria jussieui is another species which has reddish-brown plant bodies when it is stood in direct sunlight. It has up to eighteen broad prominent ribs which are sharply notched round the areoles. There are seven stout greyish radial spines surrounding a longer central upward-pointing one and all may be tinged brown at the tips. The flowers are reddish.

Notocactus

Notocacti are some of the most commonly seen cacti in cultivation and this is probably because they germinate readily from seed and are, therefore, easy to produce in large numbers. Generally they make only a few flowers each year, although some of the rarer varieties with smaller flowers go on flowering for quite a long period. The larger-flowered varieties tend to open their flowers fully for only a short period at midday and this makes it difficult for people who go out to work to appreciate them – I have had many sad letters from people complaining that they have only seen their plant in bud and when it has finished flowering. *Notocactus apricus*, *N. concinnus* and *N. tabularis* are all somewhat similar in appearance with low, rounded, green plant bodies and brownish spines. Plants thought to belong to any of these species should also be compared with the illustration of *N. muricatus* on page 142, which is slightly similar when young.

Notocactus apricus has pale green plant bodies surrounded by fifteen to twenty low ribs which are closely covered by the areoles. When young these have wool in them but with age this disappears leaving the older ones bare. The radial spines normally number between eighteen and twenty and are weak and bristle like, reddish yellow when young but becoming paler with age. There are four brownish-red, yellow-tipped central spines. The yellow flowers are produced early in the season and their presence is indicated by woolly buds appearing amongst the spines as the new growth unfolds in late March.

Notocactus concinnus is a very similar species but has fewer radial spines, normally ten to fifteen in number and yellowish rather than brownish in colour. It is a native of Southern Brazil and the yellow flowers, which are produced on quite young plants of two years of age or more, are often over 2 in (5 cm) in diameter and can completely cover the plant bodies.

Notocactus tabularis is intermediate between the two species just described with between sixteen and eighteen radial spines, about half an inch (1 cm) in length, and white rather than yellowish although they are frequently tipped brown when young. The central spines are paler than those of *N. muricatus* with which this species should be compared.

Notocactus generally require a longer resting period than other varieties of cactus and I dry them out a month earlier and water them a month later·than the other varieties. This seems to encourage the plant to produce rather more flowers than would otherwise be the case and greatly increases the chances of seeing them.

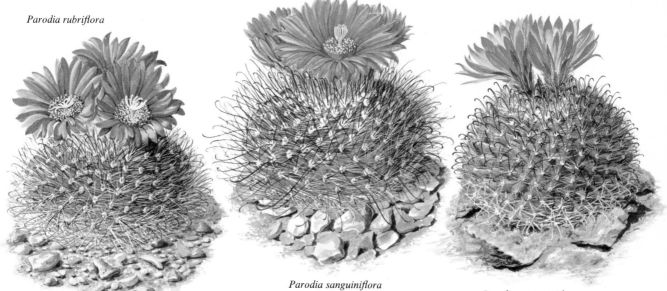

Parodia rubriflora

Parodia sanguiniflora

Parodia x *scopaoides*

I have mentioned earlier the difficulty of raising parodias from seed with any great degree of success and before leaving the genus it would be as well to elaborate on some of the instructions given on page 145. The compost in which the seeds are to be sown should be a proprietary seed compost rather than a special cactus seed compost and the seed tray should be filled slightly proud with the compost. Ideally the compost should be shaped so as to create a central mound which slopes very gradually to the sides of the seed tray. The difference in height, however, between the centre of the compost and the sides should not be more than half an inch (1 cm) or so. The tray filled with compost should be dipped in a solution of some systemic fungicide such as benomyl and the fresh seed mixed with fine sharp washed river sand in the proportion of one part of seed to about four parts of sand. This sand and seed mixture should then be strewn over the damp surface of the compost and the whole tray put into a warm propagating unit. If no such unit is available an unlit airing cupboard makes an excellent substitute, and some writers even go so far as to suggest that, unlike many cactus species, parodia seeds generally do better when germinated in the dark than when given the optimum full-light conditions of a greenhouse.

Parodia rubriflora illustrated above is very similar in most respects to *P. sanguiniflora* illustrated beside it. It is generally a much smaller plant and many authorities prefer to treat it as a variety of *P. sanguiniflora* rather than as a species in its own right.

Parodia sanguiniflora itself is one of the best loved and most widely grown of all parodias. It is a fast-growing plant when young, having a tendency (like *Notocactus leninghausii*) to split open if allowed to grow too fast in a warm, moist environment. Although not normally one of the earliest of species to come into flower it may be taken into a warm moist environment in early spring (the end of February and the beginning of March) and if water is applied, sparingly at first, so as to enable the plant to start up into growth, it is possible to have it in flower a little earlier. There appears to be no loss in vigour or profusion of flowers as a result of this 'forcing'.

It is somewhat larger than most of the parodias described and although globular during its early years it becomes more cylindrical with age attaining a height of 4 in (10 cm) or more. The stems are dark green, and the closely spaced areoles borne in the numerous warty spiral ribs are at first densely packed with whitish wool which they tend to lose as they mature. The radials are very numerous in number but weak and bristly. They are white in colour and contrast well with the dark reddish hooked central spines which number up to five at each areole. Although this contrast is very marked on the younger areoles the central spines become progressively paler with age, ultimately becoming almost completely white.

The flowers are very freely produced but unlike most other parodias the petals are narrow and give the plant a somewhat ragged appearance. This is a distinguishing feature between the true species and the numerous hybrids and varieties often wrongly ascribed the name. Many of these should probably be called *P. rubriflora*.

Parodia x *scopaoides* is a recently introduced variety and is still a little uncommon in cultivation. Its globular dark green bodies are surrounded by between twenty-five and thirty spirally arranged tuberculate ribs, which in their turn are completely hidden by the dense spreading white radial spines. The latter can grow to a considerable length compared with most other parodias where the radial spines tend to be fairly short, often attaining a length of something approaching an inch (2·5 cm). The areoles are at first filled with white wool and this adds to the snowy appearance of the plant. The centrals are red tipped with black and are about the same length as the radial spines, they number three to five and the longest is invariably hooked at the top.

The flowers are reddish orange in colour and produced between midsummer and the beginning of autumn. Although not a profuse flowerer it tends to provide a certain amount of interest in between the major batches of flowers in the collection which generally appear at the beginning and end of the summer.

Melocactus oreas

Melocactus de morro chapensis

The Cactanae

Melocactus

The *Cactanae* has always seemed to me to be a special group of cacti. It consists of a genus called *Melocactus* all of whose thirty or so members are somewhat rare in cultivation. In spite of this rarity the best-known species, *Melocactus maxonii,* has earned for itself the epithet of Turk's head cactus. As a genus they are characterized by a red woolly cephalium which forms on the top of the plant just before flowering commences but the plants as a group are slow growing and this feature does not develop until the plant is several inches in diameter. Another curious feature of these plants is their preference for coastal regions and because of this they were some of the first cacti ever seen by Europeans.

They are generally rather delicate plants and tend to need rather more warmth in winter than other cacti in spite of their hardy appearance. If you have a greenhouse it is probably worth investing in a small heated propagation unit in order to maintain at least a part of the greenhouse at a slightly higher temperature if you wish to tackle some of the rarer species of which this group is typical. They can be grown as grafted plants with some benefit as this tends to make them grow faster than they otherwise would and enables them to attain a size at which they are a little more tolerant of neglect or low temperatures.

When the plants are young it is difficult to distinguish them from any other group of globular cacti but for the sake of completeness and accuracy I have shown them separately and devoted a page to them.

Melocactus oreas makes a round globular plant with eight broad low ribs running together at the base so as to be virtually indistinguishable. The areoles are set in recesses on the sides of these ribs about half an inch (1 cm) apart and in addition to producing a small quantity of whitish wool when young they bear between seven and eight radial spines, the uppermost of which is generally very much shorter than all the others. These radials vary between nearly 1 and 1¼ in (2·5 and 3·5 cm) in length, the longer ones being on the lower part of the areole and basically straw coloured but tipped brownish red and bent over slightly at the tips, although they are by no means hooked. The younger spines are very much browner, almost purple in colour, and the radial spine which will ultimately become the lowest one is very much darker than the rest. I have never seen this species in flower but it no doubt produces the woolly red cephalium so characteristic of the group. Like *M. de morro chapensis* it is rather more tolerant of neglect and rather stronger growing than many of the other species.

Melocactus de morro chapensis is rather paler green than the preceding species but has the same globular habit which it maintains throughout its life. It has about thirteen broad ribs but these are not quite as obtuse as those of *M. oreas* and are distinguishable even at the base of the plant. The radials and centrals, like those of the previous species, are recessed in areoles in notches in the sides of the ribs and like the preceding species the radial spines are generally eight in number although the

upper one is not conspicuously shorter than the others. They are of a similar straw colour to those of *M. oreas* but are not nearly so strong, being probably only half as thick, and have the feel of stout bristles rather than thorns. The lower spine on the other hand is very much longer than those of the preceding species attaining a length of nearly 2 in (5 cm) even on quite young specimens.

The areoles are felted and the young spines are rather more brownish than purple, the colour persisting longest on the solitary central which remains brownish even after the others have turned straw coloured.

Melocacti are uncommon plants and can be recommended as something to strive for; however, they have little attraction when young apart from their rarity. Imported specimens which have already developed sufficiently in size to form the red woolly top are difficult to re-establish in Britain in a greenhouse except under the most favourable conditions and they are for this reason a plant for the connoisseur rather than the amateur.

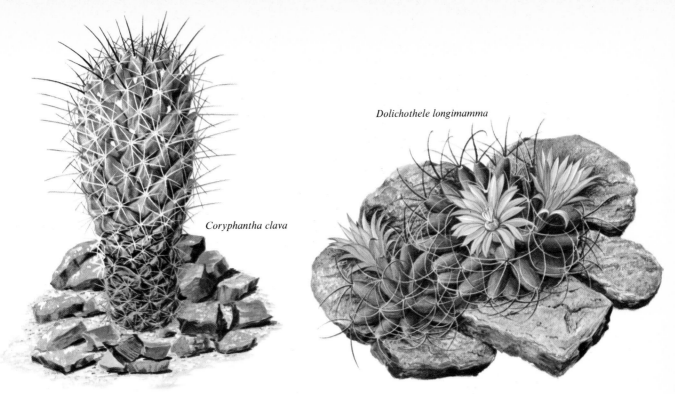

Dolichothele longimamma

Coryphantha clava

The Coryphanthanae

The *Coryphanthanae* is distinguishable from all the other major cactus groups so far discussed by the production of flowers from between the tuberculate areoles rather than from the areoles. However, because young plants of *Thelocactus* resemble mammillarias for quite a while, I have also included this genus at the end of the section on *Coryphanthanae*. Because of the relative unimportance of the number of rows of tubercles most books do not try to enumerate the spiral rows or use this as an identification. A more important feature is the actual shape of the tubercles when viewed independently, whether they are cylindrical or polygonal or rhomboidal in shape.

They are generally tolerant plants growing well on their own roots although a few species, notably *Mammillaria plumosa* and *M. schiedeana*, are a good deal easier to grow when grafted. This may have as much to do with the rather weak texture of their tubercles, and the fact that water can lie around and breed infection in them when they are grown at ground level, as with the structure of their root systems.

For ease of classification most of the authorities divide the genera into two groups, those with a milky sap and those with a watery sap. I have followed this practice and if you are currently holding the book in one hand and a plant that you suspect belongs here in the other, get a pin and prick the plant. If the sap produced is watery the plant belongs to the group described on pages 150 to 157. If on the other hand the sap is milky you should turn to pages 157 to 160.

Coryphantha

Before coming to the mammillarias which constitute the bulk of the group I should mention two attractive members of the type genus itself. *Coryphantha clava* is a fairly fast-growing plant which, although at first globular, rapidly elongates and becomes cylindrical. The plant bodies are greyish green and ultimately can attain a height of a foot (30 cm) or so, making it one of the larger members of the group. The upper tubercles have a certain amount of wool in the crevices between them but this is not a reliable indication of bud formation as it is with some members of the group. The radials are nine or ten in number, generally straw coloured and produced from areoles which, like the crevices between them, generally have a little wool at first which disappears with age. The centrals are usually solitary on cultivated plants, are brown when young but become straw coloured like the radial spines as they mature. Although fast growing, *C. clava* can hardly be called a lavish flowerer and plants normally have to attain a height of 6 in (15 cm) or more before there is any real chance of seeing the large glistening yellow flowers.

Other species of *Coryphantha* offered for sale are *C. pallida*, which has bluish-green stems like the illustrated species but is a low globular clump-forming plant and has many more radial spines, normally twenty in number and white in colour, and *C. radians* with about fifteen radials and mid-green stems.

Dolichothele

Dolichothele longimamma is an excellent species for the small collection as it provides variety of shape in a group which is otherwise somewhat similar in general characteristics. It is a native of Mexico where it is found near such unpronounceable places as Ixmiquilpan and Zimapan. It quickly forms a clump of plants and the most characteristic features are the grass-green very long cylindrical tubercles which completely swamp and conceal the plant bodies. On some wild specimens tubercles have been observed as much as 3 in (8 cm) in length although they are unlikely to grow to this size in cultivation. The radial spines are weak and yellowish in colour, not very neatly arranged and giving the plant a rather untidy appearance. The solitary central spine is rather sharper and needle like, very variable in length.

A well established plant produces the large sulphur-yellow flowers in great numbers. Unlike most of the more common mammillarias these are produced well clear of the tubercles of cultivated specimens, whereas the flowers of most varieties tend to be tucked away between the tubercles and make up for their dwarf size by their great profusion.

It is an easy plant to propagate as the very succulent tubercles can be snapped off and rooted readily on their own without the need to separate a whole clump from the main stem. These tubercles, although solitary at first, will soon start to put up additional tubercles round the base of the plant and ultimately will produce a perfectly conventional plant.

149

Mammillaria bocasana

Mammillaria bombycina

Mammillaria erythrosperma

Mammillaria

Although undoubtedly one of the most popular of cacti, *Mammillaria bocasana* is not ideally suited to cultivation on the average windowsill as it prefers full sunlight during the winter if the small flowers are to be produced in profusion. Make sure in the greenhouse, also, that the part in which it stands is not overshadowed by a brick wall or anything else during this period as flower production will otherwise be inhibited. In the greenhouse in which the cacti are grown on our own nursery I remember a disastrous crop of this variety which was grown in the shadow of a large packing hall and which completely failed to flower the following summer.

The plant bodies are low and globular and form clumps, branching in the main from the base, and single plants may often attain a height of some 6 in (15 cm). The bluish-green stems are almost completely covered by fine white hairs, which come out of the axils between the tubercles, and the very numerous long fine hair-like radial spines that come from the areoles themselves. The centrals are erect and sharply hooked and make it a dangerous plant to put at the edge of the collection as it can be difficult to detach from clothing. They are reddish brown, or occasionally yellow, in colour.

Although freely produced in the right environment the flowers are a little inconspicuous, a sort of pinkish grey in colour, but they are followed by magnificent pink seedpods which can be over an inch (2·5 cm) in length. Fresh seed from these pods germinates readily and it is advisable to save some

as the very fleshy plant bodies of this species are particularly susceptible to fungal attacks.

Mammillaria bombycina is similar to *M. bocasana* not only in appearance when young but also in its cultural requirements. It needs full sunlight and should be watered sparingly, if at all, both at the beginning and end of the season. It is not ideally suited to the windowsill and flower production may be reduced by growing it in such a position. In order to get some flowers on it the plant should be grown in a south-facing window during the summer if possible and transferred to a north-facing one at the beginning of September, then brought back on to the south-facing one again in late March. The plant bodies, which are at first globular, become cylindrical with age and form large clumps when mature. The stems are bright green below the covering of hairs and the tubercles are somewhat cylindrical. The radials are very numerous, up to forty if you have the patience to count them, and, like those of *M. bocasana*, are weak, white and hair like. The three or four central spines are normally flushed with a reddish-brown coloration and sharply hooked at the tip.

The flowers are very much more impressive than those of the preceding species being bright pink in colour and showing up clearly against the background of spines and hairs. The pinkish petals have a much darker red stripe down the centre which accentuates this contrast. It is still unfortunately a little hard to come by commercially but is worth seeking out.

Although not nearly as common as it should be in collections, *M. erythrosperma* is another excellent addition to the small collection. One of the greatest problems with members of the *Mammillaria* genus is their great tendency to cave in to fungal attacks in the late spring and autumn when they seem to be at their weakest. This is particularly common in plants of *M. zeilmanniana* illustrated on page 157, and *M. erythrosperma* makes an excellent substitute for this if you want a free-flowering red cactus. The plant has glossy-green cylindrical tubercles with a few hairs in the axils between them and rapidly forms offsets to make large clumps. The radials are numerous and are long, white and thin and at least one of the two or so russet central spines is prominently hooked at the tip. It is fairly common throughout Mexico and the flowers and fruit are bright carmine-red.

Mammillaria camptotricha

Mammillaria decipiens

Mammillaria bogotensis

In spite of its untidy appearance *Mammillaria camptotricha* makes a good addition to the collection as it flowers quite reliably even when fairly young. It is sometimes referred to as *Dolichothele camptotricha* and should be distinguished from the species illustrated beside it, *Mammillaria decipiens*, to which it has a slight resemblance.

The plant bodies are bright green in colour and grow rapidly to form large clumps, slightly pointed at the growing point in the centre. The tubercles are very long and slender, often nearly an inch (2·5 cm) in length and the axils between them carry a few bristles. The most prominent feature of the plant is, however, the interlocking net of twisted spines which is produced from the areoles at the tips of the cylindrical tubercles. These spines are four or more in number and pale yellow in colour, although there appear to be a large number of varieties and I have seen some plants with almost pure white spines which are most attractive. Although they cover the plant very densely and give it a well protected appearance the spines are not sharp, rather they are somewhat bristly in character. The flowers are a great plus for the plant, they are white and are generally produced in a circle near the base and have the added advantage of being slightly scented, a feature which is comparatively uncommon in this genus.

This variety appreciates a fairly rich soil and may, unlike many cacti, be fed regularly during the summer using any proprietary feed and following the manufacturer's instructions carefully. Watering during the summer can take place two or three times a week with beneficial results, especially if the compost is well drained. During the winter, however, it will benefit from a little more warmth than most cacti and if practicable it should be given a light north-facing windowsill on which to hibernate rather than being left in a cool greenhouse with other cacti.

Mammillaria decipiens is a more tolerant plant but lacks the very ornamental spines of the preceding species. The dark green plant bodies grow quickly and form dense clumps like *M. camptotricha* and the height of the clumps is normally similar, about 4 in (10 cm). However, the plant bodies are more globular and less obviously conical in shape. The tubercles are conical and as long as those of the previous species, but the radial spines, which number about eight, are very much shorter, normally white in colour and occasionally suffused with brown. The central spine is solitary and very much darker in colour, sometimes up to an inch (2·5 cm) in length but more commonly a little shorter, bristly rather than spiny. The flowers are produced in the same way as they are with *M. camptotricha*, that is in a ring round the base of the plants, but I have been unable to detect even the slightest trace of a scent from them.

As mentioned earlier it is considerably easier to grow than the previous species, does not need so rich a soil and can stand cold in the winter if given plenty of drainage. If the plants are grown in plastic pots in sterilized garden soil it is a good idea to mix in some coarse shingle to assist in drainage.

Mammillaria bogotensis is now regarded by some authorities as a variety of *Mammillaria columbiana* and frequently sold under the name *M. columbiana bogotensis*. The stems are solitary at first but form clumps as they grow older, although this will not normally happen until the fifth year or so has passed. Ultimately they attain a height of over 6 in (15 cm) making a comparatively tall plant. The stems are mid-green but like so many other cacti become greyer with age especially around the base. When young the axils between the tubercles are filled with wool but as they mature much of this is lost. The radial spines are very numerous, white in colour and somewhat translucent; some plants, however, have straw-coloured radial spines and varieties with this feature are sometimes referred to as *M. b. sulphurea*. The central spines are variable in number, generally one to six, at first fairly dark brown but becoming paler with age. The white wool in the areoles tends to become discoloured and turn brown with age quite naturally and this should not be taken as a sign that the plant is becoming diseased.

The red flowers are produced only on older plants with any degree of reliability and appear amongst the dense wool in the upper axils of the plant during midsummer. They are red in colour and exceedingly handsome when they form two or three rings round the top of the stems.

151

Mammillaria elongata

Mammillaria microhelia hybrid

Mammillaria microheliopsis

Mammillaria (*continued*)

The variation that can occur within a group of plants with the same specific name in the cactus family is nowhere more apparent than in the immense variety of forms of *Mammillaria elongata*. The plants are all distinguished by having long thin cylindrical stems which form clumps at the base when quite young. The commonest forms of this plant have cylindrical plant bodies about 6 in (15 cm) in height at the centre although sideshoots may be almost prostrate along the surface of the compost. The tubercles are cylindrical and the amount of wool in the axils is very small, often in fact they are completely bare, even near the growing tip of the stem. The radials are neatly arranged in a star-shaped pattern on the areoles and normally number eighteen or so. They are usually reddish in colour but this is one of the most variable features of the plant. The centrals are generally four in number and difficult to distinguish from the radials as they frequently spread out sideways like the radial spines. The true *M. elongata* has yellowish flowers but cultivated specimens may have all manner of different coloured flowers, largely I think as a result of hybridization rather than the effects of natural variation.

When grown in partial shade such as exists on a windowsill the stems will tend to become rather thinner than if grown in a greenhouse, and flower production will consequently be somewhat diminished, but the plant makes a good house plant as long as it is not allowed to become waterlogged which can cause a rapid rotting off. It is a cactus which is generally more tolerant of drought than deluge and if in doubt the best plan is not to water it.

The most commonly sold form of *M. elongata* is *M. e. rufo-crocea*, which has much more prostrate stems and a conspicuously brown-tinted central spine banded into areas of white and yellow at the centre and near the base. Another variety seen is *M. e. stella-aurata* which has much more golden-coloured radial spines as its name suggests. Plants thought to belong to this variety should be compared with the illustrations above of *M. microhelia* and *M. microheliopsis*, both of which resemble the variety in spine configuration and colour.

Mammillaria microhelia was formerly known as *Leptocladia microhelia* but the two names are synonymous. It differs from *M. elongata* and its varieties in having a solitary stem usually about 4 in (10 cm) in height. It is a native of Central Mexico where it grows near Queretaro in the Sierra de San Moran at an altitude of some 7,000 ft (2,100 m). The stems are bright green and a little wool is occasionally, but not invariably, present in the axils of the younger tubercles. The spines are the most attractive feature, the radials being arranged (as the name suggests) to form a little sun around the somewhat elliptical areoles. They are very numerous and quite short but firm rather than bristly. The true species has a solitary unhooked central spine on the upper areoles although this drops off with age and is usually lacking completely round the base of the stem. The central spine is reddish brown in colour and contrasts well with the golden radial ones.

The flowers are somewhat variable, mainly due to hybridization again, the true species having creamy-yellow flowers; plants with pinkish flowers are probably either *M. microheliopsis*, also illustrated above, or a hybrid between the two.

Mammillaria microheliopsis is not so commonly found in cultivation as the preceding variety as it is generally rather slower growing and consequently somewhat smaller in size. It is sometimes referred to as *M. microhelia microheliopsis* and it is certainly very similar to the preceding species. Some warmth is appreciated in winter although if it is in a well drained soil and given a sunny position it will be all right with the bulk of the collection in a frost-free greenhouse overwinter. It does not generally do well indoors, tending to grow even more slowly and being an unreliable flowerer in this situation.

The chief difference between *M. microheliopsis* and *M. microhelia* is the pale grey or pinkish tinge on the central spine of the former as opposed to the brownish coloration on the central spines of *M. microhelia*. Although the flower colour of the two species differs as mentioned earlier, those of *M. microheliopsis* being pinkish, this is not always a reliable guide.

152

Mammillaria gracilis

Mammillaria kewensis

Mammillaria kunzeana

Mammillaria gracilis is popular with commercial growers and amateurs alike on account of the ease with which the numerous branches can be broken off the plant and rooted. The best rooting medium I have found is pure washed river sand, and if this is kept just moist the plantlets will root rapidly into it and quickly become established in their own right. The stems are very short, seldom exceeding 3 in (8 cm) or so in height, and the branches are formed not just from the base as is the case with most mammillarias but also from the upper parts of the stem, ultimately forming small clumps nearly 4 in (10 cm) in diameter. The numerous white radial spines are pressed back round the sides of the stem and appear to cover the whole of the plant body. The central spines are rather more prominent near the top of the plant and are frequently lacking near the base of established clumps. The flowers are not so freely produced as the branches, and are yellow with a very faint orange or even pinkish stripe in them.

It is possible that *M. gracilis* will benefit from regular fertilizing, particularly where this can be done with an organic plant food which will help to raise the organic level of the soil. If this is done it is best to make the plant one of the first to receive water and one of the last to be dried out each year.

There are some varieties of *M. gracilis* which lack the dense covering of spines of the species illustrated and it is possible that the majority of these are a variety known as *M. g. pulchella*.

Mammillaria kewensis is a variety which is frequently labelled as such in the shops but is hard to find in most books on the subject of cacti. From plants which have passed through my hands there seems little distinction between the plants labelled as *M. kewensis* and those called *M. hidalgensis*, the most significant difference being in the colour of the spines and flowers.

Mammillaria kewensis forms solitary elongated plant bodies up to a foot (30 cm) in height whose dark green stems have a slight covering of wool in the axils of the tubercles on the upper part of the stem. The spines are very variable: plants which I call *M. kewensis* having no radial spines at all, the areoles supporting instead four central spines with a slightly purplish to black coloration. The younger areoles are densely packed with white wool but this disappears with age. The pale pink flowers are produced fairly freely, even on quite young plants.

Mammillaria hidalgensis, on the other hand, is a rather smaller plant, although this may not at first be obvious. The crown of the plant is densely filled with white wool produced in the axils of the tubercles, which are rather unevenly and openly arranged round the sides of the plant. The spines are like those of *M. kewensis*, extremely variable but greyish brown rather than purple. The flowers are a much darker red.

Both varieties may benefit from a little shade during the summer, especially if grown in a greenhouse, and should be stood in a position where shadows from other members of the collection fall.

Mammillaria kunzeana could at first sight be easily confused with *M. bocasana* (illustrated and described on page 150) but it differs in having only a very few occasional bristles in the axils in between the tubercles and no wool. The plant bodies are fast growing and quickly form low clusters of stems each of which is generally less than 2 or 3 in (5 or 8 cm) in height. The stems themselves, although covered with spines, are glossy green with scaly somewhat cylindrical tubercles which in turn are slightly stippled themselves. The radial spines are very numerous, frequently more than twenty-five in number, white, thin and somewhat woolly in appearance. The centrals seem very variable in colour and quantity. Plants I have grown tend to have up to four grey or occasionally straw-coloured central spines, but other authors describe this species as having solitary brown spines or up to four brown spines. The flowers are very much more ornamental than those of *M. bocasana* being larger and cream with a central pink stripe down each of the petals.

153

Mammillaria plumosa

Mammillaria mundtii

Mammillaria prolifera

Mammillaria (*continued*)

Mammillaria mundtii and *M. nundtii* are, in fact, the same variety, the misprint *'nundtii'* being of commercial origin but widely perpetrated. It is quite common to find such spelling mistakes occurring, particularly when buying from a commercial grower who may not have time to check the printing on some of his labels. A similar example is *Hariota salicornioides* which is frequently listed as *Hatiora salicornioides* but is, once again, the same variety.

Mammillaria mundtii makes a low globular plant spreading almost as wide as it is high. The dark green stems form a woolly cephalium or hat when older due to the profusion of wool growing between the axils of the young tubercles, but this feature does not normally appear on young plants below three or four years in age. The radial spines are up to ten in number and are thin, white and spreading with two brown central spines sprouting from the areoles which, like the younger axils, are woolly at first. Although a rather uninteresting plant it is very attractive when it flowers as the somewhat tubular red flowers are produced well clear of the tubercles as opposed to being hidden down in the axils, which is the case with most mammillarias.

It is normal for plants of *M. plumosa* to be grafted when sold in Britain. This is not absolutely necessary if the plant can be grown in a very well drained soil and watered carefully. It is very similar in its cultural requirements to *M. schiedeana*, described and illustrated on page 156. It is somewhat rare in cultivation, being a shy flowerer and only forming clumps at a relatively older stage in its life and thus being difficult to propagate in any quantity. During the winter it will need a little extra warmth and can either be stood right next to the thermostat or brought indoors. However, it also needs to be kept completely dry during this period, particularly if it is grafted as the most common stock is *Hylocereus* which has been already mentioned as needing a slightly higher temperature itself.

In spite of its rarity and the difficulty of cultivation it is a particularly sought-after species on account of its very ornamental spines. These are very numerous and white and arranged exactly like feathers in the areoles completely covering the dark green plant bodies which, when mature, can attain a height of 6 in (15 cm) or so. Its native habitat is Northern Mexico where it grows in rock clefts near Coahuila and this accounts for its aversion to water. If grown in a bed rather than in a pot it is as well to try and reproduce this sort of habitat for it.

The flowers, as already mentioned, are seldom produced in cultivation until the plant has attained a fair size. When they are produced they are small and white and the seedpods are black, contrasting well with the white bristles. I have never grown plants from seed, but it is probably quite a difficult variety to raise in this way and it is, therefore, a sound idea to graft them as soon as they are large enough to handle to minimize the risk of damping off occurring in the seed tray when they are young.

Mammillaria prolifera, although very much more common than the preceding species, is altogether a better plant for the amateur, being tolerant of every kind of abuse and flowering very freely. As its name suggests it has an almost uncontrollable habit of proliferating clumps, sometimes groups of plants can measure a foot (30 cm) or more in diameter. Flowers are produced very freely on plants with just a single stem and a whole clump in flower is really worth seeing. It is tolerant of adverse conditions and will do well wherever it is grown, although it will derive considerable benefit from being given the maximum amount of sunlight possible. The small offsets root readily and make this a popular plant for own-propagation enthusiasts. If grown indoors during the winter it will need a little water, especially where it is overwintered on a living-room windowsill, but if left in the greenhouse it should be allowed to dry out just like other cacti.

Mammillaria prolifera has several varieties, two of which are most commonly seen. *M. p. haitensis* has a much more dense covering of spines than the illustrated species and centrals which are yellow at first and only become white with age. *M. p. texana* is a mainland version of a variety which is otherwise a native of the Caribbean. It is rather more open in texture and forms even larger clumps.

Mammillaria rhodantha

Mammillaria schelhasei

Mammillaria pygmaea

In spite of its name *Mammillaria pygmaea* is not a particularly dwarf variety in cultivation, the elongated, somewhat club-shaped plant bodies, which are broader at the top than at the base, forming large clusters at a fairly early stage in life and generally attaining a height of some 4 in (10 cm) or so. The stems are a glossy bluish green and the whole plant resembles a somewhat small version of *M. wildii*, illustrated overleaf, with which it is sometimes confused.

In its natural habitat the plant is considerably smaller and if you want to duplicate this feature in cultivation it is probably best to give it poor soil and to water sparingly, this will also have the effect of concentrating the areoles more closely together. The radials normally number about fifteen and are white in colour. The areoles support four central spines arranged in a roughly cruciform fashion and the lower two of these are usually slightly hooked. There seems to be some variation in the flower colour as well as in the size of the plants – the flowers ranging in colour between red and cream.

Mammillaria rhodantha is another very variable species and several of the varieties more commonly seen in cultivation have been given Latin varietal names. Generally the plants are solitary and cylindrical although younger plants may be globular at first, elongating only in the fourth or fifth year of cultivation. It is also not uncommon for plants of this variety to split into two at the growing point of the stem and this should not be regarded as anything

to do with bad culture. The plant bodies are comparatively tall, often attaining a height of 12 in (30 cm) or so even in cultivation. The stems are greyish green in colour, occasionally darker, and the younger axils between the tubercles produce a fair quantity of white wool. The radial spines are normally about fifteen in number and are very variable in colour, the type normally has whitish spines but these are occasionally suffused with pale yellow. The centrals, too, are variable both in colour and number, normally three to six in the type, red or brownish red in colour and tipped with a darker patch.

Flowers are fairly freely produced in late summer and form a ring of reddish blooms round the upper parts of the plant. As with many other mammillarias with few spines it should be shielded from direct continuous sunlight if grown in a greenhouse.

Amongst the more commonly found varieties are *M. r. sulphurea,* also known as *M. fuscata sulphurea,* and *M. r. pfeifferi* which has a conspicuous covering of yellow spines but is much less free with its flowers. *M. r. ruberrima* has reddish spines and is also sometimes sold as *M. r. rubra. M. pringlei* with its very dense covering of yellow spines is also very similar to *M. r. sulphurea.*

One of the first mammillarias that any beginner should obtain is undoubtedly *M. schelhasei.* Not only is it comparatively free flowering even when quite young, but its greenish flowers are produced right at the beginning of the flowering season and it may be forced for early flowering in the

way described for *Parodia sanguiniflora* on page 147.

The plant bodies are of moderate height for this family, growing to about 6 in (15 cm) in cultivation. They rapidly expand after the fourth or fifth year to form large clusters of plants, although it is unusual to find this occurring until the central plant is well established on its own. The stems are greyish green in colour and the tubercles, between the axils of which a certain amount of wool is produced when young, are cylindrical with very slight angles on them. These tubercles are very fleshy and care should be taken when handling them as they detach readily leaving an obviously scarred part of the stem. The radial spines are normally about fifteen in number and are straight, bristly and white in colour. The centrals are hooked, which makes it easier still for the tubercles to become detached, and brownish in colour.

Although green in colour the flowers are fairly freely produced and I have always had a personal predilection for plants with greenish flowers as being a little unusual.

Mammillaria glochidiata is somewhat similar in appearance but forms clumps rather more rapidly than the illustrated species, the flowers are pale pink in colour and it is possible that plants of *M. schelhasei* which have a pinkish tinge in the green flowers are, in fact, natural hybrids between the two species.

155

Mammillaria schiedeana

Mammillaria wildii

Mammillaria spinosissima

Mammillaria (continued)

Mammillaria schiedeana has already been mentioned as being somewhat exacting in its cultural requirements and for this reason it is often grafted. However, it is considerably easier to grow than *M. plumosa* and can be raised on its own roots quite successfully if given an open well drained slightly sandy compost and if care is taken not to allow water to sit amongst the very fleshy tubercles, especially if the sun is not shining brightly enough to help it to evaporate quickly.

The plant bodies are rather slow growing and prefer full sunlight, which assists in maintaining their somewhat dwarf globular appearance. When grafted they form branches from the base in their third year or so but when grown on their own roots this branching habit may not develop until a little later. The stems themselves are dark green and are covered with very long thin tubercles which give the plant its somewhat vulnerable habit. The radial spines are weak and very numerous, often as many as thirty in number, and spread in a hair-like fashion against the outer edges of adjacent tubercles appearing to clothe the plant completely. The young spines are a clear white but as they grow older they become yellow, reversing the normal colour change which occurs in cactus spines, but contrasting magnificently with the dark green plant bodies. Cultivated specimens normally lack central spines but I have seen imported specimens which have solitary central spines at each areole.

Although it is very slow growing the plant bears flowers freely even when quite young. These are greenish yellow and are produced from the axils amongst the tubercles. They barely extrude above the covering of hair-like spines and can easily be missed. Grafted plants tend to produce rather larger flowers.

Mammillaria spinosissima is another rather variable species, the locality in which it is found in the wild having as much to do with variation as any natural tendency to hybridize with adjacent species. The plant bodies are generally solitary and although globular at first become cylindrical with age. The dark green stems produce white wool in the upper axils between the flattened cylindrical tubercles. As its name suggests it has a great many spines. The radials are about twenty-five in number and are white and spreading in the type, although these may vary in some of the named cultivars and varieties. The centrals are similarly variable but the type has anything between seven and ten of them projecting outwards and downwards slightly away from the plant bodies, giving the plant its somewhat hostile appearance.

It flowers fairly well once established, producing a ring of bright red blooms round the upper part of the plant. The varieties grown commercially tend to be very much less free flowering although more exotic in their spine colour. One of my favourites is *M. s. sanguinea* which has magnificent red central spines tipped almost purple when young.

Mammillaria geminispina is another well armed species, with spines nearly $1\frac{1}{2}$ in (4 cm) in length and pure white in colour.

M. g. nivea has even longer, pure white spines which are normally clustered in threes on the areole, as opposed to being in twos on the species.

Mammillaria wildii is a well loved and free-growing species. It makes an excellent house plant as it does not require an extended cold period in order to flower, nor does it have to have the same quantity of winter light to enable flower-bud initiation to occur. At first globular, the stems later become cylindrical, attaining a height of about 6 in (15 cm) in cultivation and branching freely at the base from the second year onwards to form fairly dense clusters. The stems themselves are bluish green but the tubercles become progressively paler towards the areoles being almost white at the tips. The radials are white or pale pink in colour and number about nine. The areoles, which are at first woolly, produce three or four straw-coloured central spines, the longest of which is hooked.

It is very free flowering, and the true species has a ring of white flowers, faintly suffused with pink near the edge of the petals. It has been hybridized with *M. glochidiata* and the resulting hybrids, although similar in every other respect to the illustrated species, have pinkish flowers. The fruits form readily on pollination but are kept hidden in the axils until the following year when the long red tubular berries appear at the same time as the current year's flowers. Easy to grow, it is best kept away from direct sunshine, a factor which makes it a valuable indoor plant, and it should be watered sparingly.

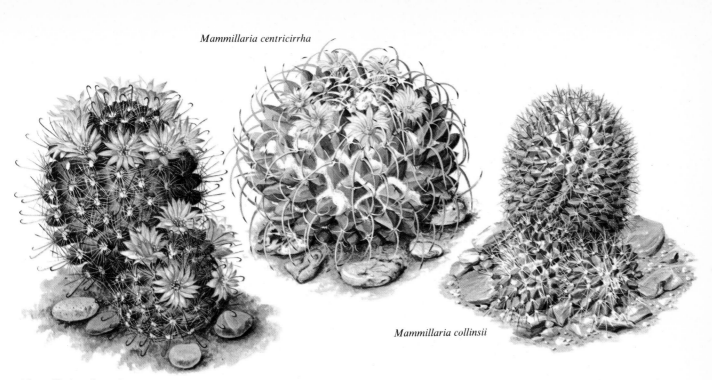

Mammillaria centricirrha

Mammillaria collinsii

Mammillaria zeilmanniana

Mammillaria zeilmanniana is, possibly, the cactus most commonly offered for sale throughout Britain. This is because it comes very readily from seed and flowers profusely even when quite young; but it is not an easy plant to grow and specimens will unaccountably collapse both in the early spring when water is first applied and the plants start to expand, and during the autumn as they are dried off prior to their winter rest. It is very similar to *M. wildii* illustrated on the opposite page but it differs in being glossy green, having pink instead of white flowers and lacking the progressive pallor of the tubercles as they get further from the main stems.

It is a freely clustering plant and even two-year-old seedlings may start to form offsets round the base. Because of its susceptibility to fungal infestations it is a good idea to remove these offsets as soon as they are large enough to handle and to root them in a tray filled with fine washed river sand. When they have established root systems they can then be potted up separately and grown on as an insurance policy against an attack of pythium or fusarium which may knock out the main specimen in the collection. Although they grow quite tall in their native Mexico they seldom attain any great height in cultivation because of this susceptibility to disease. I recommend watering regularly with a systemic fungicide such as benomyl and regular, possibly even fortnightly, inspection of the roots to make sure that the tips are still white. If the tips are brownish in colour and break away easily it is probably better to remove any offsets

and to repot the plant into fresh well sterilized soil, cutting the whole plant off above soil level and re-establishing it if the brown rotten roots extend over a considerable part of the root system. There is an attractive white-flowered variety, *M. z. alba*, which appears to be slightly hardier.

The species illustrated so far in the section on mammillarias have all had a watery sap. If you are confronted with a plant whose name you do not know but which exudes milky sap when pricked with a sterilized needle, then you should start looking for it in the immediately following pages.

Considerable confusion exists between *M. centricirrha* and *M. magnimamma*, the second name often being given as a synonym for the first. In spite of its name, *M. centricirrha* lacks any central spine and horticultural specimens sold as such which have a central spine are probably *M. magnimamma*. Having made this distinction the two species are extremely similar in habit and requirement. Although forming large clumps in central Mexico where they grow wild both species tend to remain solitary when grown in pots in this country.

The younger axils are generally hairless and plants which have very woolly tops are either about to produce flowers, or, if flowers fail to materialize, are wrongly named and probably belong to the group discussed next. Although reputedly free flowering the plants have to attain a fair size before the flowers are produced either regularly or reliably. They are pale pink to red in colour with an occasional backing of yellow in the petals. Generally the more

yellow they have the more likely they are to be *M. magnimamma*.

Mammillaria collinsii and *M. nejapensis* are very similar varieties with a mass of white wool on the upper part of the plant which does not invariably signify the onset of flowering. Both have yellowish flowers suffused slightly with a greenish coloration.

Mammillaria compressa is another species with dark green prominent tubercles and a mass of white wool in the upper axils. It generally forms clumps round its flattened plant bodies, but otherwise is of very variable habit, sometimes even completely spineless. Its red flowers are only produced on older plants but help to differentiate it from the two species mentioned above.

It is probable that considerable hybridization has occurred both naturally and otherwise amongst all the species mentioned on this page and this has clearly resulted in the confusion that confronts the amateur in trying to get a correctly named specimen. Matters are not, of course, helped by the very variable nature of the plants themselves. To summarize one could say that plants with relatively small amounts of wool in the tubercles and no central spine should be referred to *M. centricirrha*, similar plants with a downward pointing central spine are probably *M. magnimamma*. Where a considerable amount of wool is produced but few flowers the plants are either *M. nejapensis* or *M. collinsii*, which both have yellowish flowers, or *M. compressa* which has reddish flowers.

157

Mammillaria hahniana

Mammillaria heeriana

Mammillaria heyderi

Mammillaria (*continued*)

Mammillaria heyderi is one of my favourite cacti but it is, sadly, not as available in cultivation as it should be. This may have something to do with the difficulty we have found in raising it from seed and since it does not form offsets freely this makes it a problem to work up large stocks satisfactorily. However, since it is very early and very free flowering and can even produce a second flush of flowers later in the summer it is worth trying to get hold of a specimen.

In habit the plant bodies are low and hemispherical at first although in the fifth or sixth year of cultivation they start to elongate, attaining a height of about 4 in (10 cm). The tubercles are pale to grey-green and a little wool is produced in the younger axils between them. The radials are white tipped with brown and are arranged like a star, forming an attractive geometrical pattern round the plant bodies. There is usually a solitary central spine, which in spite of its small size can be very painful. Because of its low spreading habit and sharp spines this is one of the most difficult of all cacti to repot without losing one's temper. The flowers are white with a greenish tinge and are extruded through the tubercles and spines and show up quite prominently.

There are several similar species all coming from the same part of Southern Arizona, the most notable of which is *M. macdougalii* which has between ten and eleven radial spines, slightly stouter and thicker than those of the illustrated variety.

Mammillaria hahniana and *M. lanata* are two popular cacti loosely referred to as old lady cacti. *M. hahniana* is the one to which the name properly belongs and is readily identified by its long straggling hairs which protrude from the axils between the spines. There are several varieties of *M. hahniana* available, the most notable of which is probably *M. h. giselina* which is frequently sold as the true species but has much shorter hairs.

Mammillaria celsiana is very much less hairy and is a solitary plant in cultivation, occasionally forming clumps when much older. The plant bodies are round and globular when young but in the fifth or sixth year they start to elongate and eventually become club shaped, slightly thicker at the top than at the base, attaining a height of some 8 in (20 cm). The plant bodies are greyish green and it resembles *M. parkinsonii* in this respect. (*M. parkinsonii* is illustrated on page 160.) The axils between the tubercles produce a considerable amount of white wool but this hardly protrudes beyond the spines which are about twenty-five in number and rather thin and white. The central spines are short but straw coloured and show up well against the white spreading radial spines. The pink flowers are produced only on older plants among the thick wool at the top of the stems.

Mammillaria heeriana makes an upright cylindrical column with a height of some 4 in (10 cm). The tubercles are slightly angled having a faintly rhomboidal cross-section and are somewhat depressed at the tips below the areoles. The plant bodies are pale olive green in colour although in poor light this may be darker. The areoles, which have a small amount of white wool in them when young, are roughly oval to elliptic in shape and have about eighteen short white bristly radial spines, the longest of which are about a quarter of an inch (6 mm) in length. They are all tipped with a dark reddish patch when young but this fades as they become greyer with age. The four central spines are arranged in a cruciform pattern and are reddish purple in colour becoming paler as they get nearer the areole as well as growing overall rather more pale with age. The lowest of the cluster is normally hooked. The red flowers, which are tubular and extrude through the spines in a ring round the upper growing part of the plant, are very ornamental and are produced during the earlier part of the year.

Mammillaria heeriana makes a good house plant as it does not require full sunlight in order for flowering to take place. It prefers a rather open compost with good drainage and care must be taken to watch for any signs of damping off as this species, like *M. zeilmanniana*, is a little susceptible to fungal attacks.

Hariota salicornioides

Rhipsalidopsis rosea

The Rhipsalidanae

The next two pages illustrate a second group of epiphytic cacti called the *Rhipsalidanae*. The type genus is *Rhipsalis* and the botanical name is derived from the Greek word for wickerwork and is an allusion to the generally interlocking appearance of the branches of the plants. The group was one of the earliest ones to spread out of America and many of the species which are grown require rather warmer, more humid conditions than other cacti if they are to thrive. For this reason some of the less commonly available species are best left to those with a greenhouse where the minimum winter temperature can be maintained at 13°C (55°F) with a relatively high level of humidity. During the summer, too, they will need special treatment in the form of protection from direct sunlight, and since this conflicts with the requirements of the desert cacti it is seldom possible to grow the two families together in the same environment. The root systems are very scanty and the plants hardly need pots. If facilities are available they will do well when mossed on to an upright stump, although extra care must be taken with the watering under these circumstances as they will dry out quite quickly. Orchid compost makes an excellent rooting medium but if this is not available then a mixture of peat, cork, leaf-mould, sphagnum moss or anything else which is spongy in texture and organic in origin will serve as a medium.

Like zygocactus, rhipsalis are generally winter flowering although the growth is made during the summer and a short rest for some six weeks during which water should be given sparingly is normally advisable towards the end of September.

Hariota

Hariota salicornioides has been given the somewhat unkind name of drunkard's dream since the stem segments are faintly reminiscent of bottles. It makes a good house plant and is considerably more tolerant of adverse conditions than the rest of the group. The plant is frequently sold as hatiora and forms a bushy clump often producing a long main stem but otherwise branching frequently to form a densely knit mass of pale green bottle-shaped joints. The spines are very short and bristly and are hardly noticeable on the plant and the small yellowish-green flowers are produced at the ends of the short-jointed branches during late December or early January. Consequently it needs some warmth and water during this period. It is a somewhat uncertain flowerer unless grown in a warm greenhouse although its curious stems make it an unusual addition to the collection.

Rhipsalidopsis

Rhipsalidopsis rosea is frequently confused both with *Schlumbergera gaertneri*, with which it has been hybridized of late, and with *Zygocactus truncatus* and it is often somewhat misleadingly sold as the latter under the general English name of Christmas cactus. It is a somewhat delicate plant shedding its stem segments easily when allowed to get too dry, too wet or too bright. Although a rewarding flowerer it is advisable for this reason to strike cuttings as the opportunity arises to guard against the possible loss of a valued plant. It differs mainly from rhipsalis in having considerably larger, more showy flowers and forms a freely branching ultimately pendulous plant which does well when grafted on to a taller stock. The stem segments themselves are somewhat variable, some of them are flat jointed while others are broadly triangular in section. Both kinds are normally produced on the same plant and the margins of the segments are often tinged purple. Although this does not inevitably mean that they are getting too much light you should suspect it and take the necessary precautions especially where it happens during summer. The flowers are produced at the apices of the terminal segments during the late spring and early summer and although not as long lasting as rhipsalis are nevertheless longer lasting than those of most other cacti. The pale purple blooms are extremely attractive and make this a very worthwhile addition to the collection in spite of its somewhat delicate nature.

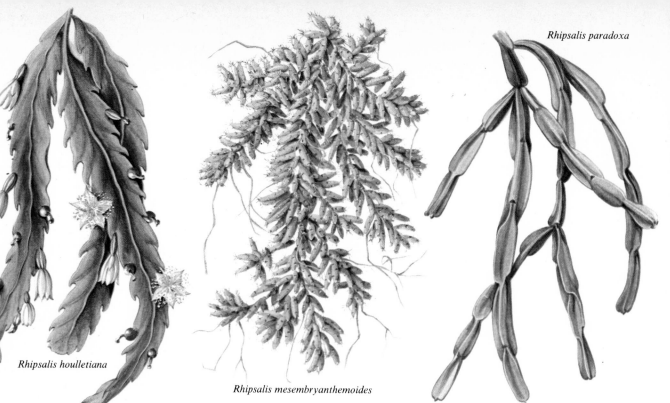

Rhipsalis houlletiana

Rhipsalis mesembryanthemoides

Rhipsalis paradoxa

Rhipsalis

Most rhipsalis have angled or cylindrical stems at least over part of the plant. *Rhipsalis houlletiana* is an exception to this in having flat, rather graceful stems with a prominent mid-rib and a conspicuously serrated margin. This edge can become reddish with full sunlight or with drought. The flowers are quite conspicuous for a *Rhipsalis* species and are followed by red berries, the flowers themselves being cream with reddish centres and somewhat bell shaped.

There are several other species of *Rhipsalis* with flattened stems, those of *R. pachyptera* are rather fatter than the illustrated species and the lower segments are often somewhat angled. The flowers are yellow, frequently with a trace of red, and the mistletoe-like fruits are white.

Rhipsalis coriacea is another species with white fruits which resembles *R. houlletiana*, and *R. warmingiana* lacks the prominent mid-rib of the illustrated species but has scented white flowers and black fruits.

Rhipsalis mesembryanthemoides is, as its name suggests, highly reminiscent of a mesembryanthemum. It is at first sight rather similar to *Hariota salicornioides* illustrated on the previous page but differs from that species in being considerably more bristly.

Although *R. mesembryanthemoides* is fairly distinctive in appearance, there are several other species of *Rhipsalis* which are characterized by short rather bristly joints. These include *R. capilliformis*, *R. heteroclada* and *R. cassutha*, which has already been mentioned as being the most easterly growing of all the true cacti. *R. prismatica* is also somewhat similar in appearance but the upper branches are distinctively angled, giving it its specific name.

Rhipsalis paradoxa is typical of a group of rhipsalis with prominently angled stems, the distinctive feature of this plant being the way in which the wings of one joint are produced opposite the flattened parts of the previous joint, giving it its name. In habit it is a pendulous plant which branches at the tips although this does not necessarily occur every year. The stems are generally three angled and vary in length, some being stubby, others being up to a foot (30 cm), normally pale green in colour but often acquiring a reddish tinge, especially when exposed to direct sunlight or when allowed to suffer from prolonged periods of drought. It is one of the hardier species mentioned so far, its thicker stems and greater degree of succulence enabling it to tolerate adverse conditions such as cold, lack of humidity and drought more effectively than the less succulent species already mentioned.

Although all *Rhipsalis* have areoles, the distinctive feature of the cactus family, *R. paradoxa* has very inconspicuous ones. The bristly spines are normally only found on the younger areoles which also have a certain amount of wool in them. Flowering is somewhat erratic and only older plants can be relied on to produce flowers at all. They are carried at the tips of the joints and are white in colour.

Various other winged or ribbed *Rhipsalis* are common in collections; *R. gonocarpa* is distinguished by black fruits, and *R. trigona* by reddish fruits. *R. tonduzii*, which is a native of Costa Rica, differs in having four- or five-angled stems.

As with most epiphytic species *Rhipsalis* may be grafted with good effect. Generally it is better to use stouter grafting stock such as *Trichocereus* as the plants make quite large and fairly heavy specimens with time. They are not generally suitable for the amateur and if I had to choose one to start with it would probably be *R. paradoxa*, which although one of the harder ones to flower is generally easier to keep alive.

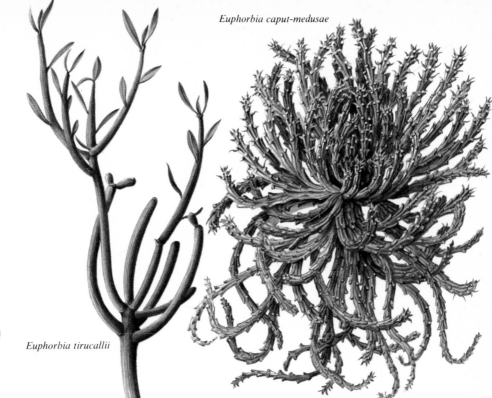

Euphorbia caput-medusae

Succulents with Milky Sap

Euphorbia tirucallii

Euphorbia

The *Euphorbiaceae*, in spite of the superficial resemblance of some species to members of the *Cereanae* and other cactus genera, is clearly distinguishable by the presence of a milky-white fluid which exudes from the damaged portions of the stems. It is a very variable family and includes our own common spurges as well as the well-known poinsettia (*Euphorbia pulcherrima*). Crotons too are members of the same overall family.

The flowers of euphorbia are really extremely small, the more important feature being the bracts or cyathophylls which are often brightly coloured as with the poinsettias and *E. splendens*. Succulent varieties of euphorbia in spite of the similarity of their flowering parts produce few or no leaves, those that are produced frequently falling during the first winter. The main exception to this rule is the crown of thorns and related species. The cactus-like varieties are particularly well suited to centrally heated living rooms since they do not require the same dry cool atmosphere during winter as do the true upright cacti. They are also very much faster growing and rapidly reach the stage at which they look to the uninitiated precisely like the columnar branching cacti.

Propagation can be carried out by seed, in which case it is advisable to surround the young capsules with a paper bag as the seed is frequently ejected with great force when mature, or by cuttings. In the latter case the fresh cutting material should be rubbed in powdered charcoal as soon as it is cut and allowed to dry out for a day or two before insertion. If charcoal is not available it is usually sufficient to wipe the end and allow the latex or milky sap to dry naturally and form a protective surround to the wound.

Euphorbia tirucallii, or the stick cactus, is an extremely poisonous inhabitant of Africa although it has become naturalized in part of eastern India. It is aptly described as the stick plant and ultimately attains a considerable height. It is comparatively swift growing especially when cared for in a greenhouse and is almost impossible to kill. The branches are repeatedly forked and produce small leaflets at the sides and tips of the young ones although these fall off with age. There is a somewhat similar species – *E. intisyi* – from which India rubber is made. The latter is an inhabitant of Madagascar and forms a sort of brownish bark on the sunny side of the stem in its native state. The main difference between the two species lies in the slight protuberances on the sides of the stems of the latter species from which the leaves are produced. It is possible that some confusion between the two species has occurred in commercial practice.

Medusa's head is a very accurate description of *E. caput-medusae* which in its mature state is reminiscent of something from a science fiction story. It is a native of Cape Province where it forms a club-shaped basal stem with very numerous semi-erect branches up to 30 in (75 cm) in length and 2 in (5 cm) thick which spread snake like from the centre and give the plant its Latin name. The stems are a pruinose green and produce little leaves which may be up to an inch (2·5 cm) in length on older stems but are normally much shorter. These fall off as the stems grow older, normally during the first winter. The flowers are produced at the tips of the spreading branches and the old flower stems remain even after the flowers have died. There are also attractive cristate forms of this variety.

Propagation is normally done by seed as stem cuttings tend to grow in a somewhat one-sided fashion never making a proper head of stems as the true species does. When buying a plant look for signs of this all-round growth. Winter temperatures should be slightly higher than for most other succulents and it may be advisable to bring the plant indoors during the cold period; this warmer environment should be accompanied by a little more water to prevent shrivelling.

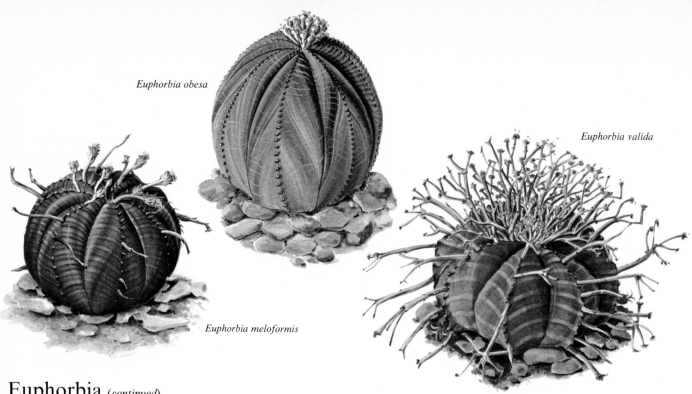

Euphorbia obesa

Euphorbia valida

Euphorbia meloformis

Euphorbia (continued)

The group of euphorbias on this page could all be mistaken for spineless barrel-type cacti such as *Astrophytum*. They differ, of course, in having the milky sap so typical of the euphorbias. They are all quite difficult to obtain and are relatively uncommon in cultivation, one reason being that they have to be raised from seed and, as explained later, this presents problems with some varieties, notably *Euphorbia obesa*.

Euphorbia meloformis is one of the more common sorts and makes a neat hemispherical plant, usually single but occasionally forming clumps from the base in its native habitat in Cape Province although I have never seen this happen in cultivation. It tends to have a somewhat flattened appearance being generally broader than high and can ultimately attain a size of about 4 in (10 cm). The root, as in the other globular *Euphorbia* species, is thick and turnip like and the mid-green stems have between eight and twelve ribs which are normally vertical but may occasionally be twisted slightly to form a gradual spiral. As mentioned earlier, the top is very much flattened and looks just as though someone had stepped on it. The sides of the ribs are banded obliquely and slightly furrowed and the old leaf cushions give the appearance of miniature areoles but lack the felting of wool which is peculiar to the true areoles of cacti. The leaves are very small and produced for a short time only at the growing tip of the plant, falling off before they have a chance to reach the sides. The flowers are fairly freely produced even on quite young plants and the old stems, which are re-peatedly brancned, remain even after the flowers have fallen and give the plant a slightly spiny appearance.

Propagation of this variety is by seed but both male and female plants are required for this, the difference being only really apparent in the flowers.

Euphorbia obesa is similar in that it requires both male and female plants in order to produce viable seed and it is quite difficult to obtain female plants. Unlike *E. meloformis* the plant bodies, which are hemispherical, are not flattened so sharply at the top although the apex is slightly depressed. The ribs are very broad with only shallow furrows between them, they are normally eight in number and have a row of minute leaf cushions on the edges. The plant body is grey-green but develops an almost purplish-brown coloration especially around the top of the plant.

There are a number of hybrid forms, one, which is a cross with *E. submammillaris*, has a curious branching habit, a feature never found in the true species. It requires a very well drained soil and it is a good idea to mix a little extra sand into the potting compost to assist with this; as a general rule do not water the plants unless you are certain that they need it as they are difficult to replace if they die.

Both the preceding species are characterized by a thick turnip-like root; *E. valida*, which is thought by many to be a natural hybrid between *E. meloformis* and *E. obesa*, lacks this feature. Although broadly spherical when young, as it grows older it assumes a more cylindrical shape and can attain an ultimate height of a foot (30 cm) or more and occasionally branches from the base. Superficially, on the other hand, it is almost exactly halfway between the two species – the body being furrowed as in *E. meloformis* but not quite so deeply. The dead flower stems are even more persistent than those of *E. meloformis* and may last for several years before ultimately falling off.

The three species illustrated on this page are quite unique in appearance amongst the euphorbias although another species with a turnip-like root is *E. pseudoglobosa*; however, this has oblong shoots rather than hemispherical ones and is seldom offered for sale on a commercial scale.

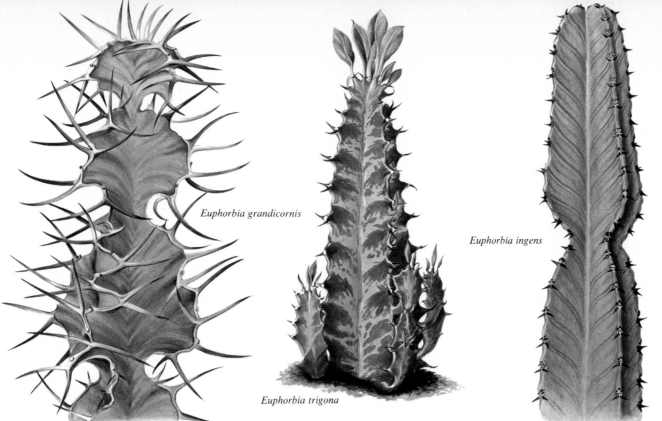

Euphorbia grandicornis

Euphorbia trigona

Euphorbia ingens

In contrast to the species described on the opposite page these three form large tree-like plants and have a distinctly cactus-like appearance. The absence of any form of felting in the areoles and the tendency to produce rudimentary leaves from the growing tips of the plants, especially if cultivated during the summer in a warm, moist atmosphere, clearly differentiate them from the true cacti. In fact the areoles at the base of the spine are not areoles at all but leaf cushions or tubercles.

Euphorbia grandicornis makes a magnificent plant with a really savage appearance, I often wonder if it was dried, cut into sections and used as a weapon by primitive man. It is a native of Natal and Zululand, Kenya and Tanzania and there it forms an immensely spiny succulent shrub with many three-angled stems branching upwards from a low trunk. Pot-grown specimens normally branch less freely and seldom before they are five years old or more. Each year's growth is clearly identified by the segmented character of the stem as it tapers towards the base. The margins are wavy and carry tubercles each of which produces two long hard spines opposite one another at the tips. The margins seem to be specially hardened and are not soft and fleshy like the rest of the plant. The flowers, which are fairly freely produced, appear between these spines at the top of the plant and are somewhat inconspicuous, hardly rising above the level of the greyish-green stems, although subsequently attractive rose-coloured fruits are produced which show up more clearly. Propagation is best carried out by means of cuttings following the drying out and healing procedures given at the beginning of this section (page 165).

Considerable confusion seems to exist, particularly in the United States, between *E. hermentiana* and *E. trigona*, and this arose as long ago as 1858 when Lemaire, the famous cactus collector after whom *Lemaireocereus* is named, wrongly identified some plants he brought back from Gabon. The most important distinguishing feature of *E. trigona* is the white variegation down the sides of the three-angled stems and the well developed leaves that often persist for 6 in (15 cm) or so down the sides of the stems. It is a native of Southwest Africa and although it normally has three angles to the stem some are reported with four. It branches freely even when quite young making an attractive plant for display in the corner of a room or at the back of a succulent bowl. In commercial horticulture the species normally sold as *E. trigona* which lacks the white marbling of the true species and the persistent leaves referred to above is known as *E. hermentiana*, a very fast growing kind which maintains its rather more slender appearance. It is possible that it is really *E. antiquorum* in many cases.

Euphorbia ingens is one of the most impressive of all succulent species in its native habitat on the west coast of Africa. It forms a large tree up to 30 ft (9 m) in height with numerous spreading branches and a tall stem. It is considered by some to be synonymous with *E. candelabrum*. The stems are at first three angled but as they grow older more ribs develop; this is especially true of the branches which are always four angled and are constricted into segments. The young stems often appear to have a hint of variegation about them.

All the tree-like euphorbias so far discussed need a somewhat warmer temperature in winter if they are to do well; otherwise they can develop hard brown woody patches on the stems similar to those of *Myrtillocactus geometrizans* and although this does not actually harm the growth of the plant it spoils the overall appearance, and can be prevented. There are several other tree-forming species of *Euphorbia*, the most commonly seen of which is probably *E. neutra*; this is easily distinguished by having five or six angles on the branches rather than the four of *E. ingens*.

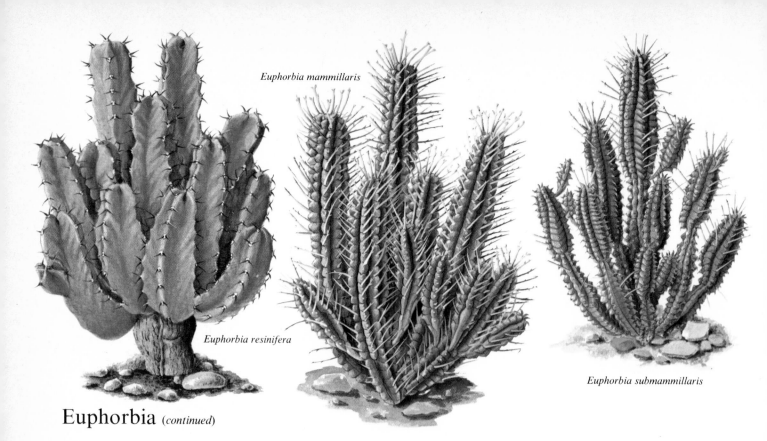

Euphorbia mammillaris

Euphorbia resinifera

Euphorbia submammillaris

Euphorbia (continued)

In contrast to the species illustrated on the previous page the ones on the present page tend to produce shorter more compact plants which branch more readily when much younger.

Euphorbia resinifera is a cactus-like species which seems to be very popular. It grows on the Atlas mountains south-west of Marrakesh where it makes low spreading clumps. This habit is not too obvious in pot-grown specimens which normally have a central upright column round which rudimentary branches seem to form, mainly at base level. In the course of time these fill out and grow round the main stem, packing themselves closely in so as to give the plant its humped appearance. The stems are an attractive grey-green colour even when older with four broad angles which give the plant a geometrical appearance. The ribs are notched a little in between the leaf cushions or tubercles and the spines, which are fairly short and brown in colour, are produced in pairs from the tips of the old leaf cushions.

A drug is produced from the plant, which is one of the few species of *Euphorbia* which is not poisonous. The name of the genus is, in fact, derived from that of Euphorbus who was physician to King Juba II of Mauretania. It is related that the plant was actually named by King Juba in honour of of the physician and he subsequently wrote a treatise on the herbal properties of the plant called *De Euphorbia Herba*. It is one of the oldest names in botanical Latin, and *E. resinifera* was almost certainly the species about which King Juba wrote.

Euphorbia mammillaris has joints which resemble corn on the cob in shape if not in colour and for this reason it is often referred to as the corncob cactus. It is, however, quite definitely a euphorbia and is not related to either of the plants which it is supposed to resemble. It is a somewhat ungainly plant and those with limited space at their disposal should grow the dwarf version illustrated beside it. It is normal to see commercial specimens growing upright, frequently supported by a cane; however, in Cape Province where it is naturally found, it forms a low sprawling ground cover, seldom more than 6 in (15 cm) in height with a short trunk and suckers sprouting up round it near the base. The stems are mainly unbranched although when supported by a cane they may often appear to be branched, this is merely the effect of trying to grow the plant upright. The stems are surrounded by flattened rows of tubercles, giving it the appearance of having numerous ribs. These are often twisted a little to form shallow spirals. The flowers are produced on twiggy stems near the tips of the sideshoots and the dead stems persist for some years (as do those of the globular euphorbias described earlier) to give the plant a slightly prickly appearance.

Those who do not have the space to grow a sprawling plant such as *E. mammillaris* can always opt for its 'dwarf' version *E. submammillaris*, which is also a native of the Cape Province. In spite of its name it differs substantially from the true *E. mammillaris* in having acutely angled stems with nine or ten ribs rather than the spirally arranged rows of low tubercles characteristic of that species. The stems are very slight, seldom more than half an inch (1 cm) thick, and the plant branches freely from the base rapidly making a small neat clump even in a 3-in (8-cm) pot. The branches have fewer angles with rather more prominent ribs than the more rounded stems. The predominant colour is a pale greyish green, the ribs of the branches are sharply notched and the sides are sharply furrowed. Like the globular species it produces small flower shoots at the tips of the branches whose dead stems persist for some time. They are in themselves quite attractive as they have a reddish colour when young.

In a greenhouse it is wise to keep this variety on a slatted shelf in the winter as it is particularly susceptible to damp cold weather and appreciates a good flow of air round the branches which helps to ripen and harden them against any possible infection.

Euphorbia milii splendens

Euphorbia milii

Considerable controversy exists over the exact nomenclature of the species illustrated on this page and commercial growers seem undecided as to which plant is a subspecies of which – if any.

Euphorbia milii is now sometimes sold as *E. milii milii* and it forms a graceful little shrub. Strictly speaking it is not succulent at all but since it tends to drop its leaves in winter and is always grown alongside other succulent plants I have seen fit to include it here. The variety illustrated is a native of Madagascar and has thin somewhat weak spines seldom more than quarter of an inch (6 mm) in length and about a tenth of an inch (2 mm) thick. The leaves are the most succulent of all those in the group being tough and leathery and conspicuously narrowed towards the point where they join the stem. The flowers, as mentioned in the introduction to this section, are the inconspicuous yellow things in the centres of the so-called 'flowers' which are, in fact, a type of bract known as a cyathophyll.

The best variety to grow has been raised by Koëniger, the noted cactus specialist at Aalen, near Stuttgart, and called in honour of the town and its river *E. m.* Aalbaeumle. This has very weak rather flexible spines and flowers almost continuously throughout the year. The slender branches grow into a compact pyramidal shape and make it especially suitable as a pot plant.

The much larger *E. m. splendens* is frequently referred to commercially either as *E. splendens*, or as *E. s. bojeri*, or even as *Euphorbia bojeri*. Like the preceding species it is a native of Madagascar and the name

which has been colloquially given to it of crown of thorns is almost certainly theologically and botanically inaccurate. As a description, on the other hand, it is very good as the shrub, which can attain a height of over 6 ft (2 m), is well armed with long hard spines up to 6 in (15 cm) or more in length and nearly half an inch (1 cm) wide at the base. It is generally much larger than the preceding species and the leaves although bigger are less succulent. The flowers are produced in branched clusters on sticky stems that grow out of the side of the plant near the tips of the branches but also occasionally from older wood. They are much larger than those of *E. m. milii* and although they are produced almost as continuously during the year the main flowering period is definitely in the spring and early summer.

It bleeds extensively when cut and the instructions on propagation on page 165 should be followed. Care should also be taken not to allow the milky latex to come into contact with the eyes, lips, or blood as it can cause considerable discomfort and swelling. If you feel some puffiness after potting or handling the plant it is advisable to call a doctor and explain what has happened. It is hardly fatal but some people seem more allergic to it than others and given the right treatment the swelling will quickly subside.

Even if adequate precautions are taken propagation is difficult on account of the woody nature of the stem and the rapidity with which it drains, and it should not be attempted on any scale without mist cultivation and a special propagator unit capable

of maintaining the humidity round the plant without allowing it to rot off.

Euphorbia milii Tananarive, also referred to as *E. splendens* Tananarive, is easily distinguished by its yellow cyathophylls, which are slightly tinged with red when given full sunlight, and its more sprawling appearance; normally it requires staking and judicious pruning if it is to make a shapely plant. There is also a variety with pink flowers called *E. m. hislopii* which is otherwise similar in appearance.

All these xerophytic or woody species tend to drop large numbers of leaves whenever they are disturbed. This means that not only does the high-street retailer lose a few leaves but that the ultimate consumer will also lose some leaves when the plant is first brought home. There is absolutely nothing wrong in this at all and the plant will rapidly make fresh leaves as soon as growth starts up. The main indication of trouble is a shrivelling of the stems and if this is noticed it is best to cut off the affected portion since the shrivelling normally starts at the growing point.

Conophytum albescens

Conophytum bilobum

Living Stones

The Aizoaceae

The plants on the following four pages are all members of the mesembryanthemum family which is one of the largest families of succulents in cultivation and whose Latin name is *Aizoaceae*. They vary enormously from the well known living stones or lithops to succulent shrubs such as *Aptenia cordifolia* which is best known in its variegated form. A detailed treatment of the group is well beyond the scope of the present volume. This section is restricted to the former type of stone plant amongst which the variation in colour and texture is only matched by the differences in cultural conditions. The rosette-forming mesembryanthemums such as *Faucaria* are dealt with in the following section, which although botanically inexact makes it easier for the amateur.

The species in this section are all extremely succulent and mostly stemless and the plant bodies have been developed from a single pair of leaves. Propagation is usually by means of seed, but where offsets are freely produced these may also be rooted as cutting material.

They are generally natives of South Africa where they inhabit the very dry Karoo and normally produce only a thick succulent turnip-like tap root. When water is applied in the wild, small fibrous hair roots are produced round this which rapidly die off when the rain passes. The best soil mixture to use is a conventional cactus compost with the addition of crushed brick or coarse gravel to help drainage. The seeds remain viable for many years, instances have been recorded of seeds from herbarium specimens germinating after decades.

Conophytum

It is not uncommon for collections of these stone flowers to be offered growing together in a bowl, but it is not wise to buy such collections unless you intend to divide up the bowl or unless you are buying from a specialist, as even within a genus such as *Conophytum* many plants have different growing cycles and consequently different cultural requirements.

Conophytum albescens is one of the easiest of all the stone-type flowers on which to obtain blooms. It belongs to a group of conophytums which have cylindrical or heart-shaped and distinctly elongated plant bodies with two quite distinct lobes as opposed to the more spherical types discussed later. It is a native of Cape Province and the bodies are flattened sideways, appearing slightly two dimensional rather than being evenly round. The tips of the lobes are rounded and there is a clear fissure in the centre just over an eighth of an inch (3 mm) in length from which the flowers are produced. The specific name is derived from the very fine white hairs which densely cover the light grey-green plant bodies. The flowers which are produced between May and October are yellow. With this variety the resting period occurs during March and April and as soon as flowering has finished in October growth starts and this growing period during which water may be given lasts through until February.

Conophytum bilobum is another species in this group of twin-lobed conophytums and has similar cultural requirements to those of *C. albescens*. In the wild this grows in the same places as the previous species

but unlike it older plants will form branches and thus a large mat of growth. The bodies are similarly compressed to those of *C. albescens*. The plant bodies are greyish green in colour, but lack the fine white hairs of the preceding species although they do have some white meal on them. The edges of the plants are slightly reddish.

Because of its eventual size it makes a good plant for the amateur and shows up well when it produces the daisy-like yellow flowers. If a collection is required to be put together in a bowl I would recommend *C. cauliferum* which has almost orange flowers, and *C. frutescens* which has deep orange-yellow flowers as suitable companions since they all come from the same part of the world and have similar habits and growing requirements.

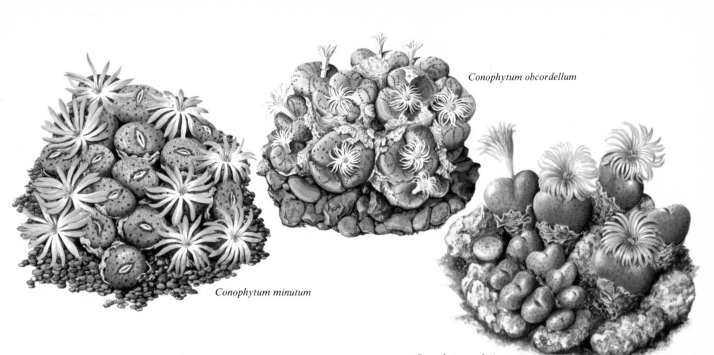

Conophytum obcordellum

Conophytum minutum

Conophytum velutinum

The species illustrated on this page should not under any circumstances share a pot with those on the opposite page as their growing conditions are quite distinct. *Conophytum minutum*, for example, requires watering during March especially when there is an early spring. At this point water should be given generously since the new plant bodies are being formed. Between April and May watering should come to a complete standstill even if the plants shrivel a little as this is the normal resting period for these species. New growth begins to show through in June when more water may be given and the flowers of this group start to appear from July through to November. From December through until February water may also be given and the temperature should not be allowed to drop below 10°C (50°F).

Conophytum minutum forms a roundish mat and has pear-shaped bodies with none of the lateral flattening that characterizes the species on the opposite page, also the upper surface is somewhat flatter and the presence of the twin lobes is not so obvious. As might be inferred from its name it is a very small species seldom exceeding half an inch (1 cm) in height and the central fissure is also very small. The flowers, which are produced freely and regularly even on the small plants, are up to half an inch (1 cm) in diameter and are pale lilac in colour.

A good species to grow with this variety if a mixed collection is desired is *C. pearsonii*, which is a rather larger plant forming cushions with age and having much darker pink flowers nearly 1 in (2·5 cm) in diameter.

Conophytum gratum, which has red flowers, taller pear-shaped bodies and a dense covering of small grey dots, can also be grown with the previous two species.

Conophytum obcordellum forms a densely tufted and matted plant with the separate plant bodies seldom exceeding half an inch (1 cm) in diameter, but occasionally reaching an inch (2·5 cm). They are severely flattened at the top and when seen from above are kidney shaped or elliptical in section. The sides of the plant bodies are a pinkish-red colour but the upper surfaces are normally bluish green, although, as this is a plant which mimics its wild surroundings, these colours may vary a great deal in the wild. The spots on the upper surfaces of the plant bodies are arranged as a series of branched lines and this distinguishes this species from the similarly named *C. obconellum* which has confluent lines of dots on the top. The latter species, which has white, or slightly yellow, scented flowers, can be grown alongside the illustrated species if required since they will both benefit from a certain amount of shade during our British summers when they should not be left on the upper shelf in a greenhouse.

Conophytum parviflorum in spite of its name makes an attractive companion to both *C. obconellum* and *C. obcordellum*. The dotted tops are slightly raised where the blackish dots occur and on some forms the spots grow so close together as to appear to form almost continuous semi-transparent lines on the top of the plants.

Conophytum velutinum is one of the species in which the old leaf sheaths persist

and remain round the developing new plant bodies. It branches freely and generally two plant bodies are produced on a single stem. They are only slightly compressed on top but are very much flattened sideways. The plant bodies have a soft velvety feel and this is given by the minute hairs which grow on the sides and help to trap the dew in their native Cape Province. The flowers are extremely spectacular, purple and nearly an inch (2·5 cm) in diameter.

Other good species to grow with this which also have a velvety covering to the plant bodies are *C. puberulum*, which ultimately forms a low shrub producing up to twenty plant bodies and has yellow flowers, and *C. papillatum*, which also has yellow flowers but whose plant bodies are densely covered in soft meal and even support a few longer hairs near the top of the fissure.

Lithops spp.

Dinteranthus puberulus

Lithops

Dinteranthus

Lithops are the true living stones whose name is derived from the Greek word for stone. The name is often used to signify the plural but *Lithops* is in fact the generic name.

They make excellent house plants and are especially popular in the Far East where they seem to be admirable companions to the art of the miniature so carefully practised with Bonsai trees. The stem is below ground and forms a long thick fleshy tap root. Frequently in periods of drought this can contract and shrivel drawing the plant bodies even deeper into the surrounding soil until they are practically invisible. The dead remains of the old leaf bodies should be left on, especially if the plants are to be grown in a sunny position in the greenhouse or on a shelf as they help to protect the new leaves which rise up from within the central fissure. The flowers, when they are produced, are frequently larger than the plants and mark the finish of the year's growth.

Even in Britain lithops do well when surrounded with stones which help to give shade to the plant bodies. The only parts of the plant which actually receive any light for any purpose are the extreme tips, and some species have small windows in the tips to enable the light to reach through. This is, however, most marked on another genus called *Ophthalmophyllum*.

Watering should stop in September after the flowers have died down and any seeds have been set and harvested; watering can be started again in April although if the winter has been mild it may be better to leave it until the end of April if flowers are required. Once watering commences the old bodies die off exposing the new ones in the centre so do not be alarmed if it appears at first as though the plant is dying. The emerging plant bodies start to grow and keep on growing until flowering begins, generally in August.

Although their watering requirements are similar to those of cacti they need a higher temperature in winter, ideally around 10°C (50°F), and during this period they will want full sunlight. If only one greenhouse is available it is a good idea to bring the plants indoors and grow them on a south-facing windowsill, although care should be taken not to leave them on the windowsill at night when the curtains are drawn but to bring them into the room; otherwise there is a real danger that they can become too cold.

Do not bury the plants too deeply in the soil. If they want to get down further into the soil they can do so of their own accord, but it is not likely in this country. Also it is a good idea to try to find some of the long extremely conical clay pots, which used to be available, to grow the plants in as this helps in the formation of a good tap root when the plant is still quite small.

Plants are best raised from seed, which germinates readily, and many varieties can be induced to flower in their second year, but where offsets are produced these may also be struck as cuttings. No attempt has been made to differentiate between species for which the reader is urged to consult specialist works.

Dinteranthus puberulus is recorded as growing amongst quartz stones so an authentic surrounding for it may be hard to come by. It is unusual amongst this group of succulents in having normally at least two sets of plant bodies, one on top of the other. The upper surface of the spreading leaves is quite flat but the lower surface is sharply keeled and bent round towards the apex giving it the appearance of a piece cut from a globular cheese. Although the Latin name suggests the presence of hair on the plant bodies these are so insignificant as to be only really visible with the help of a magnifying glass but the velvety feel is there. The flowers are produced in October and are a beautiful golden-yellow. The resting period lasts from November right round until May.

Pleiospilos bolusii

Rhombophyllum nelii

Rhombophyllum rhomboideum

Pleiospilos

In contrast to the preceding members of the *Aizoaceae* described in this section the plants on this page are generally quite large and are unsuitable for mixed plantings on account of their fairly prolific growth. They are sufficiently stone like, however, to be included in this section, having the vaguely chunky-shaped leaves which one expects of this group of plants.

Pleiospilos bolusii is named in honour of Dr H. M. Louisa Bolus who did a great deal of work on the whole family at the beginning of the present century. It is at first solitary but as it grows it develops a straggly branching habit with age. The plant bodies usually comprise a single pair of leaves but sometimes there are two pairs. They are almost vertical in habit and the flattened surfaces which face each other are often wider than they are tall giving the plant a very wide appearance. The plant bodies are a greyish green and become tinged with red if exposed to full sunlight, especially if they are allowed to become dry during this period. The leaves are covered with numerous much darker green spots although these are not, as frequent on the inside-facing surfaces of the leaves as they are on the other surfaces. It flowers freely during the late autumn, after which it should be rested until the end of March.

Pleiospilos nelii is far less common than the preceding sort. It is very similar to *P. bolusii*, the main distinction being the absence of the pronounced keel so characteristic of the latter species.

Rhombophyllum

Rhombophyllum rhomboideum is one of a group of plants in which the growing period follows the flowering period. The species forms a mat of prostrate rosettes with eight to ten thick very succulent leaves varying between 1 and 2 in (2·5 to 5 cm) in length and just under an inch (2·5 cm) in thickness. As its name suggests the leaves are rhomboidal in shape with the upper surface carrying a shallow groove down the centre and the lower surface having a pronounced keel near the tip. Most varieties have plain white-rimmed edges but these also occasionally carry a few teeth. The whole plant is covered with numerous whitish dots and the flowers are produced between June and September, often three or more on the same stalk. They are a magnificent golden-yellow colour, about 1½ in (4 cm) in diameter with a reddish outside.

As mentioned earlier growth continues after flowering has finished and the species will appreciate a warm sunny position and continued watering right through until November when the resting period starts again. During the winter resting period, which should last until growth is started up again in June, *R. rhomboideum* requires an open well-lit position but does not need the high temperatures that some of the other species require, being quite content with a minimum temperature of 7°C (45°F). Propagation is best carried out by seed which germinates readily but some of the offsets may also be removed and rooted as cuttings.

Rhombophyllum nelii is not to be confused with *Pleiospilos nelii* although they both carry the same specific epithet in honour of Professor G. C. Nel who was director of the Botanical Institute in Stellenbosch. It has distinctly two-lobed leaves which are joined on the back surface to form a united leaf going down to the base. The leaves are bluish green and have some rather inconspicuous darker dots completely covering them. The flowers are much larger than the preceding species, nearly 2 in (5 cm) in diameter and bright yellow.

Lampranthus aureus appears vaguely similar to *R. nelii* when young but the difference quickly becomes apparent as it starts to grow and form its characteristic stem which is clearly visible between the leaves.

Adromischus cooperi

Faucaria tigrina

Rosette-forming Succulents

I have grouped together on this and the following four pages a miscellaneous group of succulents other than cacti which have little or no obvious stem and form rosettes at ground level. In this there is little botanical difference between these and the preceding group of mesembryanthemums but these plants are less singular in appearance and widely differing in their requirements. Related plants are described in the section on succulents with stems other than euphorbias, for example aloes and agaves. There are also various rosette-forming crassulas, or plants whose stems are so inconspicuous that one tends to overlook them.

It is impossible to generalize about the culture of this group. They nearly all produce offsets, although *Agave americana* may have to be very well established before it does so, and these can be rooted easily. The most frequently seen are the rosette-forming echeverias, described at the end of the section on pages 177 to 178, which are widely offered for sale as cheap pot plants and even occasionally used for bedding out by parks departments. Some succulents, such as the sempervivums, are completely hardy in Britain and can form a useful bridge as it were between the glasshouse succulents and the garden. The closely related *Orostachys spinosus* is hardy in sheltered locations only.

Adromischus

Adromischus cooperi, in spite of its appearance when young when it closely resembles a lithops, is a member of the *Crassulaceae* and this becomes apparent as soon as its flower is produced. Although always sold as *A. cooperi*, and therefore illustrated and described under this name here, it is more probable that it is really *A. festivus*, the *A. cooperi* of botany being now unknown in cultivation. *A. festivus* has short, wedge-shaped leaves, flattened and slightly crenellated at the tips. They are grey green in colour and flecked and mottled heavily with darker reddish markings. A curious feature of this plant is the production of aerial roots from the stems which clearly differentiates it from the mesembryanthemums.

Another adromischus frequently offered for sale is *A. maculatus*. This develops a stem when much younger and ultimately forms a small trunk 4 in (10 cm) in height. Otherwise it is similar in appearance to the previous species, the flowers, which are produced on a long stem, being rather small and white tipped with pink.

Faucaria

Faucaria tigrina has been given the English name of tiger jaws in deference to its appearance. It is really a mesembryanthemum and the daisy-like golden-yellow flowers are produced in the late summer and autumn. Watering should continue until the end of November and the plants should then be rested in a cool greenhouse with a maximum temperature of 7°C (45°F) until they are ready to start into growth again in May. In spite of its vicious appearance the 'spines' or teeth at the edges of the leaves are not sharp at all but very weak and easily broken off.

The leaves are crowded together to form a dense and compact rosette somewhat rhomboidal in section, and the leaf tips are drawn sharply forwards over the inner surface like a chin. Each leaf carries nine or ten teeth curved in towards the centre of the plant and ending in an almost hair-like tip. In a very light position the leaves will turn reddish and there is a special form – *F. t. splendens* – in which this reddishness is even more conspicuous.

Faucaria tuberculosa has almost tooth-like pimples erupting from the inner surfaces of the leaves but is otherwise similar in most respects to *F. tigrina*.

Although most faucarias have yellow flowers, *F. candida* has white flowers and those of *F. felina jamesii* and *F. laxipetala* are tinted pinkish and reddish respectively on the outside of the golden-yellow flowers.

Gasteria verrucosa

Haworthia papillosa

Aloe aristata

Gasteria

Gasteria verrucosa is a relative of the lily and has a flower that is faintly reminiscent of that plant. It is tolerant of shade which makes it one of the best of all succulents to grow as a house plant and it can be grown alongside cacti in winter with a winter temperature of below 7°C (45°F). Cultivation generally is similar to that of aloes to which it is closely related and it appreciates shade during the summer like *Aloe variegata* described overleaf. Propagation is best achieved either through leaf cuttings or by means of the numerous offsets, but seeds should not be used if a variety true to type is required since the plants hybridize so readily amongst themselves that it is not always possible to guarantee the purity of a particular strain. Most *Gasteria* species are very similar to one another when young and at this stage have only opposite leaves; they do not develop the rosette-forming habit until they are older.

Gasteria verrucosa never actually forms a completely round rosette as the leaves continue to be produced opposite one another. The long leaves are faintly wavy and have a pink sheath surrounding the base of the stem which they clasp. The most prominent feature is the mass of small white confluent tubercles that cover all the surfaces of the leaves and give the plant its name.

The exceptional fertility of gasterias has given rise to a number of intergeneric hybrids such as x *Gastrolea* (*Gasteria* x *Aloe*) and x *Gasterhaworthia* (*Gasteria* x *Haworthia*). These are now being brought into cultivation.

Haworthia

Haworthia papillosa is also covered with numerous white tubercles but is more obviously rosette forming in character. It does not produce offsets freely but propagation is fairly easy by means of leaf cuttings. The tubercles on the back of the leaves are much more numerous than those on the front and the flowers are produced on a long stem from slightly off-centre.

Similar to *H. papillosa* is *H. margaritifera* which is also covered in white tubercles but produces more numerous offsets. There are many varieties of this latter species of which one of the best is undoubtedly *H. m. corallina*; this species has even more white tubercles, forming an almost white mass near the base of the much more slender leaves.

Haworthia cuspidata, on the other hand, has no tubercles at all. Instead it is of interest because of the almost transparent window-like patches that occur near the tips of the thick, sharply-keeled pale green leaves. The sides of the leaves are very slightly toothed.

One other remarkable haworthia is *H. bolusii* whose leaf margins are so completely armed with fibrous white teeth that the plant appears to be covered by a dense mat of white bristles. There is an even more bristly variety of this called *H. b. aranea*.

Aloe

Aloe aristata is very similar to the white-tubercled haworthias described earlier but the leaves are far less succulent than those of the haworthias. It is a deservedly popular plant on account of its rapid growth and freely suckering habit which quickly enables such large clumps to be built up that people feel obliged to root some of the offsets and give them to friends. A succession of flowers throughout the summer will be produced even on young plants and it will appreciate a little shade if the leaves are not to start turning purple. The reddish tubular flowers are produced on long stems from just off-centre.

The leaves have small cartilage-like teeth down the sides and on the upper surfaces. It is quite normal for the tips of the leaves to go hard and shrivelled and if wished these may be cut off without jeopardizing the plant.

175

Aloe variegata

Agave americana

Crassula socialis

Aloe (*continued*)

Aloe variegata is a well known species which has acquired the English name of partridge breasted aloe on account of its distinctive markings. It is a native of South Africa and forms a stemless rosette often attaining some height but more normally seen as a fairly squat plant surrounded by dense numbers of offsets or suckers which are produced round the base in great profusion.

The leaves, which are triangular in shape and conspicuously furrowed on the upper surface, are produced in three clear rows, each new leaf arising from the base of the preceding one. They can be nearly 6 in (15 cm) in length and over an inch (2·5 cm) in width on mature specimens. The white banding is given by the regular white spots which are also typical of many other *Aloe* species, and the somewhat horny edges of the leaves have very small white teeth on them, almost imperceptible to the eye but giving the edge a rough feel when it is stroked. The flowering stem is normally solitary and can attain a considerable height, often rising over a foot (30 cm) above the centre of the plant. The flowers, which are rather pendulous, are reddish and tubular and are followed by seeds which germinate readily.

This species dislikes full sunlight which tends to make the plant bodies purplish rather than green and for this reason it does well indoors, especially where the air is very dry. However, it should be kept away from south-facing windowsills and if grown in a greenhouse it should be kept slightly dryer than most other aloes as it tends to rot off fairly readily.

Agave

Agaves are not plants for those with little patience or little space. They are commonly known as century plants and have done more to give 'cacti' the reputation of flowering only once every hundred years than anything else. Their slow growth and irregular flowering have been responsible for giving them the name of century plants, and they are familiar to many of us as the plants which produce telegraph-pole flower stems round the shores of the Mediterranean.

Agave americana is a typical species and one which is fairly readily obtained. Its grey-green leaves can attain a length of several feet and have a sharp spine at the end. There are many varieties, notably *A. a. marginata* which has magnificent broad stripes of white or cream up the edges of the sharply toothed leaves. There is also a variety, *A. a. medio picta,* which has a pale stripe down the centre of the leaf.

The variegated forms of *A. americana* are frequently confused with *Furcraea selloa marginata*, a native of Colombia. However, this latter species forms a stem up to 3 ft (1 m) in height as it grows older whereas the rosettes of *Agave americana* are always stemless. The leaves are very much narrower than those of *A. americana* which are normally over 4 in (10 cm) wide on mature plants, even at the narrower part, while those of *Furcraea selloa* are only this size at the widest point.

Crassula

Crassula socialis makes an excellent plant for the smaller collection and does well in a shallow pottery bowl which allows it to sprawl around. The stemless rosettes form dense branching mats whose individual plantlets are seldom more than half an inch (1 cm) in diameter. The light green leaves are triangular in shape, stemless, and furrowed a little on the upper surface with rather horny edges. The flowers, which are produced in February, and quite freely even on young plants, are borne on short slender stems at the top of the rosette.

Rather similar in appearance are *C. columnaris* and *C. teres,* although these are both very much more upright than the illustrated species. The leaves of *C. teres* are so tightly folded into the stem as to form a practically continuous surface, while those of *C. columnaris* have a terminal head of flowers buried amongst the upper leaves, which are far more prominent than those of the preceding species.

Orostachys spinosus

Echeveria carnicolor

Echeveria derenbergii

Orostachys

Sempervivums are well known in Britain as houseleeks and make excellent plants with which the succulent collector can carry his interest into the garden. They are generally hardy species and can be grown easily and well on a rock garden. They are extremely variable in form, much depending on the type of soil on which they are grown. The English species is *Sempervivum tectorum*.

Several species are offered by alpine nurseries, one of the most attractive being *S. arachnoideum* in which the tips of the leaves develop long white bristles which become interwoven at the top of the plant giving it the appearance of being covered in a spider's web. Although quite hardy in Britain it is a native of the Alps and Pyrenees. *S. soboliferum* (now more correctly called *Jovibarba sobolifera*) is unusual in that it produces its numerous offsets between the leaves as well as round the base of the plant.

While the sempervivums are broadly European in distribution *Orostachys* is a more Asian plant. Although hardy in most parts it makes a good pot plant, being slower growing than the sempervivums and therefore doing better than them in a pot. The most commonly seen is *O. spinosus* distributed from the Southern Urals to Japan and forming a rosette whose outer leaves are loosely arranged in a circle round the inner, densely packed leaves. The flowers of *O. spinosus* are greenish yellow and as the plants are only biennials it is best to save the seed. *O. thyrsiflorus* is a less common species with white flowers occasionally tinged with pink.

Echeveria

Some echeveria are mentioned in the following section of stemmed succulents other than cacti, but many echeverias form rosettes similar to sempervivums and these are illustrated on this and the following page.

Echeveria carnicolor is a native of Mexico and forms dense clumps with numerous offsets, the individual rosettes being between 3 and 4 in (8 and 10 cm) in diameter and being made up of spatulate or spade-shaped leaves whose upper surfaces are flat but whose lower ones are slightly keeled. The leaves are purplish pink in colour, almost flesh coloured, and have a slightly frosted appearance. Malathion should not be used with this species as it may damage this pruinose covering as it does with many other greyish members of the *Crassula* family. The flowers are orange-red, slightly tubular and are produced on stems about 6 in (15 cm) tall rising from just off the centre of the plant between January and March.

When potting up a cutting or repotting an existing plant try and incorporate either some sedge peat into the compost or some sterilized leafmould as this species enjoys a rather richer soil than most succulents.

Like the preceding species *E. derenbergii* is a native of Mexico and is usually stemless although some forms may produce a rather insignificant stem. The leaves are light green in colour with a fairly dense frosting on the upper and lower surfaces which means that the use of malathion should be avoided. The flower stems are shorter than those of the previous species and the leaves are tinged with red on the margins. Because of its very free-flowering habit this species has been cultivated for some time. It has also attracted the attention of hybridists who have sought to bring to the plant additional charms by crossing it with *E. setosa* illustrated on the next page. The hybrids between them are known as *E.* x *derosa*. These have a rather more domed effect being less like a saucer than the illustrated species, and have a light covering of hair rather than the frosted appearance of the true species.

The hybrids are even more free flowering than the type and for this reason are more widely cultivated, making it worthwhile to check the surfaces of the leaf and examine critically the shape of the rosette if the true species is desired.

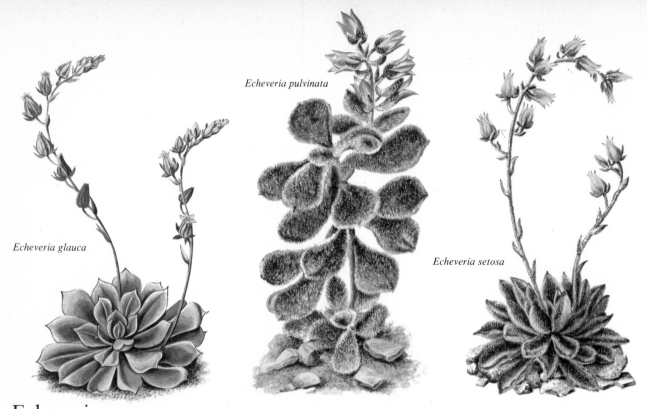

Echeveria glauca

Echeveria pulvinata

Echeveria setosa

Echeveria (*continued*)

Most *Echeveria* species will benefit from being grown outdoors during the summer as they are generally fast growers and can become straggly and somewhat etiolated if allowed to grow for too long indoors. The summer air and the generally rather lower temperatures help to keep the plant compact and by ripening and hardening the surfaces of the plant they check growth and allow flowers to develop. During the winter they do not need any great amount of warmth, 10°C (50°F) being quite warm enough for all the species, and during this time they are best kept on the dry side, watering on average once every four or five weeks. Plants may be grown easily from seed although in the case of commercial varieties these may not necessarily come true to type but cuttings are the easiest of all to take. In order to take cuttings a leaf should be broken off the parent plant and laid with its tapered end just covered by a little light loam, peat and sand compost. Within a very short period a small plantlet will form at the base of the leaf and when this is large enough to handle the whole may be lifted and planted in a larger pot. The parent leaf will grow a little at first but as soon as the plantlet becomes established it is best to remove the larger leaf as it will otherwise take some of the strength out of the younger plant.

Echeveria glauca is one of the more spectacular of the rosette-type species and forms offsets readily, only very occasionally making a short stem. The rosettes have up to fifty leaves each and attain a diameter of 4 in (10 cm) or so. The leaves are rather more openly arranged than in the species illustrated on the previous page and are purplish in colour and very much more markedly spatulate. They are covered with a slight frosting and may have a reddish margin round the sides of the leaves, especially where the plant has been grown outdoors during the summer on a rock garden in full sunlight. The leaves are also much thinner than those of the two species on the previous page and the flower stems are much taller, often nearly a foot (30 cm) above the plant, with between twelve and twenty deep red flowers produced in the spring. There is also a variety *E. g. pumila* with longer, rather narrower leaves and yellowish flowers which have a little red near the base.

Echeveria pulvinata is at first a silvery plant but as it grows older it becomes more or less densely covered in brownish felt. Although included in the stemless section it does ultimately make a short stem and may even form branches, however, it is not a fast-growing species and rather more delicate than most. The rosettes are far less regular and compact than the other illustrated species.

Echeveria pilosa is another species which is frequently stemless when acquired but which develops a short stem with age. Like the illustrated species it is also covered with soft short white down but the leaves are very much more regularly arranged and are much narrower.

Echeveria setosa has already been mentioned in connection with *E. derenbergii* with which it has been extensively hybridized. Although the two species hydridize readily in cultivation they do not appear to hybridize readily in the wild. The rosettes of this species are characterized by the blunt dark green leaves covered with white bristly hairs on both sides. It is very free flowering, producing a succession of reddish-yellow blooms on short flowering stems that arise just off the centre of the plant between April and July. The seed germinates very readily, and this characteristic may have been a feature which prompted growers to hybridize it.

There is also a hybrid between *E. harmsii* (syn. *Oliveranthus elegans*) and *E. setosa* called, appropriately enough, *E.* Set-Oliver. This has looser, neater rosettes and taller flower stems with rather larger flowers than the species.

Succulents with Upright, Arched or Hanging Stems

Aloe arborescens

Haworthia reinwardtii

In the following section I have dealt with a variety of different succulents which are characterized by having upright, arched or hanging stems. Within this category there are, of course, many different families and no attempt has been made to impose a botanical order on the species illustrated, but they have been grouped by their superficial characteristics, with the plants with upright stems or trunks forming the first and larger part of the section and those with trailing stems coming towards the end of the section.

As the plants come from such a wide variety of families it is impossible to generalize about their cultural requirements and these are dealt with in detail under the individual varieties.

Aloe

Aloes fall into two types in this classification, those with stems and those which do not form a true stem. The latter kind can be found on pages 175 and 176.

Aloe ferox requires a sunny situation as does the other commonly seen aloe of this type, *A. arborescens*. Once they become older they can be put outside during the summer provided that they are brought in before the first frosts and put out after the last ones. During the winter they should be kept on the dry side as excessive water can cause problems with rotting; in a greenhouse with cacti they can probably go all winter without water if kept cool, but in the home they will probably appreciate water once every six weeks or so. It is essential to give aloes an extremely well drained soil and it is recommended that extra sand is mixed into soil into which they are to be potted, and that the pot should be well crocked. *A. arborescens* comes from Natal where it forms a shrub. The bluish leaves develop a hard edge with teeth along the side and are curved and tapered in a very handsome way. *A. arborescens* flowers in winter but young plants are unlikely to produce flowers. *A. ferox* is widely distributed through South Africa and it tends to have more erect leaves than the previous species and the teeth are tinged slightly red. The flower stems of older plants have several branches on which the red hot poker-like clusters of flowers are produced. A characteristic feature of the species is the presence of spines down the rib at the base of the leaf and the occasional presence of spines on the upper surfaces too.

Haworthia

Haworthia reinwardtii is a very closely related species which, because of its ease of flowering and its comparatively slow growth, is an excellent plant to acquire at the start of a collection. Its cultural requirements are generally similar to the aloes just discussed but it will appreciate some shade in summer when it should not be allowed to dry out completely. Rosettes are formed at the base of the plant and these root readily; varieties may also be raised from seed but will seldom come true to type. There are very many recognized varieties of *H. reinwardtii*, the true species forms a stem up to 6 in (15 cm) in height round which the leaves are arranged densely in a tight spiral, the younger ones erect at first and flattening out with age. The upper surface has a few tubercles but the back is covered with fairly regularly spaced white tubercles which give the species its main attraction. Flowers are produced fairly readily during the winter months and the resting period is the opposite from other cacti and should be given between June and September. Because they tolerate shade they can be used as a conventional house plant and do not need the very sunny position on the windowsill recommended for other varieties.

Crassula lycopodioides

Cotyledon undulata

Crassula falcata

Crassula

Crassula lycopodioides makes an excellent little pot plant. In south-west Africa it forms a small shrub under 10 in (25 cm) in height with very slender stems round which the numerous small green triangular leaves are arranged in a very regular square-shaped pattern. The flowers are almost microscopic and are produced deep down in the axils of the leaves. The plant may be easily propagated by cuttings which root readily and can be taken from any part of the stem. There are numerous varieties as its attractive shape and great hardiness have encouraged growers to search for and propagate unusual forms. The most attractive form is undoubtedly the variegated *C. l. variegata* which has silvery leaves and again roots fairly readily as a cutting. *C. l. monstrosa* has the leaves opened up like a comb at the top of the stem. It tends to revert quite readily to the true species and it is best to cut the true stems out as and when they appear to encourage the more interesting growth. There is also a form, *C. l. pseudo lycopodioides*, with much thicker stems than the true type and greyish-green leaves. An unusual feature of this variety is the way in which young shoots are produced from nearly all of the leaf axils. The cultivated specimens differ from the wild species in having fragile, more drooping stems with rather more open leaves; the true type with more densely packed leaves is still a little scarce in cultivation.

Cotyledon

Cotyledon undulata is a very distinctive species which is very common in cultivation and which can be readily raised from seed. Ultimately plants will grow to nearly 2 ft (60 cm) in height and the young shoots are covered with a dense white meal. The leaves, shaped a little like a scallop shell and markedly wavy at the edges, are produced opposite one another and like the young stems are also covered with a dense white flocking. This flocking is quite delicate and great care should be taken when applying insecticides to check whether or not they are harmful to grey-skinned crassulas and cotyledons, and if in doubt the general rule must be not to spray these plants with anything other than water. The flower stem is very long and carries a bunch of pendulous tubular orange-yellow flowers at the top throughout the late spring and early summer.

Crassula

Crassula falcata is also frequently sold as *Rochea falcata* and is a native of South Africa. The leaves, like those of *Cotyledon undulata*, are produced in opposite rows and are joined at the base where they clasp the stem. They may be propagated by cuttings or seeds, and flowers are regularly produced in the early part of the summer. It is quite a good idea to take the cuttings immediately after flowering as cuttings taken in this way and at this time will normally flower the following season. The grey-green coloration is susceptible to various insecticides as mentioned earlier and the flowers of this variety are a bright scarlet or occasionally orange-red. Some of the true rocheas are heavily scented, two of the best in this respect being *R. coccinea* which has a hyacinth-like smell and *R. odoratissima*.

They prefer a sandy soil and cuttings should be struck in a small pot or seed tray containing a mixture of half peat and half sand. As the plants develop and become ready for potting on, a little more loam can be added to give substance to the compost. A light feed with tomato fertilizer in the autumn together with regular pinching will cause them to flower profusely shortly after watering is started up again in January.

Crassula perforata

Kalanchoe fedtschenkoi marginata

Kalanchoe

Crassula perforata is easily recognized on account of the long trailing unbranched stems which are at first quite succulent but become harder with age. The leaves are perfoliate (which means that the stem appears to grow from the centre of the leaves) and sharply pinched at the tips. The general colour is grey-green but the leaf surfaces are densely covered with tiny red spots and fine grey hairs. Like some of the species described earlier they should not be sprayed unless professional advice has been sought first. The flowers are very small and are produced at the ends of the stems in late spring.

There are several other varieties of *Crassula* with perfoliate leaves; the one most commonly seen is *C. rupestris*, which also comes from Cape Province but whose leaves are generally smaller and fatter and whose stems branch rather more readily than those of *C. perforata*. For this reason it makes a bushier plant, but lacks the appeal of the tiny red spots on the leaves. *C. brevifolia* is typical of a group of slightly similar crassulas where the leaves have become so thick as to obscure the stems completely, the ultimate kind being probably *C. arta* which makes a sort of knobbly column.

Kalanchoes (the final 'e' is pronounced) are most commonly found in Madagascar, but some have crossed the Indian Ocean to naturalize themselves as far afield as China and Malaysia. Generally kalanchoes should be given a bright position on a sunny windowsill although if space is limited the smooth-leaved species, such as *K. fedtschenkoi*, *K. daigremontiana* and so forth, will tolerate a shadier position. They should be kept cool in winter and watered very sparingly. Plants are best propagated from cuttings or in certain cases by using the plantlets which develop round the edges of the leaves of some species.

Kalanchoe fedtschenkoi is a dense shrub with numerous erect branches which can become bowed down with age. The grey-green leaves are rounded with slightly crenellated edges. Flowers are produced on long terminal stems and are tubular and brownish in colour. The variegated form, *K. f. marginata*, although seldom producing a viable or attractive flower, has a splendid cream margin round the edge of the leaves which contrasts excellently with the red band on the very edge. It tends to outgrow itself easily so it is a good idea to prune it fairly rigorously as it looks very unsightly if allowed to develop long straggly stems from which many of the leaves have fallen.

Kalanchoe blossfeldiana can now be grown on a year-round basis using artificial blackout to simulate the winter conditions essential for flowering and as a result has become a popular house plant (see page 54). Very many hybrids have been raised recently ranging from red and pink to orange in colour. They require a rather peatier soil than the previous species and a mixture of equal parts of peat, sand and loam is probably the best. During the growing period it is a good idea to pinch the soft growing tips of the stems in order to encourage the formation of a bushy plant. The short-day treatment is relatively simple and involves artificial blacking out in summer for fifteen to twenty days so as to cut the day length down to $12\frac{1}{2}$ hours. The plants can then be grown on quite normally and flowers will be produced just over three months later. Generally the longer the dark treatment period the more profusely the plant will flower and the sooner the buds will be produced. Conversely if larger plants are required growing the plant in a brightly lit sitting or dining room during the winter will encourage it to develop leaves at the expense of flower buds. For the smaller collection there is a very attractive hybrid called Tom Thumb which remains fairly compact.

181

Kalanchoe tubiflora

Kalanchoe daigremontiana

Kalanchoe beharensis

Kalanchoe (continued)

Both *Kalanchoe tubiflora* and *K. daigremontiana* are characterized by their ability to produce plantlets round the edges of the leaves. The former species is slightly less commonly seen than the latter and has slender upright stems, often attaining a height of 2 ft (60 cm) or more in cultivation, which carry numerous cylindrical leaves all round them. The leaves have a slight groove on the upper surface and are blotched or mottled in appearance. The adventitious buds (as they are technically known) or plantlets, appear at the end of the leaves furthest from the stem and soon develop miniature root systems even though they are still attached to the leaves. The flowering stem or inflorescence is produced at the end of the main stem of the plant during the winter months and the flowers hang from it on longish stalks. The flowers are reddish in colour but are not very attractive as they never open up to any extent. It is very rare for this particular species to branch and once the inflorescence has been produced in the second or third year it is normal for the plant to die back as it will have produced a good crop of plantlets by this time. Normally the plantlets will establish themselves round the base of the parent plant in the same pot but if it is wished to grow these plants in their own pots or to give some to a friend it is best to propagate plantlets either by taking the entire leaf and laying it on a mixture of peat and sand, or alternatively by gently digging up some of the young plants established round the base of the parent plant and potting them up individually in small pots.

Kalanchoe daigremontiana is, like the preceding species, a native of Madagascar, where it forms a rather more robust plant than *K. tubiflora* up to 3 ft (1 m) in height. The stems are normally unbranched and are brownish in colour supporting broadly triangular leaves which fall off with age. The adventitious buds are formed in very large numbers along the wavy edges of these leaves and it is not uncommon for these plantlets to start growing while still attached to the parent leaf and to produce their own young plantlets in turn. The upper surfaces of the pale green leaves are normally flat, but if they are allowed to become too cool in winter, small depressions can be formed on them; however, these in no way detract from the growth of the plant which will continue unchecked when heat is restored. The flowers are considerably more ornamental than those of *K. tubiflora*; not only do they open up a little more, but they are also carried on shorter stems in a slightly more tightly grouped cluster. It makes an ideal plant for children who will be fascinated by the large numbers of plantlets produced and it can safely be put outside during the summer, this will also help to keep the growth fairly short and prevent the plant becoming unmanageable.

Kalanchoe beharensis is not a very common plant, partly because it is comparatively slow growing for a kalanchoe and partly because it attains a fair size. However its appearance is most impressive. The stems can reach a height of 4 ft (1·25 m) or more and although they are smooth towards the base they are covered with a dense surrounding of woolly hairs near the top of the stem. The leaves have very wavy edges and like the upper parts of the stem are densely covered in brown woolly hairs which give the plant the appearance of being slightly rusted. Flowers are only produced on older specimens and the plant tends to shed most of its lower leaves in cultivation. It is possible, however, to cut the upper part of the stem off neatly and to root it in some fresh well drained compost and so make a more dwarf and attractive plant out of the old straggly one. Moreover, the part that remains in the pot below the cut will, in all probability, sprout again and provide a fresh source of cutting material for future use.

Sedum pachyphyllum

Echeveria harmsii

Crassula portulacea

Sedum

Sedum pachyphyllum is one of a group of sedums characterized by thin upright or semi-trailing stems and succulent cylindrical leaves, *S. pachyphyllum* itself is easily the most commonly seen and its English name, jelly beans, describes its appearance very well. The branching stems are densely covered with spirals of cylindrical grey club-shaped leaves which in the younger ones point upwards at the tips and flatten out with age. The bluish-green meal can be rubbed off and care should be taken when using certain insecticides, notably malathion, as they may cause damage to this covering. The most notable feature of the species is, however, the reddish blotch at the tip of each leaf, a feature which is lacking on the slightly similar *S. allantoides* and *S. ebracteatum*. The flowers of *S. pachyphyllum* are yellow and appear in the early spring on well established plants. One other similar species is *S. rubrotinctum* but this differs in having the whole leaf tinged red, not just the tip, and if the plants are kept during the summer in a well lit position and slightly on the dry side the whole plant will take on a reddish appearance.

Propagation of all these varieties is best carried out in the spring when mature leaves should be removed from the stem and laid on top of the soil or even with the base of the leaf stuck slightly into the soil. Young plants will then form at the base of these leaves which can later be removed when they are mature enough to be potted up.

Echeveria

Echeveria harmsii is still frequently sold under its old name of *Oliveranthus elegans* but the two plants are in fact identical. It makes one of the finest succulents for any collection and is fortunately fairly easy to obtain. The plant makes a small shrub which subsequently develops a much-branched woody stem giving it the appearance of a little tree. The leaves are broadly diagonal in shape and can be easily detached and rooted to make fresh plantlets. The flowers are produced on long stems from the side of the growing stems even on quite young specimens. Each stem bears one or two red flowers which are tipped with yellow and broadly tubular in shape. Although the bulk of the flowers are produced in spring a large specimen can go on producing more flowers over quite a period of time. It is also advisable to prune the plant occasionally, normally in the autumn, as this will encourage it to maintain its branching habit and prevent it growing too long and leggy.

Crassula

Crassula arborescens, C. portulacea and *C. lactea* all belong to a group of succulents with oval leaves and the appearance of small trees. They are known loosely and collectively as jade plants or money trees. *C. arborescens* ultimately becomes the largest of them. The leaves converge to a fine point near the stem and widen out at the further edge, which is occasionally tinged with green. It seldom flowers in cultivation and for this reason has been hybridized with the other two species which flower more readily. *C. portulacea* is similar although the leaves do not taper so closely together at the base. It flowers fairly freely and the roots are said to be edible. Some of the plants sold as *C. portulacea* are almost certainly *C. obliqua* which tends to have less rounded leaves with a slight point at the tip, but is similar in nearly every other respect. *C. lactea* is the smallest of this group and has leaves which are joined together. It is valuable as an addition to any collection since it flowers fairly freely on older plants in December and the flowers when they are produced are heavily scented. All four species mentioned in this group will benefit from a sunny position on the rock garden or a patio during the summer, as this helps to ripen up the wood prior to flowers being produced. *C. lactea* should be pruned occasionally in the late spring to encourage breaks from lower down the stem or it can become a little straggly and swamp a small collection.

Echeveria gibbiflora

Aeonium arboreum atropurpureum

Echeveria leucotricha

Aeonium

Aeoniums are generally unsuitable for the smaller collection or for an amateur. The ones most commonly offered for sale tend to make rather large specimens in time and need a maximum temperature of 10°C (50°F) in winter which it is difficult to give them indoors. In summer they will benefit from being placed outside in their pots, but, because they need a fair amount of moisture, it is a good idea to sink the pots in the soil so that the water can be conserved. The flowering branches of many species die back and some of them tend to be reluctant to produce fresh breaks below the inflorescence so it is a good idea to save the seed and sow it in August when it is quite fresh, thus ensuring a continuity of supply for the plants. The species illustrated, *Aeonium arboreum atropurpureum*, is one of the most attractive ones. The rosettes of purple leaves are carried at the top of long slender stems and it is quite normal for the lower leaves to fall off with age. There are various other forms of *A. arboreum*; a white and green variegated form called *A. a. albovariegatum* and a yellow and green form called *A. a. luteovariegatum*. There are also a few cristate forms which have a very striking appearance.

Echeveria

Somewhat similar in appearance is *Echeveria gibbiflora*. This makes a very handsome plant with erect branching stems although large plants may need a stake for support later. The most commonly seen form has large leaves more than 10 in (25 cm) in length which have a pronounced keel at the base where they join the stem. The surface is an attractive grey-green and this is yet another variety over which care should be taken with pesticides. The species is very free flowering producing numerous tubular light red to orange flowers on long stems during the autumn and winter. Young plantlets are occasionally formed at the base of the leaves on the rosette and also sometimes on the sides of the flowering stems.

In addition to the true species there are several cultivated forms which have considerable appeal. *E. g. carunculata* is a somewhat grotesque form with warty protuberances on the upper surfaces of the leaves. *E. g. crispata* has attractively waved edges to the leaves and *E. g. metallica* has bronze-coloured leaves. *E. violescens* is sometimes sold as this last variety but has more purplish leaves.

Echeveria leucotricha is very similar to *E. gibbiflora* in its general appearance but is considerably smaller and the leaves are not so neatly arranged in a rosette. However on closer examination its greyish appearance is caused by dense white hairs rather than a greyish meal. It lacks the keel at the base of the leaf that the earlier species had and has a small patch of brown hairs at the tip of the leaf. The red flowers are produced in spring.

Echeverias generally are extremely suitable plants for those with limited space available or for those who have no greenhouse. They are virtually indestructible and most varieties flower readily. They prefer a somewhat sandier soil than the general run of succulents and if you are using a proprietary brand of cactus compost it is as well to mix a little extra washed river sand into the soil to provide adequate drainage. They may be stood outside in the summer months to great advantage since it prevents them growing too fast and becoming too leggy and also encourages the production of harder wood and diminishes the need for staking. Propagation is elementary; the leaves may be broken off and laid on or slightly inserted into a seedling compost, in which case young plantlets will form at their base, or alternatively the stems may be cut through and stuck into a pot where they will quickly root into the new compost. The best time to strike cuttings or propagate is, of course, in the spring when the plant is able to produce the roots it requires for growth very quickly. They may also be raised from seed but unless you are certain that the plant you have is a true species you may be disappointed by the result, which may not conform to the original, since many commercial plants are hybrids between different species.

Caralluma hesperidum

Senecio articulatus globosus

Senecio stapeliaeformis

Senecio

Although this section is mainly concerned with succulents with stems, *Senecio articulatus globosus*, in spite of its round stemless appearance, properly belongs here. It is an unusual and intriguing plant and in its true form as *S. articulatus* it has perfectly conventional stems. The variety illustrated, which is more commonly seen in cultivation than the true species, has stems which have become so compressed and swollen as to be almost completely spherical, although it still produces a few arrow-shaped leaves near the tips of the round stems. The stems break off very easily and can be rooted quite readily, but it does make it difficult to obtain a plant of any size. It also requires just about the sunniest position in your home or greenhouse if it is to do really well, and stems which start to revert to the original cylindrical shape should be removed or they will tend to take over the plant.

Senecio is the Latin name for the common British ragwort or groundsel and these succulent varieties are an excellent example of how diverse and adaptable nature can become. The similarity between varieties is even less obvious with species such as *S. macroglossus variegatus* (illustrated on page 71), which at first sight looks remarkably like an ivy but produces groundsel-like flowers. To encourage this latter species to flower it should be regularly pinched back to prevent long straggly growth, trained round a hoop, and grown very cool in the winter, all this helps to ripen up the stems preparatory to flowering.

Caralluma

Carallumas also have British relations called motherworts or *Aristolochia*. They are very similar to the stapelias described overleaf and like them require a dwarf pot or broad pan as they have very shallow but wide ranging root systems and eventually form a good-sized clump. *Caralluma hesperidum* is the most commonly seen variety. It is a native of Morocco and has four-angled red-spotted green stems. There are small fleshy teeth on the sides of the stems and unlike stapelias it produces flowers from the tips of the stems rather than from the base. Flowering stems normally produce a tuft of flowers, up to ten in this variety, of a pentagonal shape slightly soft and velvety purplish-brown in colour.

Echidnopsis cereiformis is closely related, but, as its name implies, looks more like one of the upright cacti without spines. Like *Caralluma hesperidum* the flowers are produced from the ends of the stems but unlike it they are produced singly from the sides of the stems rather than in tufts from the tips. The edges are not nearly so sharply angled and there are many more of them with tubercles rather than spines on the edges.

Senecio

Senecio stapeliaeformis, which is frequently sold as *Kleinia stapeliaeformis*, is very similar to both the preceding species. It has slender upright stems ultimately forming a clump by branching below ground level. The greyish stems are sharply five to seven angled and are distinguished by dark green lines running down the sides. Small leaves are produced from the edges of the stems at regular intervals and the species can be induced to flower without too much difficulty if water is withheld during the summer months when the plant rests. The flowers are quite attractive, red and daisy like, and the clump-forming habit should be encouraged by growing this species in shallow pans in a mixture of loam and sand like the two previously described. There is a slightly similar variety of *Senecio* called *S. kleinia* which is sometimes confused with *S. stapeliaeformis*. This has stems which branch above the ground and can attain a height of 3 ft (1 m) or more, while the species illustrated seldom exceeds 10 in (25 cm) in height. The leaves are much more pronounced and longer, often up to 6 in (15 cm) in length on older plants.

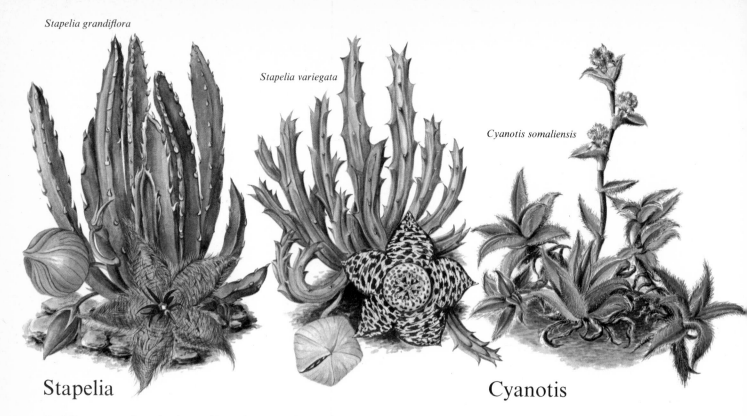

Stapelia grandiflora

Stapelia variegata

Cyanotis somaliensis

Stapelia

Stapelias are not plants for those with sensitive noses. They are pollinated by blow flies and in order to attract them in their native habitats in South Africa and east India they have learnt to imitate the smell of rotten meat. They are for this reason unsuitable for most homes as the smell is really quite powerful, and it makes it difficult to appreciate the bizarre appearance of the flowers. In spite of their unpleasant odour they are very easy to grow although they may not flower until they have reached a fair size. They need a fairly cool resting period in the winter, but a living-room windowsill will suffice as their main requirement during the resting period is a lot of light. Although they should be kept on the dry side during this period they should not be allowed to shrivel up and during the growing period they should be watered fairly generously and even damped lightly over on really hot days with a mist sprayer. If you wish to propagate these varieties cuttings may be taken from any of the stems in the spring but they must be allowed to dry out before they are struck, otherwise they will merely rot when they are inserted into the rooting medium. It is best to use a propagator to root them if one is available, otherwise you can try inverting a jam jar over the pot in which the cuttings are struck. Like the species on the previous page they require pans rather than pots if they are to grow well.

Stapelia grandiflora is one of the most impressive species and the sharply raised angles of the stems and the stems themselves are covered in soft hairs. The flowers are a fair size and have hairs on the margins of the petals which are purplish with latitudinal protuberances across them. *S. gigantea* is even more impressive and produces flowers up to 14 in (35 cm) across but is not very often found for sale.

Stapelia variegata is by far the most commonly found species and is easier to look after in summer, with less tendency to rot off. It is an extremely variable species and a great many of the forms have been given Latin names. The true species has greyish-green stems up to 4 in (10 cm) in height with somewhat flattened angles. The stems are heavily blotched all over with purple and it is this variegation which gives the plant its name. The flowers too are blotched heavily yellow and purple giving the plant an extraordinarily sickly appearance. The varieties which are available are normally distinguished by the different arrangement of the blotches on the flowers although there is a cristate form which is not uncommon.

Cyanotis

Cyanotis somaliensis is related to the better known tradescantia or wandering jew and is not an obviously succulent plant. It makes an excellent addition to any collection and can be grown satisfactorily with a winter temperature of 7°C (45°F). The stems are rather weak and somewhat arched in habit and should be pruned back slightly at the beginning of each growing season. The mid-green leaves are long and tapered away from the stem which they cover at the base with a pronounced sheath; they are densely covered in long silky grey hairs. Propagation can either take place by dividing up the matted clumps that form if the plant is pruned hard or by striking the tips that are pruned off in the spring. The species flowers fairly readily at the end of the branches in the axils of the top cluster of leaves; like all tradescantias the flowers are three petalled, they are blue in colour and produced right through the summer.

Although completely unrelated it is as well to mention here a little plant called *Anacampseros rufescens* that is fairly commonly offered for sale. It is slightly similar but has no hairs and much more succulent purplish leaves. The plant has been known since earliest times and was much valued as a talisman for bringing back lost love. It needs a very bright position in the home or greenhouse and will almost certainly need the aid of a photographic lamp once the buds are formed if they are to open, as they normally are formed and then die without opening in our climate.

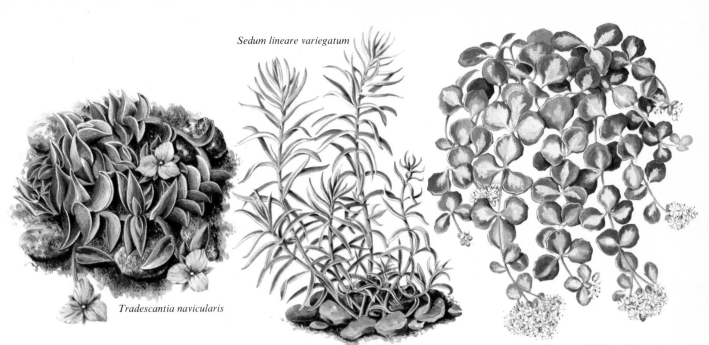

Sedum lineare variegatum

Tradescantia navicularis

Sedum sieboldii medio-variegatum

Tradescantia

Tradescantia navicularis is even more like *Anacampseros rufescens* in habit, than *Cyanotis somaliensis* to which it is related. It is a native of Northern Peru where it forms a low-growing sprawling perennial herb. In cultivation it seems to lack this clump-forming habit and like *Cyanotis somaliensis* needs to be trimmed back regularly at the start of each growing season in order to maintain a compact shape. The leaves, which are very sharply keeled and clasp the stem at the base, are borne in two rows on either side of the stem; the Latin name *navicularis* refers to the similarity between the leaves and a little boat. Although it is somewhat slow growing it is an interesting plant to have in the collection since like the succulent senecios it is a succulent example of a plant which we would not otherwise think of as being generally such. It also has attractive rose-pink-coloured flowers which are produced on short stems at the tips of the branches from the axils of the leaves during the summer and right through the autumn making it a valuable addition from this point of view. Propagation, as with all the tradescantias, is very simple when done by means of cuttings taken from the terminal shoots.

Sedum

It is sometimes difficult to know where to draw the line in discussing the cultivation of sedums in greenhouses or in the home. Many sedums are natives of Britain, particularly *Sedum anglicum* the common English stonecrop, and both *S. lineare* and *S. sieboldii* are perfectly hardy in a sheltered location. The real enthusiast should use these hardy succulents to form a bridge between his indoor collection and the plants he grows in the garden.

The variety illustrated above is *S. lineare variegatum*. This makes a most attractive plant with arched stems closely surrounded by light green lanceolate leaves which are borne in clusters of three and tinged with a white variegation round the edge. Like the following species this one produces two types of stem, flowering and non-flowering. The stems which are subsequently going to produce flowers are longer than the others, up to 6 in (15 cm) in many cases. The true species, *S. lineare*, is much more free flowering than the variegated form, and care must be taken to remove any stems which revert to the type or they will quickly swamp the weaker, variegated growth and take over the plant.

There is a slightly similar species to the preceding one without the variegated leaves, but like the preceding one coming from the Far East, called *S. bergeri*. It differs in having very much larger leaves which are spurred at the tip.

Sedum sieboldii medio-variegatum makes an excellent pot plant. It is a native of Japan and dies back to ground level during the winter when it is ideally suited to a position in a cold frame. This may not always be available, especially to people living in flats, and in this event I advise you to put it on a spare-bedroom windowsill. As soon as the warm weather comes the shoots spring up from the base surrounded at regular intervals with almost circular grey leaves, often tinged with red, and conspicuously marked with a large yellow blotch in the middle. They are borne, like those of *S. lineare variegatum*, in groups of three giving the plants a faint resemblance to a variegated clover. It can either be grown in a shallow pan or can be used for hanging baskets or window boxes. Care must be taken to remove the unvariegated shoots which detract from the overall appearance of the plant and will quickly take it over if allowed to flourish unchecked. Two sorts of stems are produced, flowering and non-flowering, the latter are longer and produce a cluster of reddish-pink flowers in the early autumn, after which the stems die back to the surface of the rootstock. During winter, water should not be withheld altogether but the plant is dormant and will only require a little water every month or so to prevent the roots from desiccating completely. Propagation is achieved by taking cuttings from the non-flowering stems, or by dividing up older plants into clumps. This latter course may be necessary as the plants tend to become a little one sided with age as parts of the rootstock become too old to carry on producing new shoots.

Pachyphytum amethystinum

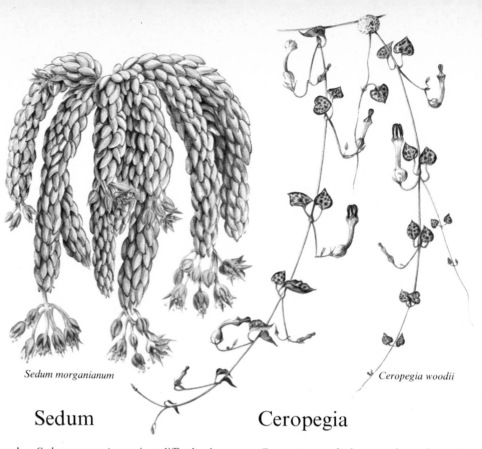

Sedum morganianum

Ceropegia woodii

Pachyphytum

The species described on this page all need some support if they are to grow upright, although *Sedum morganianum* is a naturally hanging kind. They are generally unsuitable for small collections for this reason although *S. morganianum* is occasionally seen hanging up in cottage windows.

Graptopetalum amethystinum is a good shrubby succulent closely related to echeverias and pachyphytums and is still sometimes sold as *Pachyphytum amethystinum*. Although the young shoots are quite erect they become sprawling or prostrate with age and tend to put up fresh branches from the base when this happens. The leaves are very loosely arranged round the stems and break off at the slightest touch, causing the plant to develop a slightly straggly appearance with bare stems as it gets older. The leaves are extremely thick and are heavily flattened on top and tinged with an amethyst-coloured coating over the bluish-grey undersurface which gives the plant its name. The flowering stem is produced from among the leaves out of the side of the stem and carries small pale yellow flowers on short lateral stalks during early spring.

Pachyphytum bracteosum is not dissimilar but is generally stouter with longer stems and lacks the strong amethyst colouring of the illustrated species; instead its leaves are covered with an extremely pronounced hoary coating which gives them the appearance of being slightly frosted.

Both species should be kept clear of malathion as already recommended for many members of the *Crassula* family with pruinose or hoary leaves.

Sedum

Sedum morganianum is a difficult plant to grow well. It makes a very slight root system when grown in cultivation and has a great tendency to rot off at the base. If the facilities are available it is a good idea to knock the root ball and soil out of the pot in which plants are purchased and then to moss it to a piece of bark or a large stump, completely covering the root ball with layers of moss bound in place with wires. This helps with the drainage but care must be taken to water the plant more regularly than if it were grown in a pot. It makes a spectacular trailing specimen with long stems completely covered by neatly plaited rows of bluish-grey leaves which are slightly pointed at the tips. The flowers are produced on an inflorescence at the ends of the stems and are light pink to a rich deep purple in colour and contrast well with the greyish leaves. Propagation is best done by means of stem cuttings and it is wise to have a few plants growing on behind the main species in a collection as a precaution against the rotting off mentioned earlier. It is an attractive plant but is still a little unusual and this makes the extra effort of saving a few cuttings as a precaution extremely worthwhile.

Ceropegia

Ceropegia woodii is one of my favourite plants and frequently grown by nurserymen who would not consider themselves to be succulent growers. It really requires a small greenhouse if it is to be shown to its best advantage as it sprawls all over the place and needs careful training. If space is at a premium it is best to grow it round a hoop rather than up a stick since this will encourage the formation of riper shoots by allowing greater air circulation. The long stems produce little tubers at intervals and these may be taken off and rooted to form the basis of new plants. In addition to the tubers, there are large numbers of heart-shaped speckled grey and purple leaves spaced out along the fine stems, and some pinching of the young growth may be necessary to encourage the formation of these leaves and to prevent the long trails taking over the whole of the space. The flowers are very curious and are produced at intervals along the stems; they are purplish grey in colour, tubular in shape and surmounted by five darker coloured petals which are joined together at the tip. The seeds are like dandelion seeds and the tubers can be used for grafting some of the more delicate aristolochias, hoodias and echidnopsis. To do this bury the tuber up to two-thirds of its depth in soil, slice off the top and graft the desired scion on to it.

191